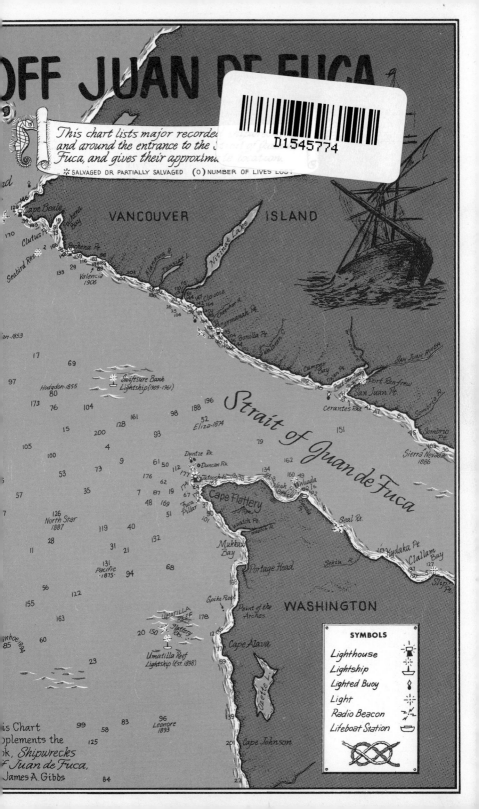

OFF JUAN DE FUCA

This chart lists major recorded ~~~~
and around the entrance to the Strait of Juan de
Fuca, and gives their approximate location.

✳ SALVAGED OR PARTIALLY SALVAGED   (O) NUMBER OF LIVES LOST

VANCOUVER   ISLAND

Cape Beale
Pachena Bay
Clutus Pt.
Pachena Pt.
Seabird Rks.
Valencia 1906
Nitinat Lake
Cloo-ose
Carmanah Pt.
Bonilla Pt.
Camper Bay
San Juan River
Port Renfrew
Pass Sandspit
San Juan Pt.
Somario R.

Swiftsure Bank Lightship (1909–1961)
Cerantes Rks.
Somario Pt.

Strait of Juan de Fuca

Hodgdon 1855
Eliza 1874
Sierra Nevada 1886

Duntze Rk.
Duncan Rk.
Tatoosh Id.
Fuca Pillar
Cape Flattery
Neah Bay
Waatch R.
Seal Rk.
North Star 1887
Mukkaw Bay
Portage Head
Sekiu R.
Kydaka Pt.
Clallam Bay
Slip Pt.
Pacific 1875
Spike Rock
Point of the Arches
WASHINGTON
UMATILLA REEF
Flattery Rks.
Umatilla Reef Lightship (Est. 1898)
Cape Alava
Ozette I.

Leonore 1893
Cape Johnson

SYMBOLS	
Lighthouse	
Lightship	
Lighted Buoy	
Light	
Radio Beacon	
Lifeboat Station	

Shipwrecks Off Juan de Fuca

BOOKS BY JAMES A. GIBBS

PACIFIC GRAVEYARD

Every great shipwreck in and around the waters of the Columbia River Bar, from early sailing ships to the present.

SHIPWRECKS OF THE PACIFIC COAST

Complete account of all known shipwrecks off the coasts of Washington, Oregon, and California.

SHIPWRECKS OFF JUAN DE FUCA

Stories of over 200 shipwrecks off Washington State's northwest tip—where the Strait of Juan de Fuca meets the Pacific Ocean.

SENTINELS OF THE NORTH PACIFIC

Histories of Pacific Coast lighthouses and lightships and the men who manned them—from Mexico to the Arctic.

Shipwrecks Off Juan de Fuca

By

James A. Gibbs

BINFORDS & MORT, *Publishers*

Portland   •   Oregon   •   97242

Shipwrecks Off Juan de Fuca

Printed in the United States of America

First Edition

CONTENTS

Skagit . . . wrecks in Vancouver Island's paradise . . . the great real estate scheme that failed . . . and the breeches buoy rescue of the Santa Rita's *crew.*

PROLOGUE

THE STRAIT OF JUAN DE FUCA

Since the days of exploration, the entrance to the Strait of Juan de Fuca has attracted commerce from the ports of the world to the rich hinterland beyond. The strait is actually a great arm of the Pacific; man has little to do to keep its entrance navigable, and he has nothing to say about problems peculiar to the area, one of the most villainous of which is fog.

Down through the years, fog has caused a grim toll in lives and property at the marginal waters of the strait—along the inhospitable shores of Vancouver Island to the north and Cape Flattery to the south. At the entrance to the strait, fog can be like a blanket of wool, or it can be spotty like a patchwork quilt —thick here and thin there, a formidable foe during certain periods of the year.

In the days of sail, the problem was more complex than today, having been compounded by the strong currents which often carried victim vessels northward to the tentacles of Vancouver Island's treacherous west coast. Until the advent of radio, radar, loran, and the radio beacon, about the only defense mariners had against fog was the simple and often inadequate foghorn. Not until modern times did man find a way to pierce these earth-hugging and impenetrable clouds with his miracle electronic devices.

The earliest information that the civilized world had of the existence of the Strait of Juan de Fuca was probably more myth than fact. From the time of Ferdinand Magellan to that of Captain George Vancouver, all discoveries along the Northwest Coast involved searching for a so-called "Northwest Passage" that did not exist—at least not in the way assumed by man.

In the year 1596, in Venice, a Greek—with the Spanish-acquired name of Juan de Fuca—told an Englishman by the name of Michael Lok that he had proof of such a great waterway. At the time, Lok was widely known for his interest in geographic discoveries. According to Lok, de Fuca gave the latitude of the strait as between 47 and 48 degrees; though later it was found to be between 48 and 49 degrees. However, de Fuca was very close. Furthermore, there are islands in the strait just as the old Greek said, and there is a conspicuous pillar he described, which we know today as Fuca's Pillar.

In view of the details of the Greek's story, he must surely be given credit for a plausible report; and it is noteworthy that greater exception to it has been taken by recent historians than by early explorers who followed in the old mariner's wake. Lok himself was so convinced of the authenticity of the account that he used it when seeking to encourage Sir Walter Raleigh, Lord Burleigh, and others then in favor with Queen Elizabeth, to undertake new enterprises of discovery.

Though Captain James Cook is generally considered discoverer of Cape Flattery, in 1778, the waterway itself was shrouded in fog—both literally and figuratively. It remained for Captain Charles William Barkley, in 1787, to discover and name it. Barkley, who was in search of furs, did not attempt to explore the strait, but sailed along its fringe and then down the coast south of Flattery.

Arriving in Canton in November of that year, he reported his discovery of the strait to Captain John Meares, a former lieutenant in the British Navy, who was then preparing for a trading voyage along the Northwest Coast. Early in 1788, Meares and another English trader, William Douglas, joined in the rush for furs that superseded the quest for the Northwest Passage.

On June 29 of that same year of 1788, Meares hove to off the island now called Tatoosh, at the tip of Cape Flattery. When Indians came out to his ship in canoes, he decided to send an officer to examine the island. The officer reported that it was a "solid rock covered with a little verdure, and surrounded by breakers in every direction."

From shipboard, Meares noted that the surface of the island "as far as the eye could see, was covered with inhabitants, who were gazing at the ship. . . . The chief of this spot, whose name is Tatooche, did us the favor of a visit, and so surly and forbidding a character we had not yet seen." Today the life-saving light of Cape Flattery Lighthouse shines out to sea from this island.

Meares also reported that they "saw a very remarkable rock that wore the appearance of an obelisk and stood at some distance from the island." To this rock he gave the name Pinnacle Rock—now Fuca's Pillar.

Meares sent his first officer, Mr. Duffin, in the *Felice's* longboat to explore the strait, the latter going as far as Port San Juan. On the basis of this, Meares later claimed that he, not Barkley, was the discoverer of the Strait of Juan de Fuca, but his claim did not hold.

Duncan Rock off Tatoosh Island is named for the English navigator and trader, Captain Charles Duncan, who reputedly did the first surveying and trading within the strait, and published the first chart in 1790.

Before the year 1788 had become history, the flag of the United States appeared in Pacific Northwest waters with the arrival of the *Columbia Rediviva* and the *Lady Washington*, at that time skippered respectively by John Kendrick and Robert Gray, and financed by a Boston fur syndicate. Captain Gray— who was later to discover the Columbia River in the *Columbia Rediviva*—traded and explored inside the Strait of Juan de Fuca for a distance of about fifty miles. He thus became the first explorer actually to navigate the strait's waters.

Early in 1789, the Spaniards—traditionally more interested in influence than trade—sent a naval force under Estevan Jose Martinez to Nootka Sound, where they claimed the surrounding country in the name of Spain, seizing several English ships. Meares narrowly escaped. The following year, a second Spanish force, headed by Francisco Eliza, took possession of the mainland at Neah Bay, claiming it in the name of Spain. The Indians were powerless to protest, but privation, cold, and rain drove the Spaniards out before a fortress was completed.

It remained for Captain George Vancouver, in 1792, to record the location of the strait—which he did very close to the area where Juan de Fuca had placed it exactly two hundred years earlier. Vancouver was convinced that the old sailor had really been there, and he accordingly re-affixed the name Strait of Juan de Fuca to fortify his belief. It is interesting to note that Barkley, Meares, and Vancouver all paid this tribute to the ancient mariner.

Today, the navigation hazards that faced these early explorers have been largely solved. A complex system of radio beacons has been set up along the Pacific Coast of the United States and the Canadian West Coast so that an offshore vessel equipped to receive their signals is never out of range. Each light station along the shore has a radio beacon radius that overlaps the next station in line, and a ship can maintain a comfortable course even in the thickest weather.

Radio beacons broadcast simple dot and dash combinations by means of transmitters giving out modulated, continuous waves. These valuable fog signals are also available for navigation in clear weather. Average range for radio beacons is 250 miles, but the more powerful ones are often picked up 500 miles away. Beacons are strategically located about the approaches to the strait—at *Umatilla Reef Lightship*, Cape Flattery, and at major light stations on the west coast of Vancouver Island.

Two other powerful, modern aids are used in the unceasing fight against fog—radar and loran. All of today's ships are equipped with radar sets; and certain navigation aids such as buoys have special devices known as radar reflectors which increase the radar echo. These echoes are picked up aboard ship to give accurate location.

Loran can also determine position accurately and quickly, day or night, and under practically any condition of weather and sea. The loran "line of position" is determined by measuring the time difference in receipt of synchronized electromagnetic wave pulses from two transmitting stations. A position "fix" may be determined by crossing a loran "line of position" with another loran line, sun line, star line, or other normal "line of position." The reliable average daytime range of loran is 700 miles, using ground waves; and the nighttime range 1,400 miles, using sky waves.

So advanced have these modern inventions become that already the extensive establishment of coastal radio beacons and other electronic aids to navigation along the Pacific Coast has eliminated the necessity for retaining medium frequency, 300-to-500-kilocycle direction-finder stations.

Strange to say, with all the advances in the fight against fog, the old foghorn dressed in modern garb still remains. Ships are still required to blast their whistles at frequent intervals when the ceiling is zero. Likewise, light stations along the shores call back with massive diaphone and diaphragm horns, affording individual sound signals for identification.

Unlike the entrance to the Columbia River—also a graveyard of ships—the wide, deep waters at the entrance to Juan de Fuca offer safe navigation channels. However, the flood currents at the entrance break with considerable velocity over Duncan and Duntze rocks. According to the *United States Coast Pilot*, these flood currents do not run in the direction of the channel, but rather have a continued set toward the Vancouver Island shore. These flood currents also have more velocity on the northern shore of the strait than on the southern. Currents attain velocities of two to four knots, varying with the range of tide—and they are influenced by strong winds.

Tide rips are particularly heavy off Cape Flattery. There are also many turbulent waters off the principal Canadian landmarks of Cape Beale, Carmanah, Bonilla, and Pachena. Just as the fogs are heaviest during the summer months, so are the driving winds and rains most prevalent during the winter months. The ten-knot average summer breeze climbs steadily up the Beaufort's scale during winter, and on some occasions sends wind gusts scudding across the entrance well in excess of 100 miles per hour.

Borne on the wings of such winds are often sleet and wet snow, but mostly rain. During such storms some of the world's greatest waves have been measured off the strait—waves of the type that undoubtedly caused the foundering of many overladen ships lost without trace around the turn of the century. Rain totals from Cape Alava north to Cape Beale range between 85 and 200 inches a year, the heaviest downfalls occurring during December, January, February, and March.

Though the entrance to the Strait of Juan de Fuca is no different today from what it was during the age of exploration, man's ingenuity in marking it with safeguards for the mariner has ended much of the fear felt by the early sailors—justified fear that long ago dubbed this area Graveyard of the Pacific.

Shipwrecks Off Juan de Fuca

Captain Charles William Barkley, credited with the discovery of the Strait of Juan de Fuca in 1787, named the waterway for the old Greek mariner who claimed discovery in 1592.

Victoria, B.C., Provincial Archives

South part of Cape Flattery showing fabled Fuca's Pillar at right—which has given support to the old Greek navigator's claim of having discovered the Strait of Juan de Fuca, which now bears his name.

Star of Lapland, a huge bark, is virtually hidden in a voluminous swell off Cape Flattery around the turn of the century.

In 1857, the HMS *Plumper* was dispatched to Esquimalt, B.C., to do charting work around the entrance to the strait and along the coast.

PART 1

SHIPWRECKS SOUTH OF FLATTERY

Including the strange adventures of the crew of the Russian St. Nicholas in 1808 . . . the arrival of the Uninvited Orientals in 1834 . . . "Dynamite" O'Brien's historic ordeals . . . and the harrowing details of a score or more of other dramatic sea disasters below the snout-nosed promontory of Cape Flattery, flanking Juan de Fuca's southern entrance.

The lonely, virtually unknown Pacific Northwest Coast was completely void of lights and foghorns one hundred and fifty years ago, and they could have been counted on one's fingers as late as a century ago. About the only aids to the earliest mariners were such primitive navigation instruments as the cross-staff and the compass for determining geographic location. Later came the astrolabe, the quadrant and, in the early eighteenth century, the sextant. As commercial sail developed, the situation improved but little. Charts were unreliable—if at all available—and sailing by dead reckoning in thick weather was like playing a deadly game of chance. The successful old-time sailor needed a built-in sixth sense to guide him when landmarks were blotted from view. He had to be able to sense the whims of the currents, smell an approaching gale, feel the approach of land, and understand every capability of his ship in any given circumstance.

Perils of the seas are often terrible today, but in those early years they were far worse; there were no search and rescue

1

planes, no helicopters, no motor lifeboats. Ships had no radio, radar, or wireless. Once a vessel crashed ashore there wasn't even such a primitive conveyance as a breeches buoy available, and frequently the natives did not take kindly to survivors. On becoming castaways their lot—if by chance they survived—was usually death or slavery.

Very few sea tragedies during the age of exploration on the Northwest Coast are a matter of record, and even their record is fragmentary.

WRECK OF THE ST. NICHOLAS

One of the earliest recorded shipwrecks on Pacific Northwest shores was that of the Russian brig *St. Nicholas*, gored by rocks south of Juan de Fuca in 1808. The castaways were traded among the Indian tribes and many ended up among the Makahs who inhabited the lands around Cape Flattery. Among the survivors was Anna Petrovna, the first white woman to set foot on the Northwest Coast.

She was an attractive, adventure-loving lady and the wife of Captain Nikolai Bulygin, master of the *St. Nicholas*. Just how she managed to become part of this Russian expedition organized at New Archangel (Sitka), in the fall of that fatal year, was never fully determined but her persuasive ways with Russian nobility and her husband's insistence that his bride be allowed to go along evidently secured for her a berth as a passenger. Had not Bulygin been held in such high respect as a naval officer, his request would probably have been refused.

For eighteen-year-old Anna, however, it was to be the highlight of her young life; at least she thought so at the beginning of the voyage. Bulygin was deeply in love with his young bride; nor did he doubt for her safety as he had great confidence in himself as a navigator despite the little-known shores for which the expedition was destined. The purpose of the voyage was to locate a site for a fort in the Columbia River area. With relatively few men, the Russians had within a few decades settled Alaska and planned colonization as far south as California and also in Hawaii. In short, they were challenging the Spanish power in the Pacific.

While Bulygin was in charge of the voyage, Timothy (Timofei) Tarakanov was given chief responsibility for the land part of the expedition, and he also served as the ship's supercargo. He was one of Baranof's most trusted men, an experienced soldier who had been with the garrison of the initial fort constructed at New Archangel, capital of Russian America in 1799. Tarakanov had miraculously escaped death in the revenge-inspired uprising of the Tlingits in 1802. He had been taken captive and made to witness the death by torture of two of his comrades. He would have suffered a similar fate had he not been rescued by Captain Henry Barber of the British ship *Unicorn*, assisted by an American, Captain John Ebbets.

Tarakanov, the genuine Russian frontiersman, had learned the language of the Tlingits and studied their ways, at the same time becoming a good friend of the Aleuts, who often took him on their fishing voyages.

Bulygin's expedition left New Archangel at about the same time that Ivan Kuskov and his men in the ship *Kodiak* set out to survey a location for a fort in Northern California. The two parties were later to rendezvous at Grays Harbor. The *St. Nicholas* carried a complement of twenty persons, seventeen men including four Aleuts, plus three women, Anna Petrovna and two Aleut squaws. The Aleuts were taken along because of their ability to converse and trade with the natives along the Northwest Coast.

Captain Bulygin was supplied with copies of Captain George Vancouver's charts and his command was a fine little 200-ton, Yankee-built sailer. He anticipated a routine expedition, discounting any thoughts of trouble along the way.

As the *St. Nicholas* took to the open sea, the first anchorages were made in little coves indenting the Queen Charlotte Islands, where the Aleuts proved invaluable in striking up trade with the natives. The officers made brief land explorations and crude charts of each area they visited. The *St. Nicholas* fired her gun when in sight of native totem poles at the small settlements along the way. Before she could drop her hook, the natives would come out by the score in their graceful canoes, eager to trade otter skins which would more than pay the cost of the expedition. The crew were on shares and their craftiness and cunning in trading could assure a profitable voyage.

The voyage continued on down the west coast of Vancouver Island, the weather holding good most of the way. Tarakanov, who was wise in the ways of the natives, would only allow three aboard at a time as he was aware of their sometimes hostile reputation.

As the brig approached the latitudes of the Strait of Juan de Fuca, the favorable weather suddenly came to a halt. Gales began blowing out of the South, making irascible seas that hampered the progress of the craft. Under shortened sail the vessel tacked off the strait entrance, unable to get inside. When the wind finally subsided, a great gray mantle of fog draped itself across the deceptive entrance and Bulygin wisely stood offshore, setting a southerly course.

One night in late October, the *St. Nicholas* reached latitude 17° 56′ north, in the vicinity of Destruction Island. There was a dead calm and the canvas hung limp. While the crew was engaged in sounding, the officers sketched the shoreline and surrounding landmarks. The current was strong and the shore pockmarked with hidden rocks.

So engrossed were all hands in their duties that little attention was paid to a southeast gale in the making. The traditional calm before the storm had deceived them and almost before they knew it, the *St. Nicholas* was in trouble. Though Bulygin ordered more canvas, contrary winds were against him. The vessel would not respond but was swept ever closer to destruction—carried northward like a piece of drift in a swift river.

In an effort to halt the shoreward drift, Bulygin ordered all three anchors dropped. The men, in desperation, were quick to respond, but despite the dragging of the hooks, the vessel was drawn as though by a magnet. The strain caused one of the halyards to snap, and some of the sails were blown to ribbons. The anchor cables, snagged on sharp rocks just under the surface, held for a brief moment and then snapped.

Throughout the black night the vessel was flung against one barrier after another, twisting and turning like an unarmed live thing trying to escape a relentless pursuer. It was so dark that none of the pitiful band could see two feet in front of them. The sea, the beach, the trees, and the lofty mountains, all had become invisible, and the feeble oil lamps aboard the vessel had flickered into nothingness. The panic-stricken complement awaited the end.

Miraculously the ship weathered the night and when the sickly dawn of November 1 finally broke over the jagged Olympics, the vessel, with her holds full of water, was impaled on a rocky crag jutting out from the mainland, a little south of the mouth of the Quillayute River.

Bulygin knew that, in 1787, between their present location and the Hoh River, a boat crew from the East India ship *Imperial Eagle*, while seeking fresh water, was massacred by the natives. Bulygin was concerned for his own wife and party. After surveying his ship's punctured hull and the tangled mass of wreckage on her decks, he ordered his comrades to abandon ship and set up camp on the beach. The seas had calmed and the survivors managed to struggle through the surf while a pelting rain added to their miseries. Later they removed what they could from the wreck. That night they slept, exhausted, among the salvaged goods that lay on the beach.

The following morning Tarakanov and Bulygin discussed their chances of survival. Both were hopeful that they could traverse the seventy miles between their location and Grays Harbor for an eventual rendezvous with Kuskov. Guns were issued and feeble shelters assembled. All hands had been warned of the danger of hostile natives and a sharp lookout was maintained day and night. Bulygin and his beloved Anna stayed close together and, despite the misery, the young Russian girl remained undaunted.

Now ashore, Tarakanov's role became more prominent. He was a hunter, a carpenter, and a metal worker, and was wise in the ways of the natives; furthermore he had the utmost respect of the Aleuts. He had studied available notes on coastal exploration and was aware of John Meares' report of July 1788, telling of the location of a stockaded Indian village near the vicinity where they had been cast ashore. It was referred to as the village of Queenhithe and was situated on a high, perpendicular rock joined by a narrow and impregnable causeway—leading to a great forest, a natural barrier against the enemy.

Indeed it was not long before the Russian sentries reported seeing half-naked, barefooted natives curiously stalking their encampment.

Tarakanov, seeing that the savages carried spears but no guns, endeavored to converse with them. They were Quillayute Indians, more primitive than the Tlingits, but they spoke a language not too far divorced from the northern Indians, permitting partial understanding. Among them was a chief who insisted his men were only curious, not hostile. Momentarily the barriers were let down, and at a sign from the Indian chief, many ascended from the forests. They invaded the camp, curiously eyeing the people from the sea and especially the golden-haired, blue-eyed Anna Petrovna. To them she was like a goddess from another world; they wanted to touch her strange, fair skin—much to the annoyance of Bulygin.

The natives greedily pawed over the salvaged goods. Tarakanov had warned his men against provoking them, but when they began dragging some of the goods into the forest, tempers flared and some of the Russians struck the intruders. Suddenly mayhem broke out, and the outnumbered Russians found themselves amid a hail of flying spears and stones. Tarakanov was knocked to the ground, and Bulygin was bleeding. Guns were fired, killing three natives outright; others fled to the tall timber.

Fearing for his wife, early the next morning Bulygin insisted that the party begin their seventy-mile trek to Grays Harbor as soon as possible. The injured were patched up and for the remainder of that day, while some stood guard, others continued to salvage items which could be taken with them on foot. The *St. Nicholas* was beyond repair and the only hope of survival was by land—and a rendezvous in December with Kuskov.

The following day every man was issued two muskets and a pistol, while slings were made in which to carry gunpowder. Both men and women were garbed in the warmest skins and parkas available for the long journey. Each of the women was also given food and supplies to carry. One of the last acts before abandoning camp was to destroy everything from the wreck that the Indians might use as a weapon against them.

Even as the procession moved southward along the beach, an angry powwow was being held at the nearby village. The Indians were pledging revenge for their murdered brothers, but despite their anger they had not forgotten the golden-haired Anna. Already they were thinking in terms of the fancy price she would bring as a slave.

The natives fanned out above the beach in large numbers, stalking the southward trek of the Russians. They kept their distance but occasionally would harass the band with a stone or a spear. Bulygin and his comrades were in constant fear of an all-out attack but burdened as they were did not fire. They kept away from the forest and lived, ate, and slept on the beach until, in the midst of a driving rain on November 7, they reached the Hoh River—an impasse.

They would have to have boats to ford the swollen stream. The wise natives had taken this into consideration at their council and here they would have their revenge. The natives on the opposite side of the river had already been alerted. Tarakanov was unaware that among the some two hundred Indians on both sides of the river were several members of the band who had visited their camp.

He called across the river and the natives responded by bringing two canoes over to him. It would take several trips to get the entire party and their gear across the river. Both Bulygin and Tarakanov—on whom Bulygin was becoming increasingly dependent—decided they would cross over last. Anna and the two Aleut women, along with a young Russian student, Filipp Kotelnikov, went over in a small canoe with a single Indian paddler. Nine men with two Indian paddlers followed in the larger craft, their muskets loaded and ready to protect the women when they reached the opposite shore.

In midstream the Indians pulled plugs from the bottom of the larger canoe and leaped overboard, leaving the men virtually helpless. Once again a volley of spears and arrows whizzed over, around, and into the Russians, who tried in vain to paddle against the rising water. Their muskets and powder were soaked and they could not fire back at their attackers. Meanwhile the Indians rushed into the stream and seized the women and ushered them off into the forest as treasured prizes. Suddenly there was a terrible scream from the sinking canoe as one of the Russians was hit in the groin with a spear. The others too were wounded but leaped from the boat and struggled to the river bank from which they had come. Cursing, the Russians picked up the dry muskets and fired, bringing down two natives on the opposite bank of the river. Their badly wounded comrade, pulled from the water, soon died in terrible pain. Bulygin seemed to go to pieces—they had his wife captive and the men were helpless to act. Most of their supplies and armament were gone.

Hastily the Russians collected what guns they could and prepared for the next encounter with the savages. Meanwhile the Indians had gone upriver and crossed back over, intending to massacre the intruders. All the while rain fell in torrents.

Soon the natives approached, two of them with guns, and the battle resumed. The Russians fought with vengeance, making every shot count. Presently the savages retreated and there was a temporary lull in the battle. The Russians used the break to seek shelter in the forest; most of them were suffering from injuries.

Along the way one of their number, writhing in pain from an arrowhead in his stomach, begged to be left behind to die. So Khariton Sobachnikov was abandoned at his own request and his friends hurried deeper into the forest for protection and food. Despite their wounds they struggled on, farther and farther away from the sea. They became exhausted, desperate, and famished. A faithful dog that had remained with them became an evening meal.

Finally another of their number joined Sobachnikov in death. By the time they had reached the high country in the shadow of the Olympics, Bulygin had asked Tarakanov to head the party. Tarakanov got the word in writing and the men voted to go along with the plan. The rendezvous with Kuskov could not now be made, and the men resigned themselves to a winter of hardship on the upper Hoh River.

As they neared their intended encampment they met two Indians who, claiming friendship, offered to sell them whale blubber. They also asked what ransom would be paid for the white lady. Bulygin, overjoyed, offered everything they possessed including their guns and the epaulets on his tattered uniform. But first he would have to see Anna. Then they would decide.

A meeting place was arranged. Anna was brought upriver and the Russian party went downriver, but the rendezvous was on opposite banks. Amid mutual tears Bulygin and his wife talked back and forth across the stream. She assured him that she was unharmed and had been treated well. Bulygin begged his comrades to give the Indians what they wanted that he might get his wife back, but they knew if they surrendered their guns they had no chance of survival.

Bulygin begged, but the best the wiser Tarakanov would do was to offer the demanding chiefs one damaged rifle, whereas they wanted four. Dissatisfied, they took Anna away, and the Russians went back upriver for long, hard weeks of survival in the mountain foothills. It was not until ten months later that they abandoned their isolated home. In February 1809, they came back downriver, this time in a crude river boat they had constructed at their campsite. They planned to cross the Quilla-yute River bar and go out to Destruction Island to keep a vigil for a passing ship, or take their chances in going to the Columbia River.

The building of the boat had helped Bulygin come out of his despondency, and Tarakanov gave him command on the down-river trip. Bulygin supported the plan to get back to civilization until they got near the river mouth; then his burning desire to find his wife changed his mind. The men, however, did not want to risk another battle with the savages. Bulygin finally prevailed and mapped a plan for capturing two natives and holding them for ransom until Anna was returned. (One report claimed that two native women were captured, another, a man and a woman.) The father of one of these natives was of considerable importance in the tribe and begged for a few days' time in which to produce the white woman. He said she had been traded to a chief of the Makahs at Cape Flattery.

The Russians agreed, setting up a breastwork on a side hill with their captives. There they impatiently waited. Finally, on the eighth day, they were informed that a party of Makahs were a mile downstream awaiting a parley. There were fifteen of them including tribal chief Utramaka. Anna was with them. Tarakanov was to be spokesman, while the excited Bulygin remained at the breastwork. The chief was dressed in European clothes with a fur cap which he had acquired from a shipwreck, or through trading with fur buyers.

Tarakanov was startled to see that Anna was as beautiful as ever. She appeared in good health, was well dressed, and was wearing moccasins. Her golden hair was neatly groomed and she appeared in excellent spirits—undoubtedly the favorite wife of the chief. She informed Tarakanov that she had no intention of relinquishing her role for one of suffering and privation. Instead she pleaded with Tarakanov to tell her husband and the others to give themselves up to the Makahs; she said they would be treated kindly as she had been and that ships would eventually come to the Cape Flattery area to ransom them.

Tarakanov returned to the breastwork to inform Bulygin. On hearing the report, Bulygin fell to his knees sobbing. He begged Tarakanov to speak again with Anna. But Anna remained firm; she no longer feared death nor the threats of her husband. Again Tarakanov returned to his camp to impart the final word to Bulygin, who, now in despair, began sobbing afresh and would not be consoled.

Meanwhile Tarakanov had considered Anna's advice and decided that it might be the only way to survive. In the discussion that followed, some of the men sided with Tarakanov but others elected to continue on with the boat. Each man was allowed to make his own decision, and the favored report is that Bulygin finally sided in with Tarakanov. The two groups separated amicably, each wishing the other God's help.

On the following day the Indian captives were returned and the Makah chief assured Tarakanov that his men, if they surrendered, would be treated as Anna had said. After Tarakanov and his followers had departed with the Makahs, the others launched their boat and made a run across the river bar toward Destruction Island. A strong wind prevailed and en route the boat was carried on the rocks and capsized. The men were thrown into the vortex and all their provisions lost. Pursuing Indian canoes plucked them from the water and took them captive. This time there was no escape and all the remaining Russians were now in the hands of the natives. The Quillayutes sold one Russian and an Aleut to Indians on the Columbia River and the others to Makahs.

Tarakanov was taken to a village near Cape Flattery called Koonistchat and Bulygin was delivered to a village at Ozette. At first all the captives were well treated but the fickle Indians soon tired of their charges and began trading them about from one tribe to another.

Only Anna and Tarakanov remained with their original owners. The latter had become indispensable because of his skill in making tools, knives, and toys; he even invented a signal for warning the tribe of battle. Meanwhile months passed and no ships came.

Then, one sad day, Anna was traded to another and became the property of a cruel and demanding chief. Her dignity and spirit finally broke, and she is believed to have committed suicide. The chief to whom she belonged had her body dragged into the forest and left there without burial.

When the tragic news reached Bulygin, he had lost his will to live and in February of the following year, in poor health, he too died; but not Tarakanov. He never gave up hope and with the knowledge that the season was near when the ships sailing from New Archangel would be passing off the entrance to the strait, he devised a crude kite and told the natives that he was sending messages to the great white father. They were so impressed that some thought he should be a chief; his kite could even top the fog banks.

Finally in May of 1810, the Boston brig *Lydia*, skippered by Captain J. Brown, entered the strait and anchored off Neah Bay. Tarakanov managed to get aboard, only to meet his comrade Afanasii Valgusov, one of his old shipmates who had been ransomed from a tribe on the Columbia. Valgusov told Tarakanov that one of the Aleuts from the *St. Nicholas* had also been rescued earlier by Captain George Ayers of the *Mercury*.

For each captive of the Russian ship, the master of the *Lydia* offered the Indian chiefs five blankets, twelve yards of cloth, a saw, a mirror, two knives, five bags of powder, and five of shot. Within a few days, gaunt survivors straggled in. Some of the chiefs tried to hold out for more ransom but the captain put an end to this practice by seizing one of their number and putting him in irons. In short order the original agreement was adhered to and most of the survivors were freed. There was great rejoicing at New Archangel on their return.

Of the original twenty who sailed aboard the *St. Nicholas* under Captain Bulygin, all but seven survived—each with his own tale to tell of fear and sufferings in a raw wilderness among savage natives.

ORIENTAL JUNKS

It was indeed an historic occasion when, in the year 1853, Commodore Matthew Calbraith Perry opened Japan to the world at large. Prior to that time Japan had for centuries been a "hermit nation" whose trade with other countries was closed by Imperial edict: "Let none, so long as the sun illuminates the world, presume to sail to Japan . . . on pain of death." Except for a few uninvited Portuguese and Dutch traders, the doors to Japan had remained sealed.

Trade with Japan, however, was rich in potential and the United States Congress authorized an expedition there in 1845. Although even friendly visits from England, France, Russia, and Portugal had been rebuffed, the United States decided on a show of force; the dangers of an appeal to the Emperor were risked by armed vessels. Commodore Perry's expedition was the third attempt under Congressional authorization. American war vessels had first entered a Japanese port seven years earlier, under Commodore James Biddle, who had been sent over with the *Vincennes* and the *Columbus*. His proposals for a treaty were rejected and his ships towed out of Yedo (Tokyo) Bay. In 1849, however, when Commodore James Glynn sailed into the bay for the purpose of freeing American prisoners, he frightened the Japanese into meeting his demands.

Aboard his flagship, the steam frigate *Mississippi*, Perry sailed from Norfolk on November 24, 1852. On April 6, 1853, in Hong Kong, he gathered the rest of his fleet: the frigate *Saratoga*, the storeship *Supply*, and the sloop-of-war *Plymouth*. These ships were joined by the steamer *Susquehanna*, which became the flagship, and the sloop *Vandalia*. This formidable fleet arrived in Yedo Bay off Uraga, Japan, in July. To the Japanese the vessels were the black ships of evil omen, but these same vessels were largely responsible for opening Japan's "closed door."

Prior to this time, Japanese sailors, though unsolicited and unwilling, had been swept across the mighty Pacific by a phenomenon known as Kuroshio, the Japanese Current. Literally scores of Japanese junks and a scattering of Chinese junks became disabled off their respective shores and were carried by this great "black stream" within the ocean on a one-way voyage to Pacific Northwest shores. Many of these craft deposited crews of dead men. A few others left survivors, but privation, exposure, disease, and starvation took a heavy toll and often, if there were survivors, these were either murdered or taken into slavery by hostile savages.

Though the ancient migration of Orientals undoubtedly was across the top of the world, where Siberia and Alaska almost touch, there were many castaways who evidently survived and intermarried with the natives of North America.

One of the rare recorded incidents of this type which happened within the shadow of Cape Flattery was reported in the *Journal of Occurrences* kept at Fort Nisqually in 1834. The *Journal* records the efforts of Captain William McNeil, master of the British brig *Llama*, who was instrumental in ransoming the survivors of this wreck from the Makah Indians.

This particular junk was a large cargo-carrying type which had filled her holds at Yokohama with rice, nankeen, and porcelain destined for merchants in other Japanese ports. Just after her departure, she was struck by a typhoon. Gale-like winds and devastating seas damaged her sails and rigging and carried her rapidly out of the bay into open water. The junk drifted away almost unnoticed while the land was buffeted with the fury of the storm. She was swept far to sea as her crew tried in vain to make repairs. But the rudder had been damaged and with every passing day she was carried farther and farther away from her homeland.

Her crew knew nothing of the lands that lay beyond and all were stricken with fear. They were able to sustain life by dipping into the great quantities of rice in the cargo and catching an occasional fish, but during the long months that followed, disease broke out among them, to add to their miseries. For over a year the vessel drifted ever eastward with the current. When land was finally sighted only three of the crew remained alive.

A few days later their frail craft was driven in among the breakers just south of Cape Flattery, where it partially broke up on the rocks before being carried up on the sands. The three Japanese struggled ashore and were quickly taken as slaves by the Makahs. The savages then swarmed over the wreck removing everything of value.

The terrified souls from the land of Nippon eventually made some friends among the natives, who helped them smuggle out a piece of paper containing a crude drawing of the wreck with stick-figures of Indians swarming about it. This was passed from hand to hand until it eventually found its way to principals of the Hudson's Bay Company at Fort Nisqually. Undoubtedly the junk was wrecked in 1833, as it was not until January 27, 1834, that an Indian finally brought the news that a strange vessel had been wrecked near Cape Flattery and all on board lost except three.

William Ouvrie, a French-Canadian who was the most trustworthy man about the place, was immediately dispatched with an Indian companion to rescue them if possible. The first day after he had started on the canoe journey he was overtaken by one of the most severe storms ever known in the Puget Sound country. The oldest Indians could not remember any to parallel it. Part of the palisade at the fort was blown down, and much damage done to the buildings. For some days considerable anxiety was felt for Ouvrie and his companion, but they were experienced canoemen and suffered no harm. The two men returned on

February 7, to report that since the Clallams near Port Discovery had heard of no wreck, there probably had been none.

The truth was not learned until four months later. The *Journal of Occurrences* records that on the afternoon of June 9, about 2 p.m., a cannon shot was heard at the fort from the neighborhood of the Narrows, and that a Hudson's Bay official named Heron put off in a canoe with six men and went on board the *Llama*. There he "had the pleasure of taking tea with Captain McNeil, who pointed out two 'Chinese' (Japanese) he had picked up from the natives near Cape Flattery, where a vessel of that nation had been wrecked not long since. There is still one [survivor] among the Indians inland, but a promise was made of getting the poor fellow on the coast by the time the *Llama* gets there."

This promise the Indians kept and the third Japanese survivor was eventually rescued.

It was not until later that Captain McNeil, who had actually seen the remains of the wrecked junk, was informed that the survivors were not Chinese, but Japanese. The third survivor had been traded to tribes away from the cape and it was some time before McNeil was able to rescue him after paying ransom. The three were taken to Fort Vancouver and placed in the charge of Dr. John McLoughlin and Thomas McKay, who treated them well and even tried to school them in the English way of living. They were eventually placed aboard a ship bound for England. Subsequently they were sent back to their native country but were not allowed to land because the Japanese law at that time forbade any resident who should leave the country from returning to it. Finally, however, through diplomatic channels the men were allowed to go home.

In 1639 the Japanese government decreed that all junks must be built with open sterns and large square rudders, which were actually unfit for ocean navigation. Once the junks were forced from the coast, the rudders washed away. The Shogun ruler of the nation, Iyemitsu, also commanded the destruction of all boats built in the foreign style.

How many hapless Japanese were thus swept across to North American shores in early times is, of course, impossible to know, but it may be assumed that happenings of this kind were not infrequent. Up till 1875, some hundred Oriental junks are known to have been found adrift, or castaway on Pacific shores—not unusual when one considers that almost 23,000 junks ranging up to 400 tons were registered in Japan's coasting trades in that year. These junks carried mostly fish and rice and were manned by crews of from eight to twelve men. Down through the ages thousands of junks must have been lost in the Pacific.

There is an account of the arrival on the California Coast many years ago of a Japanese vessel containing a man, a woman, and a Buddhist priest. Hawaiian history records that a long time ago, probably as early as the thirteenth century, a Japanese craft reached those islands at Kabului Bay, and her crew remained there, inter-marrying with the natives; also that a Spanish ship, probably one of those sent by Cortez, was wrecked there, the only survivors having been the captain and his sister. These survivors were welcomed by the natives and elevated to the rank of chiefs.

Countless numbers of castaway Japanese are believed to have taken up life among the coastal Indians of British Columbia and the Northwest Coast in ages past. History tells of enslavements and infusion of languages among the tribes.

Evidence in the present decade was uncovered by two anthropologists working with the Smithsonian Institution regarding evidence that Japanese landed in the New World as early at 3000 B.C., or even before. Their evidence was based on a discovery by Emilio Estrada in 1961, an Ecuadorian amateur archeologist working in an excavation near the town of Valdivia, Ecuador. His finding was only a fragment of reddish pottery but there was something very distinctive about it; it had an oddly marked protuberant rim.

According to the Smithsonian scientists, in an article in *Scientific American*, that pottery fragment was found in a site calculated to go back between 2300 and 3000 B.C. They wrote, "At a time as early as that, this form of pot rim is rare anywhere in the world except Japan. There it commonly occurs on pottery of the prehistoric Jomon period." From that clue, the scientists began looking at other shreds of pottery at the Valdivia site and found a large number of additional similarities between Valdivian pottery and Jomon pottery from Japan.

These scientists—Betty J. Meggers, research associate of the Smithsonian's division of cultural anthropology, and Clifford Evans, curator—speculated that a fishing craft, caught in a typhoon off the coast of Japan, was swept away in the prevailing ocean currents, swinging first northeast, then southeast, on an 8,000-mile arc across the Pacific to what is today the coast of Ecuador. They believed that the Japanese probably never returned home to report their discovery, probably having become victims of ill winds and ocean currents. There appears to be ample evidence, according to this report, that the Japanese were in the Americas as long as five thousand years ago.

RYO YEI MARU

The Japanese Current has never changed its course; this same massive sweep of water annually casts Oriental fish floats, burial urns, and flotsam and jetsam of every description upon our Northwest shores. As late as October 31, 1927, it cast a helpless Japanese vessel into the watery acres off the Strait of Juan de Fuca. Had she not been taken in tow by a passing freighter she too would have crashed ashore.

The vessel was sighted by the lookout aboard the transpacific freighter *Margaret Dollar*, Captain H. T. Payne. The ship's master immediately dispatched a boarding party to the derelict to investigate. The scene that greeted them was not a pleasant one. There was not a living soul aboard, only the grim remains of some dead men—victims of disease, exposure, and starvation.

She was the Japanese motor fishing vessel *Ryo Yei* (Ryoei) *Maru,* an 85-foot, 100-tonner from Misaki, Japan. Carrying a crew of twelve, she had departed on a fishing junket from her homeport on December 5, 1926. Nearly a year later she was sighted south of Cape Flattery by the *Dollar* and taken in tow for Port Townsend. The crude Japanese-inscribed log recorded that the vessel had developed engine trouble a few days after leaving port. Before this could be corrected, a typhoon caught the craft, sending it on its months-long, 4,000-mile drift across the Pacific. At Port Townsend the quarantine officer said there was little doubt that cannibalism had been resorted to in the face of starvation.

A smooth board found on the vessel bore the names of the crewmen. At the bottom of it the captain had written, "Our last hope is gone. We have no more food. We are lost." A small wicker trunk on the vessel held a diary recounting some of the grim experiences during the long drift. The entry for December 15 stated that a ship was sighted coming from the north and that all flags were hoisted but the ship passed without noticing them. On the following day, the *Sumi Maru* of Toyo Kisen Kaisha was noted as coming toward them from the south. Considering this as Heaven's special grace, they hoisted two flags and made a fire, but the vessel sailed away.

Though the occasion was not recorded in the diary, Captain Richard Healy of the American freighter *West Isom* reported that he crossed paths with the distressed *Ryo Yei Maru* on December 23 and offered to remove the men from their craft, but they refused to abandon ship and asked to be towed to port. Because of the course of the freighter this request was denied and the Japanese elected to remain with their troubled vessel.

The next significant diary entry occurred a week later. On the first day of January 1927, the crew celebrated the new year with a meal of rice mixed with red beans, and conversed till midnight.

The days dragged on, according to the account, and the sails were blown almost to ribbons. On January 27, they passed near a foreign liner and signaled her with fire but she continued on without acknowledgment.

On February 13, one of the fishermen, by name Hatsuzo, was reported in his eighth day of sickness; and on March 9, Dinjira Hosoi, the engineer, died. That same day, Tsunetaro Naoe and a man called Gennosuka were confined to their bunks, too weak to move. Three days later, at noon, Naoe died and on March 17, Suteji Izawa followed him in death.

The diary skips to March 27, when there is the terse announcement that fishermen Terada and Yokata have succumbed. Two days later, Tokichi Kuada, the mate, perished at 9 a.m., and by noon the next day Torakichi Mitani, another fisherman, expired.

On April 5, the master of the vessel, Captain Tokizo Miki, caught a large bird, which was served as an evening meal; but it proved of no help to Ryoji Tsujiuchi, who died about midnight after several days of suffering.

A note of hope appears on April 14, when the wind ceased and in the calm they landed a shark for food. That same morning Yukichi Tsumemitse perished, followed five days later by a crewman named Kamite. On May 6, Captain Miki was reported seriously ill. On the following day the writer of the diary complained bitterly of his ailment beriberi and said that he had ceased to take food. By the next day the disease had attacked his left hand and he was unable to move it.

Three days later the vessel was reported drifting without a helmsman; only the skipper and the writer remained alive and both were very ill. The last entry was made on May 11: "Wind northwest, weather cloudy, wind fresh, sea rough, drifting with sails hoisted." The diarist mentioned that he was worried about the scolding of Captain Miki but did not elaborate. There was no more, but imagination will suffice.

When the *Dollar* took the derelict in tow, her hull was encrusted with four inches of barnacles and seaweed, and only a tattered fragment of sail hung from one of her two masts. At the request of the vessel's owners, the partially decomposed remains of the dead were cremated in Buddhist rites at Seattle. The vessel and what it contained were burned on March 28 at nearby Richmond Beach, ending a grisly tale of horror with overtones of cannibalism.

EARLY BRITISH TRAGEDIES

The winter gales that whip across the entrance to the Strait of Juan de Fuca are something to behold and to respect. The British were soon to learn this, for such storms exacted a large toll from their early ships. Driving rains from the south or stinging sleet and snow from the north can quickly churn these waters into a frenzy.

In the mid-nineteenth century, two fine British trading vessels came to grief in the area of Cape Flattery. The first, lost in 1851, was the brigantine *Una,* one of the Hudson's Bay Company's coasting vessels of about two hundred tons. In the previous year, following gold discoveries in the Queen Charlotte Islands, this company had sent the *Una* there from Fort Simpson to investigate. The yield had been grossly exaggerated and on her return passage from the north, the vessel was caught in contrary, storm-lashed seas. On December 26, she was wrecked in the shadow of Cape Flattery.

Meanwhile the 103-ton trading schooner *Damariscove,* commanded by the intrepid Captain Lafayette Balch, was returning from the Queen Charlotte Islands, where he had been sent by Collector of Customs Simpson P. Moses to rescue the captive company of the sloop *Georgianna.* The *Georgianna,* commanded by Captain William Rowland during the summer of 1851, had posted the following hand-written appeal while his vessel outfitted at Olympia:

Last Chance for A Gold Strike

Early in November the safe and commodious sloop *Georgianna,* owned and operated by Captain William Rowland, will leave Olympia for the new gold fields at

Gold Harbor, Queen Charlotte Island. The sloop has accommodations for a number of miners. Terms can be had from Captain Rowland, who has rich samples showing the character of the ground. Make reservations before it is too late. If unsuccessful, your passage money will be refunded.

The 45-ton sloop had sailed in from Australia and her skipper had collected some specimens of ore said to be from the Queen Charlottes. This was proof enough to get him twenty-two passengers and a crew of five. The ill-timed voyage was beset by storms from the start and, outbound, the vessel was forced to take refuge in Neah Bay. Also stormbound at Neah Bay was Captain Balch's *Damariscove*. He, too, was headed for the Queen Charlotte gold fields. The vessels anchored side by side and exchanged greetings.

After leaving the bay, the *Georgianna* was driven eastward from her course, and on trying to work her way back was cast ashore in a gale among hostile Haida Indians of the Queen Charlottes. They quickly descended on the wreck, plundering and burning it and capturing the crew. The survivors were treated as slaves and made to supply the Indian lodges with wood and water, all the while living under deplorable conditions.

By promising to arrange a generous reward for their release, one of the survivors, Stephen D. Howe, was allowed to go to Fort Simpson. Seven Haidas took him by canoe to this Hudson's Bay post.

Meanwhile Captain Balch, finding that the *Georgianna* had not arrived at Gold Harbor, started south along the coast to search for her. He soon discovered the desperate plight of her company but was unable to offer any immediate help. He made a fast passage back to Puget Sound and informed Collector of Customs Moses of the situation. Since no United States government vessel was nearer than San Francisco, Moses on his own authority chartered the *Damariscove* and commissioned Balch to effect the rescue. The schooner was fitted with four cannon plus twenty-five picked men, in addition to the regular crew and the supplies for ransom.

The vessel sailed on December 9 and made good time to Gold Harbor. A ransom of five blankets, two shirts, one bolt of muslin, and two pounds of tobacco was paid for each captive, all of whom were finally freed after fifty-four days of captivity.

It was undoubtedly on the way back from this mission that the *Damariscove's* master learned of the wreck of the *Una.* The British vessel had stranded in the throes of adverse winds and heavy seas, and with anchors failing to hold had gone ashore west of Neah Bay under lofty Cape Flattery. The natives here— the Makahs—were friendly and helped the survivors ashore; but as soon as the tide ebbed, they considered the wreck as their personal property and began looting cargo and fittings despite the protests of the ship's master, Captain William Mitchell.

Mitchell had been long in the employ of the Hudson's Bay Company. On the West Coast since 1836, he had served as master of the company vessels *Cadboro, Recovery, Una,* and *Beaver.* Though acquainted with the ways of the savages, he was helpless in his present situation; he had no way of enforcing his wishes. From fear of retaliation, however, he held his peace and admonished the others to do the same. Even as the natives swarmed over the wreck, stripping off her copper and fittings, Captain Balch brought his *Damariscove* to anchor and rescued the survivors.

Collector Moses' fast action in sending a rescue ship for the *Georgianna* company proved an expensive undertaking, so expensive, in fact, that its propriety was questioned by the Treasury Department on the grounds that the rescue should not even have been attempted by Moses, but rather by the territorial officers of Washington or by the Navy. The cost of the rescue was $11,017.01, according to a report rendered by Moses. It was not until months later that he was finally reimbursed for his humanitarian act.

It is interesting to note that the schooner *Damariscove*, owned by Captain Lafayette Balch and Cyrus Palmer, became the first commercial American flag vessel enrolled in the Customs District of Puget Sound; it was the twenty-fourth day of May 1852. The vessel also held the first coasting license issued at Olympia, April 20, 1850.

The happy ending to the wreck of the *Una* was in sharp contrast to that of another British vessel, the bark *Lord Raglan*. This vessel had taken on a full cargo of piling and lumber at Sooke, B. C., and was outbound for England in June of 1854. Aboard the vessel were the Reverend Robert John Staines and his wife Emma. Staines had been the first minister of the Gospel at Victoria, having arrived there in March 1849, aboard the bark *Columbia*. He was also a leader of the Independents on Vancouver Island, demanding free land grants as in Oregon. He was on his way to England to place a petition before the Crown for such a measure, having retired from his preaching and teaching post on June 1 of that year.

The *Raglan* moved down the strait and rounded Cape Flattery and Tatoosh Island into the slanting rain of a high-velocity southerly gale. Buffeted by tremendous seas, the bark was last seen at dusk by another sailing vessel which reported that seas were breaking over the *Raglan's* heavy deckload when it was last sighted. By the following day the *Lord Raglan* had literally vanished from the sea.

Reports that the bark was missing with all hands including her six passengers came as shocking news to landsmen. It is believed that the vessel foundered in deep water south of Tatoosh Island. The only clues were some pieces of wreckage that later came ashore on the West Coast of Vancouver Island.

ORDEAL OF THE SOUTHERNER

In that same year of 1854, troublesome seas caused two other ships to come to grief, and both times Cape Flattery served as the tombstone. History has little to say about the first of these, the sailing vessel *Duchess San Lorenzo*, lost in March; but the other, the steamer *Southerner*, received widespread publicity, having been the first steam-powered vessel to be lost in the area.

The coastline south of Cape Flattery to Cape Alava on the Washington Coast has virtually no permanent population, and even the savages who once inhabited the coastal slab-board villages are gone. Much of the area is still Indian reservation land, and some is under jurisdiction of the Olympic National Park. For the most part, it has remained a wilderness area. To learn how this region looked back in 1854, one has only to hike several miles through the surrounding virgin forests and along the rugged beaches.

Late that year, the steamer *Southerner* was methodically port-hopping up the coast from California. The 339-ton vessel, her two sidewheels beating the water, had departed San Francisco in command of Captain F. A. Sampson. After dropping in and out of the ports of Eureka and Crescent City, she continued northward with a disappointing passenger list of twenty-eight and a crew of nineteen. The reputation of the North Pacific during winter months was well known in those early years, and the bulk of the tourists awaited spring and summer for sea travel. But the *Southerner's* schedule had to be maintained, and what cargo could be garnered en route helped defray the expenses.

Because of worsening weather, the stops at Port Orford and Umpqua on the Oregon Coast had to be eliminated; the bars were impassable. As the fury of the seas mounted, seasickness kept the passengers' staterooms occupied and the dining saloon empty. The steamer pitched and rolled so violently that her ancient timbers creaked in every joint. The years had told on her and she was far removed from the days when she had served under the name *Isthmus* on the Panama Canal run.

By 10 a.m., Christmas Day, she was in the latitude of Tillamook Bay, and Captain Sampson hoped to get across the bar to find refuge for his passengers. Holiday greetings were completely ignored and the cook had only a few members of the crew to taste his culinary efforts, created under the most difficult circumstances. Finding Tillamook a solid mass of breakers, the *Southerner* pressed on northward to the entrance of the Columbia River. At this point a nervous jingle was heard from the engine room. When Captain Sampson picked up the speaking tube, a voice said, "Clayton calling . . . Skipper, we got a bad leak down here."

The captain gravely counseled: "Do the best you can, Chief, we'll try to get across the bar."

Through the rain-smeared pilothouse windows the bar appeared a foaming, hissing mass. Sampson waited till 6 p.m., but the seas did not improve. Then, trusting to blind luck, he headed for the Strait of Juan de Fuca. He signalled the engine room and asked, "How's it going down there?"

"Not so good," came the answer. "Pumps can't keep ahead of the inflow. If we don't get some relief soon, it'll be up to the boilers."

The following day, as the vessel labored up the Washington Coast, the engines were barely turning over, and the passengers were as sick as they were terrified. Many had begged the captain to run the ship ashore. He, however, was one step ahead of them, having ordered the quartermaster to bring the steamer in as close to the rock-ribbed coast as he dared. He was aware that the engine could go out at any time and that water was beginning to flow through the vessel's seams like a small river. She was settling ever lower in the water.

As eerie dusk formed on December 26 and leaden clouds sent wind-driven rain against the hapless ship, which by this time had the appearance of a submarine. The water was already filtering into the boilers, and hissing white steam was driving the black gang topside. The pumps were chocked. The passengers grew more insistent that the captain put the ship ashore. Some even made outright threats. As a precaution, Officer J. L. Foster was ordered to keep a gun handy.

None was more aware of the tight predicament than the shipmaster. He was responsible for his passengers, his crew, and his command—and at this point the odds were stacked against him. What should he do?

With the steamer's forward progress all but stopped, he was forced to drop anchor in seven fathoms, ten miles southeast of Cape Flattery, off Mukkaw Bay. Still open to the full fury of the gale, the stricken steamer began dragging anchor, and the stern started to drop. As the ship settled, huge seas swept over her decks. At this point some of the passengers threatened the captain. The mate reached for his gun and harsh words were exchanged. "The next man that crosses this line will be put in irons," the captain warned.

The *Southerner's* engine had now ceased to function and her feeble sails had been blown to rags. As wind-scoured seas mingled with pulsating ground swells, the half-sunken vessel began to list badly. Mild panic broke out. Then suddenly the laboring ship was elevated by a massive sea and swept broadside onto the beach. As the fury of the breakers lashed her wooden sides, what kept her from being smashed to kindling was nothing short of a miracle. The quick thinking of the captain and the fast action of the crew—chopping down the masts, dismantling the stack, and throwing overboard heavy pieces of cargo and gear—permitted the craft to gain some stability. She was lightened enough for the breakers to push her higher on the sandy beach, and by morning she rested up among the driftwood, the tide having ebbed away from her battered timbers, recoiling for another assault. The survivors could hardly believe they were alive; all had been spared.

The prospect of the rugged overland trip ahead didn't seem quite so bad now. Trudging over rocks and fallen trees and through ravines, they came at last to the Indian settlement at Neah Bay, where they found refuge until the arrival of a rescue vessel.

The old *Southerner* had remained intact just long enough to spare her grateful company. There was, however, no such sentiment in the hearts of the Indians. On report of the wreck, the Makahs raced to the site. Pioneer writer and historian James Swan, who lived among the tribe for several months, recalls how the wreck afforded a rich harvest of iron, copper, and engineers' tools. He recorded that the wreck lay thirty miles south of Cape Flattery, farther south than listed by the survivors—which leads to the assumption that likely more than one wreck was involved; perhaps some of the remains of the missing *Duchess San Lorenzo.*

DISAPPEARANCE OF THE BRIG HODGDON

In the fall of 1855, construction men were working on the urgently needed Cape Flattery Lighthouse at Tatoosh Island. One day they saw the abandoned wreck of a vessel slip by in the murk and crash ashore on the mainland near the island. It appeared to have been thoroughly pounded by the seas—a ghost ship stripped of masts, rigging, and housing, and piloted by unseen hands. The vessel was not identified, nor was a guess made as to what she might be. Unfortunately the men could not leave the island because the supply ship was away and the sea was too angry for a small boat to venture out.

On the arrival of the supply vessel, the islanders told about the ghost ship. Gradually pieces of the story began to fit together. The brig *Hodgdon* had earlier sailed from Victoria en route to San Francisco. After rounding Cape Flattery, she had run head on into a full gale and was never again reported. And the description of the waterlogged brig that was seen passing Tatoosh closely matched the *Hodgdon.* The same gale was also responsible for the near-sinking of the passenger steamship *California,* which limped into port half full of water and badly damaged from the onslaught.

FOG PLAGUES THE LIZZIE BOGGS
AND THE HATTIE C. BESSIE

South of Cape Flattery in 1867 and 1871, dense fog was responsible for the loss of two fine early-day American sailing vessels.

The four-masted American bark *Lizzie Boggs,* 445 tons, was feeling her way up the coast from San Francisco bound for Port Discovery, Washington, in early September of 1867. An almost impenetrable shroud of fog hung over the coast. As the bark approached the Strait of Juan de Fuca, Shipmaster Captain Townsend reckoned he was about ten miles south of Cape Flattery, but just how close he was to shore he could not determine. The wind had slackened and the sails hung limp. The crew had their ears trained for the sound of breakers or the drone of a ship's foghorn. There had been much agitation for a fog signal at Tatoosh Island but unfortunately this aid was still four years off, and the island continued to be a dangerous barrier marking a vital turning point in this area. It was always a worry to the navigator when the weather thickened.

Now, with the *Lizzie Boggs* alone in a blotted-out world and an almost silent sea, the stillness was suddenly split by the distant roar of breakers. At the captain's orders the crew swarmed about the deck and into the rigging in an effort to bring the ship about. The helm was put hard over but the lack of wind to fill the canvas and the inward sweep of the current soon had the vessel thumping on the shoals and heaving crazily with each thundering comber. Her timbers shivered and groaned, the deck buckled, and the masts canted at grotesque angles. When the rigging pulled loose the men panicked.

Captain Townsend ordered all hands to lower a boat on the lee side away from the raging surf. Then, after checking to see that all his men were in the boat, he himself jumped aboard and lowered away. The little craft shot upward on a convulsive, mountainous swell that for a moment threatened to smash it against the faltering sides of the *Lizzie Boggs.* With herculean effort, backs and arms straining, the men pulled at the oars and finally got clear of the ship.

Unable to make a landing through the wild surf, they passed around the stern of the *Boggs* and put out to sea. The captain steered, hugging the shore as closely as he dared. He stayed just

within the sound of the breakers until he had rounded Cape
Flattery. When finally inside the strait and into safe harborage
at Neah Bay, all were picked up by the Hawaiian bark *Ava* and
taken to Victoria.

Almost a carbon copy of the *Lizzie Boggs* tragedy was that of
the American bark *Hattie C. Besse,* on November 20, 1871. The
loss was regretted especially by the marine people on the Columbia River, for the *Besse* had the distinction of being the first
commercial four-masted wind ship to enter the Columbia.

In command of Captain James H. Gragg, the ill-fated sailing
vessel was en route to Burrard's Inlet to load lumber for Shanghai. She was well known for transporting Chinese coolies to the
West Coast from the Orient, and on several voyages had carried
more than 385 in her cramped 'tween decks. She also carried
some back; two years before her loss she departed for Hong
Kong with a cargo of "old iron," broken glass, Yankee notions for
Chinese use, bones of defunct Celestials, and nearly two hundred
Chinese passengers. Then, in 1870, she brought 387 coolies from
the Orient to join Ben Holladay's all-out effort to complete the
historic Oregon and California Railroad. Other square-riggers
imported railroad iron for the job which, on completion, did
much to open the West.

On her ill-fated voyage, the *Besse* was dangerously near the
shore, about twenty miles south of Cape Flattery. The vessel
drifted ever closer to the fog-shrouded land, and at the sound of
roaring breakers, her anchors were dropped. The motion of the
sea snapped the anchor cable and the ship came down suddenly
on top of an inundated rock which tore her bottom planking
amidships. It was as if floodgates had been opened. Two seamen,
caught in the maelstrom as water rushed over the decks, were
seriously injured.

A heavy sea was running and the frantic crew did not even
have time to gather their personal belongings. They did, however, get the injured seamen into the boat. Then hurriedly pulling
away, they watched through murk as the *Hattie C. Besse* broke

in two. Resting on their oars, they drifted in the sea of fog. Many hours later they were picked up by the passing southbound steamer *California* and safely conducted to Portland, Oregon.

Meanwhile news of the wreck had reached Port Townsend by word of mouth and the Revenue Cutter *Lincoln* was dispatched to the scene. The wreck had come ashore twenty miles southeast of Tatoosh Island but by the time the cutter arrived it had been well broken up by the pounding surf. The rescue vessel carefully hunted the area for survivors, unaware that they had been picked up by the *California*. The *Besse* was valued at $40,000 but was insured for only $15,000.

WRECK OF THE STEAMER PACIFIC

In the mid-1870s, occurred one of the most important advances in Pacific Northwest water transportation: securing regular steamship service between Puget Sound (Seattle) and San Francisco. The initial vessel placed on the run was the veteran steamship *Pacific*, of the North Pacific Transportation Company, commanded by Captain Jefferson Davis Howell. Howell was a near relative of the President of the Southern Confederacy, Jefferson Davis. Howell's nautical experience had begun on the privateer *Alabama*, when Captain Raphael Semmes was engaged in exterminating American commerce on the Atlantic Ocean.

Puget Sounders were elated over their dependable link with San Francisco after years of hit-and-miss water transportation, but the *Pacific* had made only a few voyages on the new run when there occurred one of the most regrettable sea disasters in North Pacific history. The date was November 4, 1875.

The *Pacific* was berthed at Victoria, B. C., after arrival from Seattle. It was almost sailing time and there was much excitement on the dock as the ship prepared to depart for San Francisco. As many times as Captain Howell had witnessed this scene it never ceased to thrill him. For a late fall voyage his vessel carried a sizable load of eager, lighthearted passengers and a goodly shipment of freight. A colorful serpentine wound from the steamer to the dock as the time for departure neared.

Captain Howell walked into the pilothouse and picked up the speaking tube for word from his chief engineer, H. F. Houston. "How's it down there?" he asked.

"Got a good head of steam and raring to go," the chief answered with his usual joviality. Howell glanced at the clock. It was 9:25 a.m. Just then the quartermaster pulled the whistle cord as a warning to all remaining visitors to go ashore. The skipper went into the chart room to look over his course. After a few minutes he hastened to the bridge and, using the megaphone, ordered the deckhands to stand by the lines. First officer, McDonough, then informed the shipmaster that the gangplank had been hoisted; second officer, Wells, reported that the cargo had been properly stowed.

As the deep droan of the whistle echoed along the waterfront, black smoke filtered through the stack and the vessel was under way. The lines were dropped and she quietly edged out from the dock. Soon the calls of the crowd faded and the skyline of the little port grew smaller. Tugboats and sailing craft in the bay were quickly lost to sight.

The skipper ordered half ahead as they moved out of the harbor and into the strait. Leaving the pilothouse, he went below for consultation with the purser. Going over the passenger list, he became confused as to just how many persons were aboard. There had been a number of last-minute tickets purchased by miners out of the Cassiar district, anxious to get home. Purser O. Hyte, Jr., showed the captain a list of about 132 persons who secured tickets from the Victoria agent, plus another list of thirty-five who had embarked at Puget Sound ports. There were, in addition, another twenty or more persons to whom Hyte had sold tickets at the last minute without bothering to get their names. While the captain censured the purser, one of the deckhands entered the cabin and informed him that several stowaways had jumped aboard just as the steamer pulled away from

Walter P. Miller

Left: Picked up by the tug *Angeles* off Cape Flattery in 1926 was the waterlogged schooner *Alice Cooke,* victim of a storm in Juan de Fuca's graveyard.

Right: Here off Cape Flattery is one of the last of the square-riggers to fly the American flag—the *Tusitala* breasting a swell in 1929.

Pounded into submission in a gale some 50 miles off Cape Flattery, in December 1894, the American bark *Southern Chief* was abandoned at sea.

Japanese SS *Canada Maru* grounded in a heavy fog just south of Cape Flattery, February 31, 1918, with 176 passengers aboard and a $4-million cargo of raw silk.

Victim of driving winds and turbulent seas, the Chilean bark *Carelmapu*, in November 1915, was first in distress off Pachena Point.

After weathering a terrific gale off the west coast of Vancouver Island, the Panamanian MS *Beulah* arrived at Victoria on a 31-degree list. Shortly thereafter she sank at dockside—December 27, 1937.

Diving into a mountainous swell off Cape Flattery is the powerful Canadian tug *Lorne*, towing the British ship *Thistlebank* into the strait around the turn of the century.

Stranded on Waada Island off Neah Bay, September 1, 1910, the SS *Watson*––a coastwise passenger and cargo ship––was a victim of heavy fog.

In recent years, the yacht *Phoebe* was driven ashore south of Cape Flattery and became the target of a salvage controversy. The vessel was ashore on Indian reservation land.

the dock. They were believed hiding below where forty coolies were accommodated in steerage.

Captain Howell was obviously annoyed by the thought of a pack of stowaways aboard but he had no intention of putting back to port.

After checking his course later in the day, he went down to the dining saloon to eat and to meet some of the more prominent passengers. Among them was S. P. Moody, principal owner of Burrard's Inlet Sawmills. Then there were several theatrical people, including Jennie (Mandeville) Parsons and her brother Cal Mandeville. Fred D. Hard, postal agent for all the Washington Territory, was aboard; also F. Garesche, a well-known Victoria banker, and a host of others. All seemed to be in good spirits and anticipating a smooth voyage to San Francisco.

After leaving the dining saloon, the shipmaster checked to learn the content of the cargo. The manifests showed 2,000 sacks of oats, 10 tons of sundries, 361 hides, 10 cords of bolts, 280 tons of cranberries, 2 cases of opium, 18 tons of merchandise, 6 horses, 2 buggies, and $79,220 listed as "treasure" from Victoria. What the last item consisted of was not revealed in the document.

As afternoon wore on, the breeze stiffened and the barometer began dropping. At 4 p.m. the ship was abreast of Tatoosh Island and the wind was blowing hard from the south, creating a heavy swell. Speed was decreased but the ship still experienced difficulty, pitching violently. Most of the passengers had now gone to their cabins, some feeling the first effects of seasickness.

Darkness came on suddenly. The captain walked through the ship's lounge, where there was a noticeable lack of activity. It was almost abandoned. The excitement of the morning hours now seemed distant, almost as if it had never happened. He could feel the increasing vibration of the sidewheels as they churned in the heaving ocean. The steamer's wake looked like a crooked path, barely visible from the afterdeck.

Captain Howell was thinking about the voyages he had made

as master of the *Pacific*. Though she was by no means the largest nor most luxurious ship on the West Coast, he was satisfied that she was making a fair profit for her owners. The vessel was nearing twenty-five years of service since her construction at a New York shipyard. The *Pacific*, registered at 875 tons, earned a bad name at the end of her first decade of service when she rammed into Coffin Rock on the Columbia River and almost became a total loss. It was then that persistent rumors about her being tender and in poor condition got started and never eased. She was laid up in 1872, and somewhat neglected. When business picked up, however, she received a face-lifting and was returned to operation. Call it pride or whatever you will, Captain Howell considered his command wholly seaworthy though maybe lacking the luster of more prosperous days on the Panama run. Evidently the bad rumors about his ship hadn't hurt her popularity because many prominent persons had been aboard virtually every coastwise voyage.

About 10 p.m. that evening, the shipmaster felt the need of sleep and after checking the watch on the bridge headed for his cabin. On the way he noted the faint beam from the lighthouse on Tatoosh Island bouncing off the low-hanging clouds. Though somewhat concerned at the poor rate of speed his vessel was logging in the wind-whipped sea, he shrugged his shoulders, breathed deeply, and started down the companionway. Just when he opened the door to his cabin, a shrill blast sounded from the whistle. As he did a turnabout, a sudden impact threw him to the deck. While struggling to his feet he saw a number of passengers hurrying down the passageway, clad only in night clothes. Half running, he scurried toward the bridge; as he went he could feel the ship convulsing.

The deck was a scene of confusion. Off the starboard beam he could see the dim running lights of a sailing vessel slowly drifting away. It was only then that he realized that the two ships had collided.

Trying to round up his officers and restore some kind of order, the captain was hampered by the ever-increasing droves of passengers flocking to the boat deck. As the ship began to assume a list, panic broke out. Water was rushing into the forward hold unchecked, and the steamer was settling lower by the minute. *Why hadn't the ship that struck them stood by?*

The officers tried in vain to get the boats into the water but the terrified passengers crowded in against them, thwarting their every effort. Fists began to fly. There was screaming, weeping, and wild shoving—a shocking scene of confusion. And the *Pacific* was going down fast. She had been struck in a vital quarter and was starting to heel over, shuddering, as if trying to catch one last breath. A paddle box dipped deep into the water; then the stern began to rise monstrously. Everything loose went tumbling.

"Let go!" an officer shouted, trying to free a lifeboat. The davit lines were released and the boat swung crazily. Passengers leaped into it and it dropped rock-like into the black, pulsating vortex. A breaking sea caught the little craft and pounded it to pieces against the side of the steamer, throwing its occupants in every direction—bruised, bleeding, and dying.

As the *Pacific* began to slip under, massive geysers of live steam arose, and there were weird rumblings from deep within. Then a huge cavern opened in the sea and the ship dropped out of sight, sucked down in a vast whirlpool. All around were bits of wreckage and people fighting to keep their heads above the maelstrom.

Captain Howell found himself on a piece of decking that had supported the pilothouse. With him were the second officer, the cook, and four passengers. Those clinging to the piece of wreckage were soaked to the skin. The wind drove against and around them and the seas washed over their makeshift raft.

It was now 1 a.m. None of them spoke a word but just held tight. Some three hours later a big sea struck with vengeance and over went the second officer followed by two passengers, a man and a woman. Then Howell lost his grip and he too was deposited into the open sea. He was last seen by those left on the raft trying to keep the unconscious woman afloat. Now only four dazed individuals still clung to the wreckage.

At 9 a.m., the cook could stand it no longer. He went mad and rolled off into the sea. At 4 p.m. the following afternoon, the haze cleared away and the three survivors caught their first glimpse of land, about fifteen miles away. They also sighted another piece of wreckage with two men clinging to it. An hour later, a second tortured individual expired, and by the following morning, a third died, leaving Quartermaster Neil Henley alone on the raft. What kept him going will perhaps never be fully understood.

When a box drifted by him, he was able to reach out for it. This he used as a protection against the wind. Finally exhausted, he fell into an uneasy sleep. Early on the morning of November 8, he was sighted and rescued by the Revenue Cutter *Oliver Wolcott*. The only other survivor of the *Pacific* was a passenger, Henry F. Jelley, who was rescued after clinging to an overturned section of lifeboat for forty-eight hours. Four others originally with Jelley perished, one after the other. Jelley himself was rescued by a tugboat from Port Townsend. Afterward he recalled how Chief Engineer Houston and Freight Clerk Bagley succeeded in getting the one lifeboat over the side of the sinking *Pacific*. Tears filled his eyes as he told of its being smashed; his mind was haunted by the memory of a baby which Jennie Parsons carried in her arms. The tiny infant was crushed to death before its mother could enter the boat. Jelley died a few years after the *Pacific's* loss—partly as a result of his ordeal.

While the world lamented the fate of the *Pacific* and its personnel, another side of its story was being enacted. This involved the ship *Orpheus* (Captain Charles A. Sawyer), which had collided with the *Pacific*. The plight of the *Orpheus* is best told in the words of Captain Sawyer as he related it at the hearing of the disaster:

> The *Orpheus* was steering about north, keeping close in to the land, with the wind from the southward and blowing

fresh with fine rain—the ship going about twelve knots. Her head yards were braced sharp up by the starboard braces, her main and after yards, square, thus leaving the ship in such a position that she could be hauled off shore on a moment's notice, if anything came in view.

At 9 p.m., I left the deck in charge of second mate, Allen, with orders if he saw anything, to starboard the wheel and keep her head to the northwest off shore. I went below to consult the chart and had just seated myself at the table in my cabin with my oil clothes on and was looking at the chart when I heard the second mate tell the man at the wheel to starboard his helm. I looked up at the telltale compass over my head and saw that the ship's head was rapidly coming up toward the northwest.

I immediately went on deck and asked the officer what was the matter, and he said there was a light on the port bow; said it was Flattery Light. I told him it was impossible to have Flattery Light on that bow, and just then I saw the light on the starboard bow. I let the ship come up in the wind until she headed to the southward of west, and the after sails aback. My ship was now comparatively at a standstill, in just such a position as I would be if I were going to take a pilot on board. This brought the steamer's light a little forward the starboard beam. I stood looking at her with my glasses.

I did not then think there was going to be a collision, but as I looked and saw no change in the course of the steamer, I said to the second mate, "She will be into us"—though I did not think she would, for I thought she would see us and keep off. . . . Shortly afterward she blew her whistle and immediately struck us on the starboard side in the wake of the main hatch. The blow was a light one. She had evidently stopped her engines and was backing and gave us a glancing blow, for she bounded off and again struck us at the main topmast backstays, breaking the chain plates, car-

rying away the backstays and bumpkin, main and main
topsail braces, leaving me comparatively a wreck on the
starboard side.

Before she blew her whistle, my wife came on deck and
stood by my side. We could plainly observe the steamer's
deck from the pilothouse to her bows, and not a soul was to
be seen there as she passed the stern. I hailed her and
asked her to stand by me, but she made no reply. My wife
attempted to jump on board her, and would, had I not
grabbed her.

The vessels drifted apart, and I gave my attention to my
ship, and gave orders to the mate to cut the lashings on the
boats, and to the carpenter to sound the pumps. My rail
was broken from the fore rigging to the main rigging. The
first report the carpenter made was that the ship was half
full of water.

I told him to take a light and go down the fore hatch and
see. In the meantime I found there was no water in the
hold. I then gave orders to the mate to never mind the
boats, but to take all hands and secure the backstays and
repair damages. All my starboard braces had been carried
away with the blocks, and so forth.

Now, while I was attending to the condition of the ship—
it certainly took from ten to fifteen minutes—I never looked
after the steamer. Neither did anyone else that I know
of. . . . We were all busy attending to our own necessities.
When, after I found I was not seriously damaged, I looked
for the steamer, I just saw a light on our starboard quarter,
and when I looked again it was gone.

There has been a great deal said about the crying and
screaming of the women and children on the steamer. Not
one sound was heard from her by anyone on my ship;
neither was anyone seen on board of her. Neither did anyone on my ship think for a moment that any injury of any
kind had happened to the steamer, for at 1:30 that night,

as the sailors were furling the spanker, they commenced to growl, as sailors will, about the steamer, after running us down, to go off and leave us in that shape, without stopping to inquire whether we were injured or not.

The 1,100-ton *Orpheus*, with an over-all length of 200 feet, was a famous ship in her own right. She had been built as a clipper ship by Rice & Mitchell at Chelsea, Massachusetts, in 1856, and had some highly creditable passages to her credit, including one made in 1859 from New York to San Francisco in 114 days. She had been trading on the Pacific for several months at the time of the tragedy.

After the *Orpheus* collided with the *Pacific*, she sailed on into the inky night, hardly able to maintain a proper course. Out of San Francisco she carried only ballast; she was bound for Nanaimo for coal. A few hours later she found herself in jeopardy off Cape Beale. Her master mistook the beacon at the new lighthouse there for the beam at Cape Flattery. Not possessing the latest charts marking the recently established light, the *Orpheus* blundered blindly toward Vancouver Island and struck a jagged reef that soon reduced her to a total wreck.

The twenty-one-man crew escaped in boats, along with Captain Sawyer, running the surf to the beach. They were cared for by Captain A. D. Laing, owner of a nearby Indian trading post.

In the wild excitement following the disaster, Captain Sawyer was accused of casting his ship away. He was later arrested on the charge of barratry at San Francisco, but a thorough investigation acquitted him of blame. He explained that Cape Beale Light had been illuminated for only a few months and that he had no light list or charts showing its existence. He went on to say, "My sailing directions gave Cape Flattery as the most northern light, and the negligence of the second mate in not calling me when he found he could not steer the course given him caused the loss to the *Orpheus*."

Sawyer further produced a letter from Captain Gilkey of the ship *Messenger* (which picked up survivor Henry Jelley from the tug), saying that he also had mistaken Cape Beale Light for Cape Flattery, and that had he made the light earlier he would have been in the same fix. Fortunately he did not sight it until daylight when he could see by the land that it could not be the entrance to the Strait of Juan de Fuca.

There was hardly a Pacific Northwest home that was not saddened by the loss of a friend or relative in the sinking of the *Pacific*. The death toll, as close as could be ascertained, stood at 275.

The accusations and insinuations wore heavily on Captain Sawyer. Though his friends stood by him, his name, until the time of his death, remained synonymous with the disaster. Furthermore, he had the reputation of being a hard master, and many who had sailed under his strict code unjustly used it as a fulcrum against him. Until the *Pacific* disaster, though, he had always been considered a worthy shipmaster who ran a tight ship with strict discipline.

The fact that corpses kept washing up on beaches as much as 150 miles away from the scene of the wreck did little to erase the tragic memories or the public agitation. The fact that Henley was rescued off the Strait of Juan de Fuca and that the bodies of several victims were found weeks later on San Juan Island indicates that the current inward through the strait, when the tide comes in, is much stronger than that outward, when it is receding. This is probably due to the fact that a large part of the water which comes in through the strait passes out through the Gulf of Georgia and the channel east of Vancouver Island.

At Victoria, during the inquest held on the body of Thomas J. Ferrill, it was recorded—

> that the said steamer *Pacific* sank after a collision with the American ship *Orpheus*, off Cape Flattery, on the night of November 4, 1875; that the *Pacific* struck the *Orpheus* on the starboard side with her stem, a very light blow, the shock of which should not have damaged the *Pacific* if she had been a sound and substantial vessel; that the collision

between them was caused by the *Orpheus* not keeping the approaching *Pacific's* light on her port bow as when first seen, but instead putting the helm hard to starboard, and unjustifiably crossing the *Pacific's* bow; that the watch on the deck of the *Pacific* at the time of the collision was not sufficient in number to keep a proper lookout, the watch consisting only of three men, namely one at the wheel, one supposed to be on the lookout, and the third mate, a young man of doubtful experience; that the *Pacific* had about 238 passengers on board at the time of the collision; that she had five boats, the utmost carrying capacity of which did not exceed 160 persons; that the boats were not and could not be lowered by the undisciplined and inexperienced crew; that the captain of the *Orpheus* sailed away after the collision and did not remain by the *Pacific* to ascertain the damage she had sustained.

Despite his terrible experience on the *Pacific*, Quartermaster Neil Henley continued a nautical career. He lived to celebrate his fiftieth wedding anniversary at Steilacoom, Washington, in 1935. At the occasion, the eighty-year-old Henley again related the oft-told story. He died some months later.

To this day the loss of the *Pacific* is still talked about. The disaster was one of the worst in the annals of the North Pacific Ocean and probably the most publicized.

DEAD END FOR THE CAMBRIDGE

An American sailing vessel of ancient vintage, probably operating long after her appointed time, fell victim to the wrathful moods of the Pacific off Cape Flattery in 1877. The *Cambridge*, which in her latter days was registered out of Astoria, had started life in 1858 as a crack 255-ton bark at Charleston, Massachusetts. She was a fast-sailing vessel but small for her rig. Shortly after her completion she came to the West Coast, where for many years she was owned by her master, Captain N. C. Brooks. In

1866, however, steamers began to cut in on the sailing-ship monopoly in the Columbia River-Victoria-Sandwich Islands (Hawaii) run—and that was where the *Cambridge* had proved so successful. Big steamers like the *Pacific, Orizaba, Sierra Nevada,* and *Del Norte* could undercut the sailing ships on rates, thereby getting the mail contracts between the Islands and the mainland. Unable to compete, the *Cambridge* was withdrawn and relegated to the coastal trades. She was the last of the regular traders to quit the Hawaii run, though sailing vessels continued to operate on the route for many years thereafter, carrying out lumber and returning with sugar, or occasionally copra from some of the other islands.

During her coastal days, the *Cambridge* deteriorated. Always shipshape before, she now became a mongrel among deep-sea vessels, and perhaps would have failed the simplest of inspections—which were practically non-existent in those early days. The condition of a ship was strictly up to its owner, or master. So the *Cambridge*, aging and tender, on June 12, 1877, took on a cargo of lumber at Port Ludlow and put out to sea, bound for San Francisco. With sails filling, she signalled the lighthouse keepers on Tatoosh and started down the coast. The glass had been dropping for several hours when the vessel plunged into a tumultuous sea racked by relentless winds. Her loaded decks were struck by the full impact of the storm fifteen miles southwest of the cape. Taking it green over the bow and leaking like a sieve, the *Cambridge* shouldered one sea after another while the crew jettisoned cargo to gain more freeboard. Suddenly the bark heeled over on her beam ends and the lumber slid into the water like so many jackstraws.

The frantic Chinese cook was trapped inside the galley and drowned. The others, struggling amid a mad array of runaway timbers, somehow managed to get a boat into the water. Tossed about on the wild ocean and constantly shipping water, all of them baled by hand in a desperate effort to stay afloat. Exposure might have claimed the entire crew had not the barkentine

Emma Augusta sighted them and, in a neat piece of seamanship, plucked them from the sea. They were transported to San Francisco, grateful to be alive.

The old vessel probably floated for as long as her lumber cargo remained with her. She was valued at a mere $8,000, but if the owner, N. C. Brooks, who still had a controlling interest in the vessel, collected the insurance, he certainly came out a winner.

THE SAGA OF THE UMATILLA

Three miles northwest of Cape Alava, the black, breaker-washed rocks of Umatilla Reef jut grimly westward. Even in fair weather, spume from crashing waves obscures these offshore rocks, making them the greatest danger to navigation along the northwest coast. Two and a half miles southwest of the reef is *Umatilla Reef Lightship*, one of the loneliest vigils off coastal United States. The mariner puts his trust in her light, fog signal, and radiobeacon. Should the lightship drift off station in a gale, he gives the area a wide berth.

Ironically, the first large vessel to run afoul of these rocks managed to escape, but she bequeathed her name to them. When the *Umatilla* struck, February 8, 1884, there was no guardian lightship and there wouldn't be for another fourteen years. She was a virtually new steel steamer carrying fore-and-aft canvas with a squares'l forward, and she was one of the finest coal-trade vessels on the West Coast in the latter part of the 1800s.

The nationally acclaimed hero of this shipwreck was one "Dynamite" Johnny O'Brien, whose name tops the Pacific rim's hall of fame. "Dynamite" joined the ship as chief mate in 1883, and on the first voyage from San Francisco north to Puget Sound the trouble began. Lashed on deck were several hundred carboys of muriatic acid and a cargo of railroad flatcars.

Off Cape Blanco, Oregon, the 3,069-ton, 310-foot *Umatilla* was battered by a fierce southeast gale and her decks were swept by heavy seas. One huge wave set free several large cases of acid.

Then two rail cars broke loose. O'Brien hurried sailors down the slippery decks to secure the multi-wheeled ramrods that threatened to knock out the bulkheads. At the order of Captain Frank Worth, O'Brien and several others set to work to get the acid-spilling carboys overboard. The salt water which drenched the men served as a protection for their skin. Afterward O'Brien found that his clothes were in shreds, eaten through by acid, but neither he nor any of his cohorts was burned.

No sooner had the strain of this ordeal ended than that of another began. Early the following morning, weird noises issued from the recesses of the ship. Lantern in hand, O'Brien went down to investigate. He found that a huge safe had broken loose and was battering against cases of dynamite. He called for mattresses and ropes. A possible explosion was averted when the safe was finally lassoed and secured to a bulkhead.

The *Umatilla* seemed jinxed. She finally reached Seattle, but her return voyage was even more unfortunate than her voyage north. It was early dawn of February 8, and a northern gale was driving ominous seas into flying silver as the black-hulled steamer passed Tatoosh Island on her southerly course. Now a blinding snowstorm came up and coated the ship with slush.

"Dynamite" O'Brien was on the bridge keeping a sharp watch. He suggested to the skipper that they might be closer to shore than they should be, but the captain shrugged off the warning: "We're at least twenty miles off Flattery Rocks."

O'Brien hunched his collar up around his neck, held his tongue, and waited.

When eight bells struck, O'Brien got blessed relief; he was replaced by the second mate. While the latter peered out into the white mass of whirling snow, O'Brien gave him the course, then started below for a cup of hot coffee. As he hurried down the companionway he noted that the captain was still on the bridge wing, keeping a vigil despite the cold. Suddenly a shrieking call sounded from the ship's forepeak:

"Rocks and breakers ahead!"

O'Brien turned abruptly and ran forward, grabbing the rail to keep from sliding. He looked over the side just in time to see the threatening rocks before a huge wave washed them from sight. The spume shot up in his face. He heard the frantic, repeated command of the captain to the quartermaster to put the helm hard over. Too late. The ship struck with a terrific, jarring impact.

O'Brien was knocked off his feet and ended up in the scuppers. He regained his footing and rushed to the bridge where the second mate was getting a dressing-down from the captain for not going inside the reef—a dangerous course even for small boats. At that moment the engine-room telegraph began clanging wildly.

The captain held fast to the bridge rail; the engines rumbled full astern, and the vessel shook convulsively. Startled crew members now crowded the forward deck. Soon O'Brien joined the throng.

As the ship slowly backed off the reef, there was a call from the hold: "The cargo's afloat!"

O'Brien shouted up to the captain: "Put 'er back on the reef, Sir, before she sinks."

Again the telegraph clanged as the *Umatilla* dropped slowly by the head with a shuddering movement. Once more she scraped over the reef's black rocks, then suddenly became motionless—all but her canvas, which flapped wildly. O'Brien ordered the men aloft to furl the sails.

Inch by inch the *Umatilla* heeled over until she reached a considerable list. As wind and sea relentlessly pounded against her hull, fear spread throughout the ship. Boats were ordered over the side, manned, and lowered away. O'Brien tossed into the captain's boat the chronometer, the navigating instruments, and some of the ship's papers.

The only woman aboard was the steward's wife, who had taken passage as a stewardess. She was in the skipper's boat clinging tightly to the thwart. O'Brien, now alone on board, grinned down at the frightened lady and asked if there was any food cooking in the galley. She looked at him in amazement and pleaded for him to get into the lifeboat before the *Umatilla* sank. O'Brien replied coolly:

"First I fill my stomach. I'm hungry."

He then proceeded to the warm galley to appease his hearty Irish appetite while those in the boats waited impatiently. As he ate he thought: *What a shame it would be to abandon this fine ship. Who knows . . . she might not even sink. She certainly won't go down as long as her nose is on the reef.* The possibility of spending several days on cold, watery shores didn't appeal to O'Brien. In any case, he could ready a raft and make his escape should the vessel go down.

When he came out on deck, the snow was blowing as hard as ever and he saw one of the engineers climbing back over the railing to get his wallet, which in the excitement he had left behind. O'Brien asked him to help launch a life raft from a rack on the afterdeck—a 6 x 10-foot conveyance with two airtight cylinders. The engineer agreed. O'Brien then made the painter fast to the ship and went to his cabin for his pocket watch and seabag.

All this time the boats in the davits were swinging crazily in the gale and their crews were growing more impatient. As the boats were lowered Captain Worth shouted angrily:

"Are you crazy, O'Brien? Shinny down the rope and we'll pick you up."

The Irishman nonchalantly waved them all away, lowered himself to the raft, and lashed his equipment to its wooden frame. The irritated shipmaster snapped:

"O'Brien, what do you mean by going onto that raft?"

In his gentlest Irish brogue, barely audible above the roaring sea, O'Brien replied that he would be perfectly safe. Red-faced and obviously enraged, the captain shouted:

"The ship's going down, O'Brien. Have you taken leave of your senses?" O'Brien was obdurate:

"We're in the shipping lanes and it would be a devil of a note if she slipped off the reef and floated with nobody standing by her."

The captain had now lost all patience; he ordered his boat to come alongside the raft and pick up O'Brien. Two oarsmen reached out for the obstinate mate on the rolling raft. O'Brien stood up and grabbed them, then lunged powerfully backward and all three sprawled out on the raft.

"You're safer with me," O'Brien told seamen Hanlin and Hardness. Then, in direct and deliberate insubordination, with his foot he shoved the lifeboat away.

The captain cursed but his profanity fell on deaf ears. O'Brien was determined to save the ship and with his two shanghaied assistants he figured his chances were greatly improved.

Soon the lifeboats faded away into the driving snow, leaving the three to their fate. The trio then scrambled aboard the ship to get food and blankets for their long vigil. Back on the raft, which was fastened to the wounded ship by a single line, they began their long, tormenting wait. Getting as comfortable as possible, they tied themselves securely, but soon they were numb with cold. The thermometer stood at about twelve degrees.

The hours slipped slowly by while the uneasy *Umatilla* lurched first one way, then another, bringing the men to their feet, their bloodshot eyes straining. They didn't dare go back on board now; the vessel might suddenly roll over.

O'Brien did everything he could think of to keep the men awake. Then when it seemed their very joints had frozen, the ship showed signs of lifting off the reef. The towering walls of steel trembled, and with two great heaving swells the *Umatilla* floated free, on a list but still afloat. Down by the head, with her propeller blades breaking the surface, she drifted away from the reef toward Flattery Rocks, etched in dark outline in the falling snow. The raft, still tied to the ship, was cut loose.

When the ship showed no signs of sinking, "Dynamite" Johnny considered reboarding. He knew that the steam pumps had been working before the vessel was abandoned; perhaps enough water had been sucked out of the forward ballast tank to counteract the water in the holds. Whatever the reason, the ship was still afloat.

So cold he could hardly stir, O'Brien tried to rally the younger men. "I don't think she's going down," he told them. "I'd like to try getting back aboard." He paused a moment, then: "If only I can make it up her sides I'll drop you boys a Jacob's ladder." The others seemed dazed by the cold, but O'Brien was adamant. He again made the raft fast to the ship and tried to climb the perpendicular steel wall, but his arms and legs just wouldn't respond.

One of the others suddenly reached under a mattress and pulled out a flask of whiskey. "I was saving it for the last," he said. "Maybe it'll warm you enough to try again."

O'Brien took a healthy swallow. "If only we could get aboard, I think maybe we could rig what's left of the sails and pull her away from those rocks."

Again he tried the painful ascent. He dug his fingertips into the overlapping plates and porthole frames and slowly inched higher and higher. Exhausted, he grabbed the railing. The ship suddenly lurched and he tumbled onto the deck, almost senseless from the cold and physical strain. His watersoaked clothes anchored him to the deck.

When he regained his strength he went to the midship house for the Jacob's ladder and dropped it to the seamen in the pitching raft below. He told them to grab hold and climb fast if they wanted to keep the ship from going back on the rocks. After they were safe on deck, O'Brien hustled them forward to unfurl the main sheet. Only the wind could edge the *Umatilla* away from disaster. The big sail sputtered and slatted but failed to pick up enough breeze to stem the drift.

"Hoist the fore-topmast stays!" O'Brien ordered as the men staggered toward him. "Sheet her to windward! We've got to get her head to pay off."

With superhuman effort, the exhausted men jumped the stay-sail halyards hand over hand as the rocks reached out for the ship. Then scarcely a hundred yards off the ragged boulders, the vessel suddenly swung off toward open water. Once again the *Umatilla* was a free agent.

The life raft which had floated free was soon far astern, and the wretched little crew was now dependent on the ship alone. How far would she drift? Where would she go? How long would she last? There were no answers.

With the prevailing northerly wind, O'Brien set a course for the mouth of the Columbia River. Several hours later the men sighted a small sealing schooner dead ahead. They immediately inverted the *Umatilla's* ensign to attract the sealer's attention. The schooner came alongside and her captain asked if they wanted to be taken off. "No!" O'Brien said indignantly.

"What do you want then?"

"All the men you can spare."

The schooner's crewmen eyed the mangled hull of the big ship and her precarious position in the water. They wanted no part of her, and after a short consultation reported this to O'Brien.

Still insistent, the Irishman cupped his hands to his mouth, "Fifty dollars a day to every man who'll come aboard!"

At this promising offer the sealers gathered forward on the pitching schooner. Sealing had been none too good, and for that kind of pay it might be worth taking a chance. The crew was made up almost entirely of Indians. There were only three Caucasians, including the captain.

Suddenly a dory was swung overboard and three sealers jumped in and started for the steamer. The seas had moderated and the snow was only intermittent. Before long the men were hoisted aboard and the dory made fast. O'Brien could now get the squares'l properly set and add a half knot to the present three-knot gait. He brewed a huge pot of coffee and filled the bottom of the cups with whiskey to perk up his new recruits. Meanwhile the sealing vessel faded slowly into the murky seas.

Night came on with added cold as the injured steamer pushed southward.

Toward midnight one of the men sighted a ship's running lights to the southeast. The lights grew brighter as the ship approached. When the *Umatilla's* motley crew gathered excitedly at the railing, they were able to make out a large collier. Even as they watched, a boat was put over the side and some hardy sailors rowed the watery stretch to the *Umatilla's* side.

"Ahoy, there, what ship are you?" called a voice from the small boat.

"Steamship *Umatilla*," bellowed O'Brien. "We struck a reef near Flattery Rocks and we're trying to make the Columbia. Can you take us in tow?"

"How much is it worth to you?"

"Tell your skipper he'll be handsomely paid if we're towed to port safely," O'Brien answered.

Though not over-anxious to accept a tow, neither was O'Brien foolhardy enough to think the *Umatilla* was beyond sinking. He was taking a calculated risk in endeavoring to reach the Columbia, but even with a tow he figured on a handsome profit for all involved."

The small boat returned to the collier. Thirty minutes later she was back.

O'Brien ordered his crew to break out the manila hawser, but when the boat came alongside, a strident call came up, "We're the steamer *Wellington*, Captain Young. Stand by to take our line."

"You stand by to take our line!" O'Brien retorted. He realized that if he accepted the *Wellington's* line, the salvage costs would be greater. An argument ensued, and the small boat again returned to the *Wellington*.

A long wait followed. Then the craft returned. "Give you one more chance. If you want a tow, get busy and take our hawser," ordered the man in the bow of the boat.

O'Brien did not answer. He decided to wait them out. It was a risk, he knew, but much money was at stake. He sniffed the air and sensed another "blow" coming. If the winds should shift, the *Umatilla* might once more be in grave peril. As the breeze increased, the small boat found it difficult to keep abreast of the ship.

O'Brien was about to give in when to his surprise someone from the boat called up, "Heave to; we'll take your damn hawser!"

The boat jockeyed near the battered bow of the *Umatilla* and O'Brien's men lowered a light line down to them, which in turn was attached to a heavy hawser.

The *Umatilla's* helm was put hard over and she responded slowly. Within minutes the hawser was being winched aboard the *Wellington*. Two hours later, O'Brien and his ship were in tow, bound for the Strait of Juan de Fuca.

Snow began to fall and the seas mounted. The *Wellington* labored heavily towing a vessel her own size, and the unwieldy *Umatilla* nosed into each sea. O'Brien and his men wondered how much punishment she could stand. When he went forward to take an extra hitch on the hawser on the mooring bits, he was surprised to see a small boat from the *Wellington* coming alongside.

"What d'ya want now?" Johnny O'Brien demanded.

"Captain Young sent us over to help handle your ship."

The Irishman sensed another salvage trick. "We don't need any more help. All we need is your tow."

"Can't I come aboard?" insisted the man in charge of the bobbing boat.

"Who are you?"

"Chief mate of the *Wellington*."

"We don't carry any passengers but you can come aboard as my guest," O'Brien answered. "I'll drop the ladder to you." He extended his invitation in such a way that it could not be said in court that he needed more crewmen to handle his ship.

Over the rail climbed the newcomer and the boat below was soon blotted out in the murk. O'Brien showed the officer around, offering him his own cabin. Then, giving orders to his men to call him if the weather changed, he retired to other quarters, but he had slept less than an hour when one of his men was shaking him awake. O'Brien started up, rubbing his eyes.

"You better come topside quick," said the man standing over him. "I think the mate from the *Wellington* has cut away our sails."

"Dynamite" grabbed a lantern and ran up to the main deck. Squinting his eyes from the sting of the cold air, he noted that the peak halyards of the fore and mainsail had been slashed away with a knife; the sheets had been slacked off, and as a result the canvas was ripped to pieces. If anything should happen to the *Wellington* now, the *Umatilla* would drift, a hulk. And there was no more canvas to hoist.

The big Irishman was beside himself with wrath. He grabbed a piece of timber and started for his cabin, sliding and slipping as he ran along the deck. When he got to the door he banged on it so hard it flew open. He barged in. The mate from the *Wellington* was in the bunk. He tried to shield himself with the blankets as the Irishman swung the stick, but the blunt weapon caught him squarely on the side of the head. He was knocked senseless.

Still angry, O'Brien went back to the bridge. He wondered if he had killed the man. He approached the crewman who had tipped him off. "You better go below and get a bottle of brandy. See if you can get it down the fellow's throat. He's in my cabin."

The seaman quickly had the senseless man moaning and groaning and convinced that he had learned his lesson.

O'Brien later sent his men aloft to salvage a few pieces of sail in case of emergency, but the effort was useless. The *Wellington* continued her towing, and by the time a pale dawn broke, the two ships had rounded Cape Flattery and were in the Strait of

Juan de Fuca. By mid-afternoon they were near Royal Roads preparing to drop anchor off Esquimalt, British Columbia.

O'Brien was exhausted; he had been without sleep for almost forty-eight hours. Before quitting, though, he insisted that Captain Young bring the *Umatilla* in alongside the dock for safe-keeping. The captain refused: any ship that had taken the beating the *Umatilla* had would certainly remain afloat in calm water. But during the night the *Umatilla* made a convulsive sound and suddenly started settling. O'Brien had to leap from the bridge to keep from being sucked into the vortex. His men also narrowly escaped. Shortly after gaining the shore, the Irishman collapsed on the dock, to awaken hours later in Esquimalt Naval Hospital. O'Brien had sustained earlier internal injuries when clambering from the life raft back aboard the *Umatilla* and the strain had at last caught up with him.

As soon as he felt better he left the hospital and succeeded in talking a livery-stable owner into driving him to Victoria, B. C. for fifteen dollars—which he could ill afford. There he forwarded the news of the wild saga of the *Umatilla* to the agents in Seattle. They were jubilant to hear firsthand that the ship had been spared from the reef but dismayed that she was now lying in forty-two feet of water.

O'Brien arrived back at Esquimalt in time to face the preliminaries of the litigation. Owners of the *Wellington* advanced a claim of $50,000 for a towing fee and Lloyd's of London counter-claimed for $100,000, alleging that the master of the rescue ship was derelict in his duties when he allowed the *Umatilla* to sink.

The reputable Whitelaw Salvage Company of San Francisco was called in by the underwriters to raise the sunken ship. This took almost six months of hard labor. A huge cradle supported by barges had to be built during the salvage operation. After the vessel was raised she sat idle for another six months, awaiting settlement of insurance claims. Finally Captain Frank Holmes took her to San Francisco for a complete refit. Thereafter she had a long and successful career as a passenger liner, finally ending her days when wrecked in 1918 off the Japanese Coast.

Poor "Dynamite" Johnny O'Brien . . . the most he got out of all his troubles was considerable newspaper publicity, a cheap reward for the cold, wet, and miserable hours he had put in to save the *Umatilla*. Furthermore, he had made several enemies, among them Captain Frank Worth, former master of the *Umatilla*. The captain with the others had reached shore safely, but the fact that the ship had made harbor did not delight him. Then there was the mate of the *Wellington*, who was hospitalized from O'Brien's savage blow. Finally there was the master of the *Wellington*, whom O'Brien had outwitted. However, before the year was out and the case settled, the Irishman was back at sea.

At the investigation held in Seattle by Inspectors Morgan and Hinckley, Captain Frank Worth was exonerated from all blame. Testimony showed that a strong northerly current had prevailed during the thick weather, casting the ship on the uncharted reef despite any precautions that might have been taken. "Dynamite" O'Brien was praised for his heroism in bringing the vessel back.

His colorful career as master of sailing vessels, freighters, and passenger liners continued. The famous Rex Beach said of him after his death in August 1931, at the age of eighty:

> "Captain Johnny O'Brien was a true sailor, a splendid captain, a loyal friend, and a courteous gentleman. He had the heart of a boy and the soul of a Viking. God rest him!"

PORT OF NO RETURN—BARK AUSTRIA

Just beyond Cape Alava, the southerly end of Fuca's graveyard, lies the barnacle-encrusted anchor of the bark *Austria*. She was wrecked in 1887, near the Ozette Indian village. Some half-rotted bottom planks can still be found on the beach, partly burned by early Indians to recover metal for making knives and fishhooks. These grim reminders are the last evidence of the wreck of a once-proud sailing vessel.

The 1,300-ton bark was out of San Francisco and had experienced a fair run up the coast of slightly more than eight days when she gained the latitude of Umatilla Reef. At that date there was no lightship guarding the treacherous rocks. The only major aid to navigation north of the Columbia River and Willapa Harbor was the light on Tatoosh Island.

The *Austria*, which was bound for Tacoma in ballast, was riding light in the water on that twenty-first day of January 1887, when with virtually no forewarning, a gale blew up. The wind hauled around from the south and east and then came from the west. Captain George E. Delano ordered every stitch of canvas crowded on and steered his ship northwest by north—aware of the hazards that threatened her inshore.

Making leeway, the ship wore around, heading south southwest. The blast tore into the canvas with such impact that three sails immediately split down the middle. Gone were the foresail fore-topsail, and mizzen-staysail. The vessel still made leeway and was being drawn toward the dreaded shore like a needle to a magnet. The sea had turned to a mass of white-lipped mountains, the crests blowing from the top of each in huge, billowing masses.

As daylight broke, the exhausted crew, who had not had a wink of sleep, peared at their captain as if expecting him to perform some miracle. But miracles were not in the cards and the skipper knew his dangerous position only too well. With most of the canvas gone, there was only one recourse open: to worm his way the best he could through that pincushion of rocks and reefs, and run his vessel aground on the smoothest section of the beach available. The task before him was formidable, but it was either this or let the elements batter his vessel on one of the outlying reefs—which could have meant death for his entire crew.

With the captain standing beside him, the helmsman fearfully guided the *Austria* on what would be her port of no return. In past Ozette Island, countless rocks stuck their snouts above the surface, ready to sink their fangs into the tender wooden hull of the vessel. Any master of the sea would have praised Captain Delano's effort. The vessel got in respectfully close to the shore before she struck a rock and came to a sudden, jarring halt. The obstruction came right up through her bottom planks, impaling her. She was in far enough for some protection from the open sea and remained in an upright position.

It was now 7:30 a.m., and though the tide was ebbing and flowing through her hull, the shore was only a short distance away and the chilling danger of a few hours earlier had mostly subsided.

During the day the wind shifted northward and the seas quieted sufficiently to allow the *Austria's* crew to take to the boats and bridge the remaining distance to the beach. Excited Indians came out in canoes from the village, a slab-board conglomeration of nondescript houses that hung onto the weather side at Cape Alava.

With their Indian canoe escort, the survivors got in safely. They were cold and very hungry but the dried fish offered by the natives did little to whet their appetites. The sea calmed enough the next day to allow the crew to return to the wreck to get watersoaked bedding, clothes, and provisions which they urgently needed.

After a few days of hardship and inclement weather, the survivors sighted the steamer *Mexico* passing out toward the horizon. Hopefully they raised some signal flags from the askew mizzenmast of the wreck. When the steamer altered course but failed to acknowledge the signal, the *Austria's* men assumed she would proceed to port for aid. They then set about in earnest to salvage everything movable from the wreck, as it had become obvious there was no salvation for the vessel. But no rescue ship came.

They soon had the beach stacked with old sails, rigging, and ship's gear of all types; in fact, with everything but the anchors and chain. The Indians were already casting fond glances at the loot, eager to share in the spoils. Aware of this, Captain Delano decided to leave his crew to guard the salvaged materials while he trudged the thirty miles to Neah Bay. The journey was a difficult one and he suffered intensely from the cold but he kept going, following Indian paths and the lonely stretches of beach until he reached the bay. There to his surprise he found the revenue cutter *Oliver Wolcott* still at her moorings. Disturbed by this, he hastily boarded the vessel but discovered only a skeleton crew and cold boilers. The cutter, out of fuel, was awaiting coal to fill her empty bunkers.

As soon as the coal arrived, the *Wolcott* got up a big head of steam and started out to find the wreck. After a fast run against headwinds she anchored well offshore, sending in her boats for the survivors and as many salvaged items as could be lightered. Such gear as the anchor, chain, hawse pipes, and chocks could not be handled in the small boats. The Indians watched the whole operation with misgivings, having hoped that all the spoils would be left for them. After the survivors departed, the winter storms pushed the vessel higher on the beach and the Indians lost no time descending on the remains for their metal yield.

Following the wreck of the *Austria*, Captain Delano wrote his wife in San Francisco: "I frosted my face walking from the wreck to Neah Bay over the roughest ground I ever saw. I got through all right, but pretty well used up, so stiff I could hardly move the next day."

As for the wreck, he reported: "It was one chance in a thousand that anyone was saved, but we succeeded in getting on shore all safe and none hurt, although the sea was running mountains high and breaking all over the rocks." He also told how the Ozette Indians who lived along the beach kept coming back to the scene of the wreck, finding clothing which had drifted ashore from the vessel. One of the savages had selected a particular undergarment that attracted his eye. He had put it on over his own clothing and danced about with its straps and garters waving. In lighthearted manner, Captain Delano informed his wife that the boned corset belonged to her, having been left on the ship from a previous voyage.

On the sadder side, the captain owned a large share of the vessel and the loss caused him to face bankruptcy, inasmuch as the insurance coverage was a mere $7,900. Some $3,000 was recouped from the salvaged gear but the *Austria* was valued at $20,000. She had been built at Bath, Maine, in 1869, and had seen about eighteen years of service when the final entry was made in her log.

Delano later wrote his father-in-law, T. T. Weeks, in Jefferson, Maine: "I don't know what I will do now, but I guess I will have to go farming." As a boy, he had left Damariscotta, Maine, to go to sea. His family—distantly related to Sara Delano, the late President Franklin D. Roosevelt's mother—had been engaged in shipbuilding there.

Delano now considered going back home. His daughter and his wife, Edith Weeks Delano, had been awaiting his return to San Francisco, but on learning of the wreck they joined him in the Northwest. After pondering the situation at length, the erstwhile skipper finally made up his mind: he would stay on Puget Sound. In many ways it reminded him of his native Maine. In a small vessel chartered from Captain Lorenz of Tacoma, Delano cruised along the Puget Sound shoreline for nearly a month. Finally he chose—not so much with a farmer's eye as with a sailor's—a fine small harbor nine miles across the water from Tacoma. He was attracted by a quarter mile of tideflats. For a paltry sum he purchased from the federal government two hundred acres on Carr Inlet. The original purchase included the land which now is known as Penrose Point State Park. Two years after the purchase, when Washington became a state (1889), Delano deeded part of the property for school land.

Delano's tideflats were first used for careening sailing vessels, to scrape their hulls of barnacles and seagrass. When excessive tides swept away the flats, the upper land was utilized for growing hops, but without much success. Finally Delano decided to build a summer resort, which became the Delano Beach Hotel, a twenty-room structure with dining room, post office, and cabins. With its New England flavor and shipshape maintenance, it was a tribute to the Delanos. Around the turn of the century, it attracted many prominent Pacific Northwest families.

Today all that remains of the captain's enterprises are memories, except for the *Austria's* pitted and rusted anchor and a few bits of wreckage on the beach at Ozette.

THE TRAGIC END OF THE LEONORE
AND THE PRINCE ARTHUR

Two disastrous sailing-vessel wrecks occurred about the time that the Delano Beach Hotel was flourishing. Both took place near the southern boundaries of Fuca's marine graveyard and both resulted in heavy loss of life. The first was that of the Chilean bark *Leonore,* which went to her doom south of Cape Alava. Northbound, she had reached the area of the graveyard on the night of October 4, 1893, when she was confronted by a devastating hurricane. She was inbound to Puget Sound from Valparaiso when the fury of the gale struck, causing her to lose all headway.

The wind howled through her rigging, blowing the sails out of the gaskets and causing yardarms to tumble to the deck. When the lookout reported sighting a ship in the half light, distress signals were quickly hoisted, but the so-called ship turned out to be a rock jutting from the surf, the first warning that the *Leonore* had been swept near the shore.

Captain Jenaca, master of the vessel, was gravely concerned for the life of his young wife, who was making the voyage with him. The night turned black and the ship spun wildly about in the cross currents. Though wreckage was strewn over the deck, nothing could be done to make repairs till dawn. But dawn did not come in time. Throughout the night the full northwest hurricane had blown the ship farther and farther south of the graveyard. The rain came down in sheets and the wind was overpowering. Soaked to the skin and miserable, the crew became outright frightened when the bark ground over the rocks and began breaking up in a remote spot three miles north of the Quillayute River (near where the *St. Nicholas* had been wrecked). The masts came hurtling down and sent the men scurrying. For a brief moment the bark gained some stability but the water rushed into her slashed hull with the force of an avalanche.

Captain Jenaca lost all self-control; he could think only of his wife. He grabbed her and tried to throw her overboard, but she struggled wildly, aware that her husband had lost his senses. She broke free and ran to the mate for protection. The dumbfounded officer was torn between allegiance to his captain and the pleadings of the frantic woman. All the while the crew looked on in bewilderment, lacking orders. Suddenly the captain lunged at the mate and wrenched his wife free. With her clutched tightly in his arms he leaped overboard. Neither was ever seen again. The mate finally recovered sufficiently to rush to the quarter-deck and peer down into the maelstrom. All he could see was some of the ship's keel lifted by a voluminous swell.

As the vessel broke up beneath their feet, the terrified cook, carpenter, and a seaman jumped overboard, in a desperate effort to swim to shore. Only the seaman—a huge, powerful man—somehow fought his way to the beach. A tremendous breaker lifted him and flung him in a heap on the shore, half-dazed from shock and exposure.

It took less than thirty minutes for the liquid onslaught to tear the 843-ton wooden ship asunder. The remaining survivors frantically clung to buoyant pieces of wreckage. The boatswain, paralyzed with the cold, was washed off a makeshift raft by a great wave and drowned. The others, through the stormy half haze, finally gained the shore, all barefoot and with clothes mostly torn from their bodies. They realized their only chance of survival was to start immediately toward Neah Bay, many miles away through virgin timber. By day and night, with little rest

and less food, they made their way, mile after mile. It was a
gaunt and weary band of seafarers who finally completed the
three-day trek and telegraphed for help. The tug *Discovery* set
out at once to find the wreck, but by the time she arrived the
seas had completed their destruction.

An even more tragic wreck along this forbidding stretch of
coast was that of the Norwegian bark *Prince Arthur*. This live
drama was enacted twelve miles south of the Ozette River. The
grave of eighteen of her twenty-man crew is marked by a monu-
ment which reads:

Here lies the crew of the bark PRINCE ARTHUR
of Norway—foundered January 2, 1903.

The names of the two survivors, Chris Hansen and Knud Lar-
son, are scrolled on the grave marker right along with the dead,
beginning with Captain Hans Markusson.

The absence of guiding beacons along this dreaded stretch
was responsible for many tragedies, but in this case it was a
feeble light of mistaken identity that caused the wreck. The iron-
hulled, 1,600-ton bark, in ballast, was making her way up the
coast, bound for British Columbia ports from Valparaiso. She
was in quest of a cargo of lumber.

Ironically there was only one settler's cabin—inhabited by
three woodsmen—along a forty-mile coastal sweep. On the night
of January 2, 1903, a dim kerosene lamp was burning in the
single window of the shabby dwelling. Out on the murky sea,
the captain of the *Prince Arthur* was straining his eyes for the
beacon on Tatoosh Island. When he finally sighted a faint glim-
mer, he reasoned it was none other than the lighthouse. At once
he issued a course change and under shortened canvas headed
the vessel directly toward disaster—which was not far away.

Suddenly the vessel struck, tearing, grinding, and shaking violently. The initial shock went far toward breaking her up. Immediately the shipmaster gave the order to abandon. The well-dis-
ciplined crewmen—many of them young apprentices—responded

like seasoned sailors, despite their fear; but the boats were smashed into kindling against the sides of the ship. Some of the men vainly tried to make it to shore on pieces of wreckage. The master's commands faded in the howling wind, then were silenced forever. Only two survivors gained the shore: Hansen, the second mate; and Larsen, the sailmaker. They alone were left to tell the tale of terror and death. At first both lay on the cold, wet sand, too weak to move. Eventually, in desperation, Hansen mustered enough strength to crawl up over the cliff behind the beach and make his way to the nearby woodsmen's cabin.

As dawn broke, some Indians dwelling close by joined the woodsmen in bringing the other survivor to the cabin and in recovering the lifeless bodies which had since washed ashore.

News of the disaster later reached Clallam Bay and was relayed to Seattle. Here sympathetic seafaring men with Nordic background—Captain John Johnson, master and owner of the schooner *Pilot;* Carl Sunde, L. W. Sandstrom, and C. J. Johnson (a Seattle undertaker)—sailed to Neah Bay where an Indian guide was hired to take them to the scene. Reaching the mouth of the Ozette River, they made their way twelve miles southward over the rugged beach and across wooded headlands.

The Seattle men found the Birkestal brothers, Ivar, Ole, and Tom, at the cabin, the three woodsmen still catering to the needs of the survivors. With the assistance of the Indians, the woodsmen had already placed the dead in shallow graves. At the request of the visitors, however, they agreed to help disinter the bodies and carry them to the bluff overlooking the sea. Here they dug a plot fourteen feet square. Under, over, and around the corpses they wrapped canvas that had come ashore from the wreck. With ship's planking they banked the grave, arranged a carved ship's door as a headstone, and held a simple service. In later years a permanent marker was placed above the grave, and on frequent occasions since then, Norwegian seafaring folk have made pilgrimages to the gravesite.

Following their grim chores, the Seattle men returned to the Birkestal cabin to learn the details of the wreck. The two survivors told of lying on the beach for hours too weak to move. Hansen said he was driven to find assistance by the moaning cries of his shipmates perishing in the surf. The woodsmen told of hastening back to the beach and finding Larsen stretched out on the rocks, almost frozen; and other scattered dead about the beach. The ship had broken in two, only the stern half jutting from the surf.

"Lost south of Cape Flattery" had become a household phrase well before the turn of the century, as the toll in shipwrecks mounted.

THE CANADA MARU

Occasionally a ship which has fallen prey to the perils in the southern quarter of Fuca's graveyard regains her freedom, but instances are rare. One of the fortunate vessels was the Japanese steamship *Canada Maru* of the Osaka Shosen Kaisha Line.

This 5,700-ton vessel was on the final phase of a transpacific crossing from Japan, with a passenger list numbering 176. It had been a stormy passage and the tourists were more than ready for some dry land. Seattle was then less than a day away. As the vessel approached the Strait of Juan de Fuca, fog mantled the entire area, erasing all landmarks. The ship made slow headway through the quiet sea.

The captain was on the bridge peering out into the wall of gray, listening for the foghorn on Tatoosh Island. The passengers, unconcerned about the fog, were below making preparations for their approaching departure. The $1.5-million, passenger-cargo liner carried freight valued at $4 million, including many fine Oriental silks. Little did anyone aboard dream that January 31, 1918, would be a black day for this ship. Newspaper headlines had screamed the events of World War I, and the loss of many ships had been reported in the Atlantic, but the Pacific was almost as peaceful as her name implied—as far as the war was concerned.

Then, with a grinding roar that sounded almost explosive, the steamer gave a violent lurch, sending passengers sprawling. The immediate assumption was that she had been torpedoed—but no, she had struck the outlying barriers of rock off Cape Flattery. The startled passengers were quickly summoned to their lifeboat stations and crewmen stood ready to lower away on command from the captain. The ship was taking water forward and was down by the head. Wireless messages crackled over the airways. The surf was moderate and despite the water that had entered the ship's forward holds she was holding in a steady position.

The steamer's whistle kept blasting and strict vigils were maintained as all waited impatiently for rescue boats to come. Fog swathed the ship and its people. Then came new whistle sounds and the throb of powerful engines. Soon parting the strands of fog were rescue vessels; the *Canada Maru's* calls of distress had been answered. Passengers were herded to their lifeboat stations and one after another the boats were lowered away. The sea was calm, the crew well disciplined, and the passengers cooperative. All came off like clockwork. As for the steamer, it first appeared that she, like many before her, would become a total loss, scattering her bones on the floor of the sea. But this stout ship, despite her wounds, refused to surrender.

A fleet of tugs darted about, endeavoring to pull her free— the *Iroquois, Hero, Traveler, Echo,* and *Richard Holyoke,* among the most powerful American and Canadian tugs of that day—yet despite their combined maximum horsepower they could make no headway. If this ship were to get a new lease on life it was increasingly obvious that it would have to be the target of a major salvage operation.

The British Columbia Salvage Company was the successful bidder in answer to frantic calls from the underwriters; time was an important factor. Work began immediately on patching the flooded forward holds. This required divers, riveters, and ship

The coastal steamer *Henry T. Scott* is seen here a few months before she was rammed and sunk at the entrance to the strait by the SS *Harry Luckenbach*, July 16, 1922.

The coastal freighter *Skagway* was a victim of a devastating fire in December 1929, while en route to Puget Sound from San Francisco. She was grounded near Fuca's Pillar. The place today is known as Skagway Rocks.

German ship *Flottbek* in trouble between Flattery Rocks and White Rock off the rugged Washington Coast, in February 1901. The vessel was pulled free from almost certain destruction and towed to port.

Canadian tug *Sudbury* stands helplessly by as the big barge *Island Maple* breaks in two and sinks in ugly seas south of Cape Flattery in October 1963.

Dismasted and waterlogged, the American brig *Harriet G.* was towed to port after abandonment by her crew, 35 miles southwest of Cape Flattery in 1916.

Canadian motor vessel *Jessie Island No. 4* departed Chemainus for Port Alberni, B.C., December 24, 1926. Long overdue, her mangled remains were later discovered near Pachena Bay.

This photo was taken just a few weeks before the vessel—the American bark *Florence*—vanished somewhere off Cape Flattery in 1902, en route to San Francisco from Tacoma.

Powerful steam tug of yesteryear—the *Wanderer*. From the time of her completion in 1890, she towed scores of sailing vessels in from Cape Flattery to Puget Sound.

fitters; all salvage equipment had to be barged in. There were anxious moments when the weather interfered and again when the salvagers were ready to give up. These men, however, were skillful. In the past, they had performed some incredible salvage feats and their occasional failures were never caused by lack of human ingenuity or tenacity.

The salvage job on the *Canada Maru* was unique in maritime annals. That she could have been saved from such a position of exposure to the ocean was without precedent. But even more unusual was the fact that the salvagers had to actually create a second ship stranding in order to refloat the Japanese liner. The Canadian salvage steamer *Salvor* was assigned to the job and her part in saving *Canada Maru* proved to be the apex of her thirteen-year career as a salvage ship. Because of her age she was in the process of being sold during this, her final salvage endeavor. In order to complete the refloating of the *Canada Maru* they purposely ran her aground. With faith in her stout iron hull (which dated from the year 1869) her skipper grounded her upon the rocks with assurance that the old ship was up to the task. The vessel, decades earlier, had been built as the *Danube* at Govan, Scotland, to replace the tea clipper ships on the run from London to China. Among the laurels in her famous career was being the first tea-laden ship to transit the Suez Canal; also the vessel chosen in 1873 to return to England the body of the "beloved master" of thousands of Africans—explorer-missionary, Dr. David Livingstone.

From her precarious position, the *Salvor's* crew performed the final phase of the miracle salvage job. The *Canada Maru* wreck was a real challenge. The job went on day after day. Finally, on the flood tide of August 5, 1918—more than a half year after the stranding—snorting tugs pulled her free. Hastily ushered off to the nearest shipyard, the *Canada Maru* was soon back on her old run. The *Salvor* went to Australia as a freighter and later became the Spanish steamer *Nervion,* adding more laurels to her long career.

SALVAGE OF THE PHOEBE

From the time of the earliest shipwrecks along the Northwest Coast of Washington, the Indians insisted on their rights to salvage, or to claim anything that came ashore on their beaches. When prevented by the white men from doing this they often became hostile, and trouble was the result.

Even down to our present decade the Makah Indians have endeavored to claim salvage rights on vessels wrecked on their reservation lands—an unwritten law which white man's judicial practice continually tears apart. An unusual case arose in the summer of 1962, in which the Makah Tribal Council asserted their right to salvage a wrecked yacht, only to have it snatched from their grasp through legal processes.

It all began when the 42-foot yacht *Phoebe* was en route to Puget Sound from Astoria. Aboard her were Mr. and Mrs. Russell Woodruff and son Russell, Jr. Woodruff, sixty-eight, of Portland, testified to the truth in the old adage, "a chain is only as strong as its weakest link." He asserted this truth after the grounding of his yacht and the subsequent harrowing rescue. The *Phoebe* was driven almost on the beach near Cape Alava, after her main anchor chain snapped in heavy seas, June 1, 1962.

The events that led to the unfortunate accident began in the afternoon, while the craft was headed northward in the regular shipping lanes, about fifteen to twenty miles from shore. It was then that Woodruff noted how the twin 150-horsepower engines were drawing too much fuel from one tank. He started a pump to balance the load and left the wheel in the cabin to go to a second wheel on the flying bridge. Before he remembered to shut off the pump, Woodruff estimated he had inadvertently pumped fifty to seventy-five gallons of fuel into the ocean— enough to take them in to Neah Bay. After he realized he might run out of fuel he left the shipping lanes and pursued a course dangerously close to shore, where he made his second mistake.

They had passed Destruction Island and Woodruff mistook the rock formations, believing he was passing Tatoosh Island.

Seeing what he thought was the breakwater at Neah Bay, he headed in. When he was close enough to realize that he was lost, the vessel ran out of fuel and the main anchor was dropped. As the seas began to kick up, Woodruff started sending distress signals every five minutes and eventually made contact with a Coast Guard plane. It took the Coast Guard motor lifeboat five hours to reach the *Phoebe* from the Quillayute Coast Guard Station at La Push.

By this time it was night. When Woodruff detected the sound of the rescue boat's engine, he signalled with his searchlight, shut off the power on the boat, and readied his wife and son to abandon the craft. Irascible seas prevented the Coast Guard boat from getting a line aboard, but eventually it maneuvered alongside, and Woodruff and his son leaped to safety. It was different with Mrs. Woodruff—she panicked and leaped at the wrong moment. Falling between the two rolling boats, she had her legs badly mangled. Only the fenders prevented the accident from being far worse. While the rescue boat pitched and rolled violently, she lay in the cabin, her head in her son's lap, lifejackets piled over her for warmth. By radio, the coastguardsmen were advised to put tourniquets on Mrs. Woodruff's legs to stop the bleeding, and to head for Neah Bay with dispatch.

The rescue craft battled head seas for six hours and in the thick weather had trouble finding the entrance to the strait. It was another six hours before they reached Neah Bay. The three miserably cold and uncomfortable survivors finally were taken to Port Angeles, where the ailing lady was moved to a hospital.

The insurance company immediately hired two Makah Indians to proceed to the wreck and get the Woodruffs' personal belongings and loose gear. The boat had drifted northward and gone hard aground at Portage Head, six and a half miles south of Cape Flattery.

Woodruff was so troubled by his harrowing experience that he told the insurance company they could have the boat if it could be salvaged. Though some $83,000 had been invested in the craft, he doubted if he could ever again get his wife to step aboard it or any other vessel.

On June 4, Captain Loring F. Hyde, marine surveyor and well-known salvage master of Port Angeles, was contacted by the U.S. Salvage Association in Seattle to proceed to Portage Head and make a survey of the *Phoebe*. With John Sweatt and Ronald Little, prospective salvors, they went to Neah Bay, thence to Portage Head by truck over an old logging road. Then they took an Indian trail to where the wreck reposed. Hyde found the *Phoebe* partly buried in the sand and a large hole in her hull. A considerable amount of electrical and other loose equipment had already been removed by Dan Elverum and Laurence Bunn of the Indian village.

Hyde, after making his preliminary survey, reasoned that, weather permitting, there was a good chance of refloating the *Phoebe*, after sufficient hull patching. Heading back to Neah Bay, the three men held a conference at which Elverum and Bunn submitted a bid of $12,000 to refloat the vessel on a "no cure no pay" basis. Sweatt and Little later submitted a bid of $10,000.

At 9 a.m. the following day, Hyde phoned the U. S. Salvage Association and relayed the bids for consideration of the Underwriters. The parties finally agreed on a bid of $9,000 favoring Sweatt and Little.

Within two hours a truck was loaded at Port Angeles with men and equipment and the successful bidders were off to try their fortune. They planned to jack the vessel up high enough to patch the holes and then to float it over outlying rocks on a high tide, June 6 or 7. Digging began immediately and camp was set up on the beach.

Then came the crowning blow: just at midnight in this isolated, forsaken spot, the salvage crew was served a restraining order by the Makah Indian Tribal Court, to vacate operations. The case was at a stalemate until June 7, when Captain Hyde received instructions that the restraining order would be lifted by the U. S. Deputy Marshal.

On June 8, the salvagers returned but the weather was adverse and operations were halted again—all but a watchman going home. After more frustrating efforts it was decided a bulldozer was needed to move rocks from the beach. Also needed were two Alaska spruce trees for use as a cradle for the *Phoebe*, to which flotation drums would be chained.

On June 12, the necessary equipment was acquired and pre-liminary commitment gained from the Makah Tribal Council for the cutting of the two trees and for bringing more heavy equip-ment onto the property. On June 14, a tug was dispatched from Port Angeles to Neah Bay to stand by. All was ready the follow-ing day, but a strong westerly wind and heavy sea thwarted the attempt. At low tide, the bulldozer cleared more rocks and pre-pared a channel, but heavy breakers again prevented the effort on both June 17 and 18.

Finally, on June 19, at twelve noon the weather moderated. The tug arrived and got a line in at high tide. The pull was suc-cessful and the *Phoebe* floated free in her drum-buoyed cradle. The tug brought her into Port Angeles several hours later. The full $73,000 insurance carried by the owner was paid and the boat was sold on an "as is where is" basis for a new lease on life.

The Indians, as in days of yore, received no compensation for either the fallen spruce trees or the roadways bulldozed onto their land—nor were their salvage claims deemed valid.

PART 2

LIGHTHOUSES AND LIGHTSHIPS

Including the Indian troubles encountered in the survey and construction of Cape Flattery Lighthouse . . . the story of Umatilla Reef *and* Swiftsure Lightships *. . . problems at Slip Point Light . . . the novel arrival of keeper Cox and his family at Cape Beale Lighthouse . . . fire aboard the tug Haida Chieftain . . . the isolation of Carmanah Lighthouse . . . Pachena Light's establishment brought about by the* Valencia *disaster . . . and the demise of the Russian freighter* Uzbekistan *on Vancouver Island's West Coast.*

The entrance to the Strait of Juan de Fuca is international in character—the boundary running horizontally down its center. In and out of its portals on an average day pass about thirty deepsea vessels; it is one of the most important maritime crossroads in the entire Pacific Ocean.

The boundary question, historically, did not come about in serenity, for the killing of a pig on San Juan Island came very near involving two great nations in war. This island, and all others which compose the San Juan archipelago, was claimed by the United States under the treaty of 1846, in which the boundary was defined as the forty-ninth parallel "to the middle of the channel which separates the continent from Vancouver's Island; thence southerly through the middle of said channel, and of Fuca's Strait to the Pacific Ocean." But ownership of the San

70

Juan Islands remained in dispute. Both countries attempted to collect customs and taxes and English and Americans lived there in a constant state of tension.

Affairs reached a climax in 1859 when a pig belonging to an Englishman raided a vegetable garden of an American. The American shot the pig and threatened like action against any Britisher who dared disapprove.

Both the British and Americans sent ships and men who stood ready to battle, but the touchy question was finally resolved peacefully by the Treaty of Washington. Concluded on May 8, 1871, it adjusted all matters of difference between the United States and Great Britain, through arbitration of His Majesty, the Emperor of Germany.

Prior to the boundary fracas, several partial surveys of the strait and its entrance had been made by both Americans and British, perhaps the most noted having been that of British Commander Charles Wilkes in the summer of 1841. As his party was leaving the strait, a close watch was kept for that "exceeding high pinnacle, or spired rock, like a pillar," which Fuca had described much earlier. Such a rock was sighted and a sketch of it made. Wilkes' party also visited Neah Bay, where they found a few of the bricks from an unsuccessful settlement established on May 29, 1791, by Spanish explorer and navigator Salvador Fidalgo of the *Princessa*.

One thing on which the British and American surveyors all agreed was that aids to navigation were sorely needed in this remote corner of the world. It was, however, the middle of the nineteenth century before any action came to fruition. The document that initially aided the cause was the report accompanying a survey of the Columbia River by the United States surveying schooner *Ewing*, out of San Francisco, September 25, 1850. The report from William P. McArthur to Professor A. D. Bache, superintendent, U. S. Coast Survey, Washington, D. C., read:

A lighthouse is much needed also at Cape Flattery [one had been suggested for Cape Disappointment at the entrance to the Columbia River], and I would recommend that it be situated on "Tatoochi [Tatoosh] Island," a small island almost touching the Northwest extremity of Cape Flattery.

To vessels bound from seaward a lighthouse on this island would be of much assistance. It would enable them to enter the strait, when the absence of a light would frequently compel them to remain at sea till daylight. Once inside the strait, vessels are comparatively secure.

The advantage of having the lighthouse situated on the island, instead of on the extremity of the cape, is that being so situated, it would serve as a guide to vessels seeking Neah or Scarborough Harbor, a small but secure harbor of refuge four miles inside the strait. Strong contrary currents will cause navigators to seek the little harbor quite frequently.

Because of the East Coast "Moon Cussers"—a motley breed of men who caused shipwrecks by nefarious methods—the United States government by this time (1850) had been prompted to strict laws that would prevent such evil practice. The Moon Cussers were so named because they could only work on the darkest nights when the moon failed to shed its light on the shoreline. The law read:

> Every person who holds out or shows any false light or extinguishes any true light, with intent to bring any vessel sailing upon the sea into danger or distress or shipwreck, shall be punished by a fine of not more than five thousand dollars and imprisoned at hard labor not more than ten years.

Such a practice was very rare in the Pacific Northwest. A century or more ago, shipwrecks were common in the area because of natural hazards and those who desired to make an existence by plundering the spoils had but to be beachcombers. Wrecks were often sold for a paltry sum, should one wish to be legal. The problems lay in the many perilous locales and the lack of communication with centers of population. Most of the vast, empty acres and rugged shorelines skirting this graveyard of ships were frequented only by coastal Indians.

CAPE FLATTERY LIGHTHOUSE

In the year 1852, in writing of the difficulties encountered while his party was operating in the vicinity of Cape Flattery, George Davidson, pioneer West Coast surveyor and scientist, stated: "The topography has been executed at the risk of the life of every one at work on it." He was speaking of his survey of Tatoosh Island, which was the site recommended for a lighthouse at the then extreme northwest corner of continental United States.

When Davidson referred to risk of life, he was not speaking of the rugged terrain but of likely attack from hostile Indians who looked upon palefaces as intruders. When his party landed—"The only means of conveyance I could furnish was two small canoes, which were forced to land on the rocks and rocky points." He noted that the Indians there "resort in summer about one hundred fifty strong," and he considered the station to have been occupied at very great risk from the hostility of these Indians— "but a knowledge that we were always prepared for an attack, without doubt, prevented one. We built a breastwork, and could fire sixty rounds without reloading. Guard was kept six hours every night."

These defenses were for protection against the Indians who frequently stole materials and caused trouble generally. Twenty muskets were issued to the construction crew and positions were assigned at the breastwork in case of alarm. At first there were many anxious moments, but as the project continued, the natives began to tolerate the intruders, dwelling with them in a sort of tense co-existence.

These were the precarious conditions under which Davidson and his men had to work. His survey team charted out the most suitable site for a lighthouse and outbuildings at the most elevated spot on the island. The plateau was one hundred feet above the sea.

Tatoosh was initially suggested as a lighthouse reservation by a joint Army and Navy commission in 1849, when the steamer *Massachusetts* visited the area. Acting on their recommendation, Congress, in 1850, suggested construction of beacons at both Tatoosh Island and at New Dungeness (the latter, a spit well inside the Strait of Juan de Fuca). Construction, however, was not authorized until after Davidson's survey, when an appropriation was set aside for both structures in August 1854. The total amount was only $39,000.

Though much credit must be given to these early surveyors—intrepid individuals who risked their lives to do the job—the wrath of the Indians is readily understood. They had long used the island for fishing and whaling, and for growing vegetables. At one time they had much of the tillable soil, about twenty acres at the top of the island, under cultivation for raising potatoes; and they had erected crude slab-board dwellings where they resided during the better months of the year. To all intents and purposes it was their island, yet Uncle Sam took it over without the slightest consideration for them. Already the white men had brought great peril. Influenza, smallpox, and venereal diseases, virtually unknown to the Indians, had been spread among the tribes.

Access to Tatoosh Island was rugged. It rose sharply with but a single beach suitable for landing, and this was the spot from which the Indians conducted their fishing and whaling enterprises. A steep switchback trail led to the top of the island and was the only means of reaching the summit until the lighthouse crew landed a derrick through the surf. They assembled it during the construction of the station.

Isaac Smith was foreman and superintendent of construction. He was a fearless individual with a knack for getting the utmost out of his men. What he put together was built to the highest specifications, and the fact that the tower at Tatoosh stands as stout and firm today as when it was built is mute testimony to his skill.

A government vessel brought great blocks of sandstone two feet thick for the foundation of the structure. It was quarried near the present site of Bellingham, Washington. Landing the rock through the surf proved a difficult undertaking. The men, however, prevailed. The derrick hoisted the stone from the beach to the island plateau and the masons laid the foundation.

The lighthouse was soon ready for the huge iron lantern. Into it was fitted a flawless first-order Fresnel lens and oil lamps. The apparatus was made in Paris, France, by order of the U. S. Lighthouse Board, and it came around Cape Horn by sailing vessel. The scintillating glass and bronze mechanism, 10.6 feet high, remained at the station until a couple of decades ago, when it was replaced by a fourth-order triple-flashing lens. Because of the superior brilliance of modern light globes compared to oil lamps, the present apparatus casts a beam thousands of times more powerful than the original, though the lens is much smaller.

Unfortunately the original lens, after being replaced, was rudely deposited in a big crate at an old Seattle waterfront pier and almost forgotten. It wound up at the home of a Seattle glass dealer and eventually was broken up in his backyard. The lens was made by Louis Sautter & Co., Paris, in 1854, by order of the U. S. Secretary of the Treasury, the Lighthouse Board, and Lieutenant W. A. Bartlett, U. S. Navy special superintendent.

The Indians who had watched the lighthouse construction thought the station should be shared with them and they roamed about its interior without the slightest hesitation. To them, the 36x24-foot edifice and its 65-foot sandstone and brick tower was a castle. They frequented the dining room, hall, sitting room, kitchen, and even the head keeper's office. Sometimes they were found sitting in the dark cellar. They ran up and down the circular staircase and were frequently to be seen shouting from the windows of the four bedrooms on the second story—wearing out their welcome almost around the clock.

The builders had rushed completion so the station would not be left unoccupied during the winter months. Morris H. Frost, collector of customs, and in charge of government aids to navigation for the area, had the job of choosing the initial keepers for the station. Word about the troublesome Indians had become widespread and there was some concern among those considered for the positions. George H. Gerrish of Port Townsend eventually accepted the post as Flattery's first keeper. His three assistants were James Barry, George H. Fitzgerald, and William C. Webster. The light was first exhibited on December 28, 1857.

So troublesome did the natives become after the construction crew departed that three months later the keepers all tendered letters of resignation. They also complained of the extreme isolation of the place and of the difficulty of getting provisions, most of which had to come by Indian dugout from the mainland. From his very first watch, Gerrish had experienced great difficulty putting the light into operation because of the inferior quality of oil. The lamps had to be trimmed constantly and the lens looked like a smudge pot each dawn. According to early records, the final pay of keeper Gerrish and his assistants combined came to only $220.83.

The collector of customs hastily replaced Gerrish with Franklin Tucker, who originally had been slated to take the head keeper's job at New Dungeness Light Station. Tucker, however, had been out of the territory when that station opened. John Thompson and James Mutch came along as Tucker's assistants at Flattery. This trio were no more satisfied than their predecessors had been, and by the summer of 1858 they too tendered their resignations, citing poor pay and trouble with the Indians—who sometimes numbered more than two hundred strong.

Frost then lined up F. W. James to take charge of the station. The latter's trouble did not come from the Indians alone but also from ships passing in the night. Some shipmasters reported that the light was barely visible and at times inoperative. Angered by these reports, Frost promptly sent word by way of Indian mail to keeper James that he was relieved of duty. The keeper protested, vigorously claiming that he had kept the light burning to the best of his ability. He further demanded of the collector of customs a new station boat, inasmuch as the old one had become damaged beyond "reasonable repair."

After making a thorough study of all the facts, Frost felt obligated to rehire James but flatly refused to supply the station with a new boat. It was then the keeper's turn to mull over the situation. He did, and decided that if his request could not be met, he would quit; he notified his superior accordingly.

Frost was exasperated. The light station was scarcely a year old and already three keepers and their assistants had turned in their resignations. New keepers with the right qualifications were extremely difficult to find; the Fraser River gold rush had lured young and old alike to the Canadian side. In despair Frost had to turn for assistance to Lieutenant W. L. Hyde, commander of the revenue cutter *Jefferson Davis*. Inasmuch as the vessel was working in Pacific Northwest waters, Frost asked to borrow two of her company to man the light station temporarily.

When the revenue cutter arrived off the Island, the men made a landing by small boat. During their brief visit the ship's officers endeavored to explain to the Indians the "boom boom" power of the ship's guns—should they be so foolish as to interfere with the keepers.

Finally, in January of 1860, a permanent head keeper was assigned—William W. Winsor of Port Angeles. He was a determined individual and the first recruit to stay on the job for any length of time. He solved most of the vexing problems, but did complain of driving rains seeping in under the shingles of the dwelling, dampening the structure so that moss grew on the interior plaster. He also had trouble with the downwinds in the chimneys blowing billows of smoke back into the rooms.

On the credit side, Winsor established better relations with the Indians and managed to acquire a more suitable brand of oil which made the lens glow like a great star. This satisfied captains whose ships passed in the night. On March 3, 1871, Congress appropriated $10,000 for the erection of an urgently needed steam fog-signal at Tatoosh. This could have prevented several shipwrecks had it been installed earlier.

Geographically, Tatoosh Island today is little altered from those early years, except that Indians no longer frequent the place. A U.S. weather observation station was maintained on the island from 1883 till August 1, 1966, when—because of the extreme isolation—the station was moved to the site of the Quillayute Airport, nine miles west of Forks, Washington. A diaphone foghorn with a powerful voice now blasts whenever the weather thickens, and it is far more audible than the old steam whistle. There is also a radio-beacon whose signal is picked up by ships far at sea.

Unlike in the early years, the attendants at the station are permitted to have their families with them, and they live in modern duplexes instead of in the old dwelling at the base of the tower. The island is serviced regularly by Coast Guard vessels bringing supplies and mail from Neah Bay. In an emergency a helicopter can service the remote island from the base in Port Angeles. Visitors are allowed at the station by special permission of the Thirteenth Coast Guard District headquarters in Seattle, but it is a tedious and sometimes rugged trip and sightseers are few.

Before the Coast Guard took over the old U. S. Lighthouse Service in 1939, keepers put in long terms of duty with little time off. Today, the routine chores of the lighthouse no longer demand endless hours of work; everything is electronic. Coast Guard personnel are rotated frequently with generous relief periods.

In early 1961, the Coast Guard doubled the light intensity of the Cape Flattery beacon. This was accomplished through usage of a special high-intensity light globe. At the same time the three major lighthouses on the Canadian side of the strait entrance had their light intensities increased. Pachena was upped to 90,000 candle-power; Cape Beale was increased to 30,000 candlepower, and Carmanah Point was fitted with a brand new airway-type rotary beacon producing 1,770,000 candlepower.

The purpose of increasing the candlepower and adding greater range to the radio-beacon signals of these four stations was a conservative move to eliminate *Swiftsure Lightship* station, thirteen miles west northwest of Cape Flattery and ten miles southwest of Carmanah Point—after more than a half century of service.

A more recent innovation at the light stations is Loran coverage of the approaches to the Strait of Juan de Fuca, affording lines of position that intersect at greater than seventy-five degree angles. With Loran, a navigator can determine his geographical position by using signals sent out from two radio stations. The Flattery radio-beacon is audible to 150 miles at sea and the Canadian stations one hundred miles.

UMATILLA REEF LIGHTSHIP

Umatilla Reef is off a remote sector of the last frontier of continental United States. Since 1898, a lightship has anchored in twenty-five fathoms two and a half miles southwest of the reef, westward of Cape Alava.

The first vessel assigned to duty off the reef was *Lightship No. 67*. This plucky 112-footer remained at the post for prolonged periods as there were no relief lightships in those early years. Only when bottom plates became barnacle encrusted did she dare vacate her anchorage. For three decades, *No. 67* performed faithfully. In her latter years of service, relief lightships gave her more time at the repair yard. For years the vessel was almost as permanent as the reef she guarded—though she was often buffeted by tremendous North Pacific storms which caused her to drag anchor.

In the winter of 1914, *Relief Lightship No. 92* was struck so hard by a driving gale that she slipped two anchors and lost ninety-five feet of anchor chain. Her machinery and deck gear were damaged and sea water was in every compartment. A call for assistance brought old *No. 67* steaming back to take over.

In 1930, while under command of her veteran skipper, Captain Eric Lindman, *No. 67* was retired and *No. 93* was given mastery over the reef. Later the Coast Guard switched *No. 93* to the Columbia River station and *Columbia River Lightship No. 88* came to Umatilla Reef, reclassified as *WAL 513*.

Today the regular lightship at Umatilla is *WAL 196*. She was assigned in November 1961, after coming around from the East Coast from duty at Nantucket and Pollocks Rip. Built at Bay City, Michigan, in 1946, she became widely traveled for a lightship. Her voyage around from the East Coast included stops at Kingston, Jamaica, Rodman, the Canal Zone, Acapulco, San Francisco, and Coos Bay.

SWIFTSURE BANK LIGHTSHIP

Established in 1909, this was the last of five U. S. lightship stations on the Pacific Coast and the first to be terminated. The initial lightship on this station was *No. 93*, which came around Cape Horn from the East Coast in a flotilla of lightships and lighthouse tenders. The voyage required 124 days at the speed of the slowest lightship.

Swiftsure Bank is about three and one half miles in extent, with a thirty-fathom curve, and lies off the Strait of Juan de Fuca northwestward of a submarine valley, the least depth of which is nineteen fathoms.

Every year the lightship was passed by thousands of ocean-going vessels. Her foghorn blasted an average of 1,200 hours annually and she acted as a mother ship for scores of commercial fishing craft that depended on her presence in foul weather and fair. The ship was also the turning point for the annual Swiftsure Race for sailing yachts, which begins off Race Rocks near Victoria, B. C.

One of the nation's first diesel electric lightships, *No. 113* was assigned to Swiftsure in 1930. She was a product of a Portland,

Oregon, shipyard and opened a new era in aids to navigation. This vessel also had to her credit a voyage to Alaska as a naval observation ship during World War II. She is now a relief lightship with the classification *WAL 535.*

During a driving gale in December 1932, the *Swiftsure Lightship* took a merciless pounding. While dragging anchor with her engines at full speed ahead, she ducked into a mammoth sea that smashed her pilothouse windows and flattened the helmsman against the wheel with such force that he broke out three of its spokes. Knocked unconscious, he suffered a wrenched back, a broken arm, and facial cuts. The unfortunate sailor was almost drowned from lying face down in a foot of water inside the wheelhouse. The vessel received so much damage that it had to be relieved by another lightship.

On December 30, 1952, the *Swiftsure Lightship*, at the height of a sixty-five-mile gale, lost her anchor and seventy-five fathoms of chain. She was carried more than two miles off station and had to be blacked out in order not to mislead other ships by her light or radio-beacon. She finally regained her charted position and dropped a second anchor. It was all in the line of duty.

The discontinuation of *Swiftsure Lightship* on July 1, 1961, should have brought a flow of tears from a host of mariners who had been aided by its comforting light and assuring foghorn down through the years. But at a public hearing conducted by the Coast Guard in Seattle to hear protests, only two persons showed up and the lightship was promptly withdrawn.

SLIP POINT LIGHTHOUSE

The only major U. S. light established immediately inside the strait entrance was a picturesque little station located on the rocky ramparts of Slip Point near Clallam Bay, Washington. The old lighthouse no longer exists. In its stead, erected on piling, is an automatic light.

The original lighthouse was replaced in 1951 and with it went much of the maritime romance of the area. On June 6, 1900, Congress had appropriated $12,500 for Slip Point Lighthouse, but the price asked for the land was so high that it finally had to be acquired by condemnation proceedings. On June 5, 1902, damages to the extent of $2,562 were awarded the owners of the property. More problems ensued. When bids for construction were let, they were so excessive that the work had to be done by day labor.

Costs mounted and progress was aggravatingly slow. It was not until April 1, 1905, that the light was first displayed. Eventually this inferior light was replaced with a clam-shell type lens illuminated by an oil-vapor lamp which sent out a brilliant beam of light.

In the early years post lanterns were displayed to guide ships into Neah Bay: Neah Bay Light and Waada (Waaddah) Light, located on the north and south ends of Waada Island. These navigation aids, modernized and electrified, still exist today.

Buoys also roll and rock at important points on both the American and Canadian side of the strait's entrance. And each has its individual characteristics and personality—important factors in safeguarding lives and property and a far cry from the unprotected waters of yesteryear.

CAPE BEALE LIGHTHOUSE

The bright star of hope—a name affectionately applied to Cape Flattery's old beacon—was singular in meaning. The lone beacon was in urgent need of some companion lights in bygone years. Despite the tremendous increase in maritime traffic and the subsequent heavy loss of ships in the area, it was seventeen years before another major light shone out over Fuca's graveyard. Even then it was only through much public agitation that funds were finally allocated by the Canadian government for the construction of Cape Beale Lighthouse. It was to serve a two-fold purpose: as an entrance light to Barkley Sound and as a landfall and guiding light to ships entering the Strait of Juan de Fuca.

The rash of shipwrecks and resultant loss of life along the West Coast of Vancouver Island were chief factors behind the decision to construct the lighthouse. Funds were hard to come by and labor scarce. The remote area was void of white population. To economize, much of the lumber was cut on the scene from the tall trees that surrounded the cape. Local Indians were used in the labor crew. Building materials for the station had to be landed by boat and carried up the rocky cliff to the site. Construction was slow, hampered by the frequent heavy rains, but the work was pressed to completion. The forty-two-foot wooden tower was a four-sided pyramidal affair surmounted by an iron lantern, with the focal plane of the light 172 feet above the Pacific.

No fog signal was included in the scant appropriations for the station, and it was not until 1908 that a first-class fog signal was established.

The first keeper assigned to the isolated lighthouse was Emmanuel Cox. He got passage with his wife, three daughters, and two sons aboard the antiquated steam tug *Alexander* from Victoria. Cox had previously been stationed at Berens Island at the entrance to Victoria Harbor. It was indeed a challenge to him and his family to take off for the isolation of Indian country. Their experiences were to be many and varied, but their native neighbors proved to be loyal and friendly.

The Cox family's introduction to the new lighthouse proved an event in itself. The *Alexander* had landed them at an Indian village at nearby Dodger's Cove on Diana Island, inside Barkley Sound. Adverse weather kept them at the cove for nearly a week before the Indians brought them the final six miles by canoe. They passed through reefs, rocks, breakers, and a school of killer whales. The finale was piggy-back rides on the Indians through the surf to the beach below Cape Beale. The children never forgot their unusual arrival. After all the stores had been landed, housekeeping was set up.

The light was first displayed at the station on July 1, 1874. It was a catoptric (with metallic reflectors) revolving apparatus which showed a white light at intervals of thirty seconds, making a complete revolution every two minutes. To differentiate the station by day from that at Cape Flattery, the tower and its dwelling were painted a light stone color.

Whenever Keeper Cox had to go to Victoria, his wife was left in charge of the light. The children willingly helped out, and so did the friendly Indians. On one occasion when Cox was in Victoria, the revolving apparatus failed. To maintain the flashing characteristic, Mrs. Cox and all but the youngest child took turns at the lens throughout the night, turning the apparatus by hand. This routine was repeated for ten days, until Cox returned.

Except for the arrival of the government lighthouse tender *Sir James Douglas*—which came only every third or fourth month— all mail and supplies were brought by canoe from Dodger's Cove. When an Indian was needed at the light station, a Union Jack was displayed. Usually first on the scene was Indian John Mack, who dwelled not far from Dodger's Cove. For being available whenever required, the government paid him five dollars per month. If the light was defective, up went the flag, and the wise old redskin would come in for a feed, receive a letter to the marine agent, and set out immediately for Victoria in his canoe. The eighty-five mile trip took him two days and two nights, but he was always punctual and dependable. In fact, he was so loyal that several years later, in 1890, when keeper Cox suffered a fatal heart attack, John Mack refused to take pay for carrying word of his death to the marine agent.

Just prior to Cox's death, a telephone line had been strung from tree to tree along the island's coast. It was for lighthouse and lifesaving purposes, but a storm later knocked down the line, necessitating another trip to Victoria by John Mack's canoe express. When pay was forced on the old Indian for his effort, he sulked for three weeks, claiming that the trip was made out of respect to keeper Cox. During those early years, the Cox family was responsible for warning many ships away from the treacherous coast. Nevertheless, numerous vessels fell victim to its jagged rocks when the light was shrouded by fog. On July 27, 1879, the British sailing ship *Bechardass Ambiadas* was driven on a reef three miles east of the lighthouse. Some of the survivors resided at the station until the schooner *Favourite* arrived to take them to Victoria.

For beachcombers, the wreck yielded a bonanza, much of which was recovered by the Indians. The Cox family retrieved several casks of wine.

In 1958, the present steel and frame lighthouse with an aluminum lantern house replaced the old Cape Beale tower. The pioneer wooden structure had served its time and a replacement was overdue.

HAIDA CHIEFTAIN

A near tragedy that had a happy ending is among the more recent episodes off Cape Beale Lighthouse. The *Haida Chieftain* —one of the largest tugboats on Canada's West Coast—was towing a huge 344-foot barge when she was saved by the tug *La Reine*, then on her maiden voyage.

It all started on January 3, 1965. The spanking new Canadian tug *La Reine*, owned by Vancouver Tug Boat Company under command of Captain George Horton, was heading for a rendezvous with the 700-foot ore carrier *Santa Isabel Maru*, to help her into Toquart Bay. Here is the story as Captain Horton tells it:

> We were off Cape Beale when the radio picked up a conversation between the disabled 143-foot tug *Haida Chieftain* and the tug *La Pointe*. They were coming down the coast on the same course some miles apart. Ten miles off Cape Beale, near Barkley Sound, fire broke out in the engine room of the *Haida*. She was blazing out of control and they abandoned ship.

We set course for the scene, and by the time we arrived, the tug *La Pointe*, skippered by Alan "K. O." Stanley, had picked up the ten-man crew from the *Haida Chieftain's* lifeboat. The ill-fated tug was on fire and drifting abandoned.

It was midnight when we got there. We went close alongside the burning tug. She had 1.5 million feet of logs aboard her barge, with 2,200 feet of two-inch towline out. Well, we maneuvered into position. It was snowing and visibility was poor. The wind was blowing twenty-five miles an hour and gusty. There was a moderate to heavy swell and a rough sea. Our men on the stern were constantly engulfed in water—they had to hang on or get thrown over the side.

Under these conditions it was impossible to board the stricken tug and attempt to get the fire out. But with our twin screws and plenty of power, we were able to hold position. We turned on the six floodlights on our mast, as well as the two big searchlights, and the scene was a blaze of light.

After more maneuvering, we managed to pick up the tag line, attached to the float astern of the barge. This we attached to our towing winch. We brought in the line, and with it came the emergency towline from the barge's bow. Well, the barge swung around, bow first, and the tug came with it—taking the sea on the beam.

With the tug burning all the way, we worked our course up Imperial Channel and rendezvoused with the *La Pointe*, which had tied up her own barge and transferred the rescued crew to another vessel. At 0745 hours [7:45 a.m.], the *La Pointe* went alongside the still-burning craft and proceeded to put out the blaze. At 1400 [2 p.m.], we delivered our tow safely in the sheltered water of San Mateo Bay.

Captain Horton had nothing but praise for *La Reine*—her seaworthy qualities and her comfort: "A river pilot told me the

La Reine is a towboat man's dream, and he's right—she's a dream you never expect to see in real life."

What does he like about her?—"First, she has a whistle like the *Queen Mary*," he says. "Second, she has terrific pulling power, and third, the twin screws give her fantastic maneuverability—you can go from full ahead (better than eleven knots) to dead in the water in twenty-two seconds. Going full-speed through the water, you can put the helm hard over and the turning circle is almost negligible. With twin screws, you can go into confined spaces with ease; and you can do standing turns, with one screw going ahead and one going astern."

The fire out, the *Haida Chieftain* was towed to port for a complete overhaul and a new lease on life—thanks to the quick thinking and fast action of a tugboat crew and a fine new tug.

CARMANAH LIGHTHOUSE

The rotary electric airway-type beacon that shines out from Carmanah today is many times more powerful than the former Fresnel lens. The fifty-six-foot octagonal concrete tower with its red lantern house stands out prominently against the surrounding terrain.

The station was established in 1891, and modernized in 1922, 1944, and 1961. The focal plane of the light is 175 feet above the rolling combers of the Pacific. The tower is on the most seaward projection, two miles from Bonilla Point. Below the tower is a diaphone fog signal at the 127-foot level.

Until recently, H. C. Pearce and his wife manned the station. They maintained a nice garden with a highly productive strawberry patch. They came to Carmanah from Scarlett Point Light about the time a powerful new radio-beacon and high-powered light were installed, giving the station the leading role on Vancouver Island's West Coast. There are two commodious keeper's dwellings at Carmanah; and a hoist—which travels 850 feet—brings supplies up from the beach, saving many weary steps.

Despite the numerous pre-century shipwrecks between Carmanah and Bonilla points, it was unfortunately not until 1891 that a station was established at Carmanah. Like Cape Beale, it has been the means of salvation of many ships and sailors in peril on the sea. Though only fifty-five miles from Victoria, it might as well be five hundred miles. Even today there are no roads leading to the station; in fact, the trail frequently grows over with bracken. Cougar, bear, deer, and mink abound, and hawks constantly soar over the forests. It is so isolated that, in order to vote, the keeper must walk the better part of a day back and forth from the tiny Indian village of Clo-oose.

When the lighthouse tender's boat cannot make a landing near the lighthouse with supplies and groceries, these have to be packed in from Clo-oose. The trail was in much better condition some years back when a telegraph line was stretched through the forest. Today, the station radio-telephone has outmoded the line and heavy rains have caused jungle-like growth along the path.

One welcome innovation, however, is the use of helicopters. Though the Department of Transport has constructed copter landing-platforms at other isolated light stations for emergencies, no platform is needed at Carmanah because of a natural rocky plateau abutting the site. The only unofficial visitors to the station are Indians or, occasionally, a timber cruiser. Sometimes the survivor of a wreck finds refuge at the lighthouse but this is not so common as in bygone years.

Heroism was enacted at Carmanah in 1955, when the station keeper, Gerald David Wellard, waded into the surf to get a line to a stranded American fishing vessel. He braved high breakers, undertow, and chill October weather, but managed to heave the line to the boat's operator and pull him to safety. His brave deed earned him a special award from the Royal Humane Association of Canada. Two years later another fishing boat was wrecked near the lighthouse. Two survivors struggled ashore in the night and found their way to the station by the beacon light. A helicopter was dispatched from Port Angeles to pick up the men.

Many lives and millions of dollars in ships and cargo would have been spared had Carmanah Light been built much earlier.

PACHENA LIGHTHOUSE

Completing the trio of major lighthouses on the Canadian side of the entrance to Juan de Fuca Strait is Pachena Lighthouse, established in 1907. Its construction was brought about by the tragic 1906 wreck of the coastwise passenger liner *Valencia*. Unfortunately it took this wreck, with its loss of 117 lives, for the Canadian government to realize the vital need for a major aid to navigation in the locale.

The structure is an octagonal frame tower, sixty-six feet high, and topped with a red, circular metal lantern two hundred feet above the water. A fog signal is housed six hundred feet from the light tower, its mournful cry being produced by a diaphone horn. A duplex houses the keeper, his family, and assistant.

UZBEKISTAN

Though many more shipwrecks occurred near Pachena before the erection of the lighthouse, one of the better known wrecks of more recent years is that of the Russian freighter *Uzbekistan*. This stranding was not the fault of the lighthouse, however, as its beacon had been temporarily blacked out because of Japanese submarines marauding offshore during the hectic years of World War II. One had shelled Estevan Lighthouse north of Barkley Sound.

The *Uzbekistan* went aground west of Darling Creek, a little more than two miles east of Pachena Point, in the winter of 1943. She was heavily laden with lend-lease cargo loaded at Pacific Northwest ports and was destined for Vladivostok. The ship, off course by several degrees, slammed onto the sandy beach and came to a jarring halt.

First to arrive at the scene was the veteran lighthouse tender *Estevan*. When the Russian crew was found to be in no immediate danger—and since the ship was armed—the matter was turned over to the Canadian Navy. When the tide ebbed from the sandy beach, the forty crew members, including several women, walked ashore hardly wetting their feet. The ship, however, under the burden of a full cargo, worked on the sands, and the heavy surf and rising tides fractured the hull. Surveyors and salvagers were quick to announce that any chances of saving the vessel were hopeless. She broke in two in short order despite her tender age, having been built in a French shipyard as late as 1937.

When it was learned that the *Uzbekistan* had been abandoned, looters descended on the scene like locusts. Meanwhile the survivors who had set up camp on the beach were escorted by naval personnel on a twelve-mile hike to Bamfield, where arrangements were made for their return to Russia. Under the rulings of the late Joseph Stalin, the master of the freighter faced possible death for losing his vessel. It is believed that, in this case, the intervention of Canadian officials on his behalf spared the master's life.

Parts of the rusted wreck are still visible on the beach where it grounded off Darling Creek, a grim reminder of what can happen when the beam of a major lighthouse is blotted out.

PART 3

WRECKS AT FUCA'S GATE

Including the account of the first wreck to be salvaged from the graveyard of ships . . . the sad plight of the William Tell *and* Duchess of Argyle . . . *the strange tale of the* Southern Chief . . . *the storm-tossed ride of the steamer* Alice Gertrude . . . *port of no return for the salmon-packed schooner* Bianca . . . *torment and triumph for the master of the freighter* Skagway . . . *the sister ships that lived and died together . . . and the grinding crash between a little cargo ship and a giant bulk carrier.*

HECATE, FIRST SURVIVOR

Salvage of a stranded vessel at the entrance to the Strait of Juan de Fuca was a near miracle in the last century. British naval sources, however, record one case as early as August 1861. The British Government survey vessel *Hecate*, 860 tons, five guns, and brigantine rigged, went aground in a thick fog two miles east of Cape Flattery on the American side. She was commanded by Captain George H. Richards, R.N.

At first it was feared she would be a total loss. An American power schooner, name not recorded, was summoned to her aid. With the help of a flood tide, the schooner managed to pull her off and escort her to Esquimalt where damage was found to be of major proportions. The ship was temporarily patched and pumps were kept going constantly. As there was no drydock in Western Canada or north of San Francisco capable of handling a vessel of her size, the *Hecate* had to risk the voyage to the California port.

To safeguard the vessel's crew, the sloop *Mutine* escorted her most of the way to the Golden Gate. The *Hecate* later returned to Canadian waters and continued her survey work, becoming one of the most successful survey ships ever to chart the area. The vessel bequeathed her name to Hecate Strait. Captain Richards also named Bligh Island, in Nootka Sound, for the controversial Vice Admiral William Bligh, who was master of the *Bounty* during the infamous mutiny.

SAD TALE OF WILLIAM TELL

Tragedy struck one of the finest ships in Pacific trades in 1864. The ship *William Tell*, after sailing across half the world and encountering storms and fogs, was lost within a few hours of reaching her destination.

A splendid full-rigged ship of 1,500 tons, virtually new, the *William Tell* flew the houseflag of N. Y. French of Walpole, Massachusetts. It was on August 15, 1864, that she departed Simonstown, South Africa, in command of Captain Jones. After logging a fair passage, the vessel's crew sighted land to the west of Nootka Sound on December 13.

Tacking off the entrance to the strait, the *William Tell* was forced to wait three days for favorable winds before entering. She was in ballast and scheduled to load spars at Puget Sound ports for the French government. When no tugs appeared, the vessel headed down the strait to within six miles of New Dungeness Lighthouse on December 19. Then the wind shifted and carried her near treacherous Race Rocks, on the Canadian side.

Vainly trying to reach Freshwater Bay, she beat about in the strait until December 22. The following day she lost all headway and moved in an easterly direction. The weather became thick and as night approached the ship got in too close, striking a reef three miles southwest of Port San Juan. The surf was moderate, and on the ebb tide a boat was lowered to carry a line to shore. When the boat stranded in shallow water, a daring crewman volunteered to carry the line to the beach. There was a 600-foot gap between the *William Tell* and the beach, but the line to which a conveyance was attached allowed all twenty-two crew members to reach shore safely.

Last to leave the ship were the captain and the mate, but only after they had felled the mainmast so that it toppled toward the reef on which the *William Tell* was impaled. This would permit easier access to and from the wreck. Shortly after they abandoned, however, the vessel bilged and broke up.

The survivors set up camp on the beach. A couple of days later they succeeded in signalling the passing schooner *Surprise*, Captain Francis. The vessel sent in a boat for the castaways and took them to Victoria.

DUCHESS OF ARGYLE TRAGEDY

Like America's *William Tell*, the British bark *Duchess of Argyle* was one of Britain's finest merchantmen. She was operated by a Scotch-English shipping house and at 1,700 tons and 250 feet in length was large for her day. Also like the *William Tell*, the *Duchess of Argyle* was almost at voyage-end when overtaken by disaster. In command of Captain H. E. Heard, the vessel was en route to Burrard Inlet from Liverpool. It had been a good passage with favorable weather most of the way.

The *Duchess of Argyle*—which carried an effigy of the duchess under her bowsprit—neared the Strait of Juan de Fuca on October 11, 1887. The entrance was shrouded in a thick fog and the whole opening from Cape Flattery to Bonilla Point was a great veil of white. Dead reckoning told Captain Heard that he was in deep wtaer. The big four-master groped about under a persistent breeze, working in and then coming about and running before the wind. The strong currents which were carrying the ship dangerously close to the hostile fangs of Vancouver Island were forgotten in the endeavor to escape the fog. No landmarks were visible. Suddenly the vessel ground to a jarring halt, knocking the men to the deck. The wheel was wrenched from the helmsman's grip and spun wildly.

Captain Heard immediately ordered his men to stand by the boats. He had no idea of his position; the fog was so thick that the reef on which the ship was cradled could not be seen from the railing. Even as the men prepared to abandon ship, the hull opened up and water surged in unchecked. Yardarms broke loose and tumbled to the deck, the canvas tearing as it fell. All hands were gathered aft to await the final command.

Boats were lowered to the water on the lee side; they contained the entire crew, the ship's articles, and emergency supplies. All were worked through the murk into the breakers and thrown high on a sandy beach. Shortly, the fog lifted and the survivors looked out on the reef where the ship had met her doom. The vessel had been leveled; she was now a total wreck marked by a tangled mass of masts and rigging. Fate, however, was kinder to the crew. All survived and eventually found their way back to Victoria, B. C.

SAGA OF THE SOUTHERN CHIEF

In December of 1894, the 40-year-old *Southern Chief*, a tried and tested veteran of the Pacific tradelanes, departed Tacoma for Port Adelaide. She was towed out to Cape Flattery by the big steam tug *Wanderer*. There the towing hawser was dropped and the vessel, laden with a million feet of lumber, set her course for the Antipodes.

Within the hour, the *Southern Chief* was bucking a fresh southeasterly storm which soon turned into a whole gale. The aged vessel was alone on a tempestuous sea. The tug had long departed and the bark had no choice but to ride out the 75-mile-an-hour winds. Finally her tired old timbers opened and water came through the seams. The pumps did all they could but faltered before the task. The vessel's owners had worked the ship to the breaking point and it was literally years since she had been dry docked or overhauled. The neglect had begun to tell.

To gain additional freeboard, the master ordered the crew to loosen the lashings and jettison part of the heavy deckload. Soon the contorted surface of the sea was a mass of floating lumber drifting in all directions in the wake of the bark. With each roll of the ship more lumber tumbled into the sea, splintering the gunwales as it went.

The situation grew worse when two hours later the storm-tossed vessel had a section of her stern quarter bashed in by driving seas. This weakened part of the stern frame and filled the dark recesses of the ship with tons of sea water. Then the deck began breaking up. The donkey engine fittings worked free, and as the ship lurched, the cumbersome mechanism slid across the deck and plunged into the sea. Next the wheel, the binnacle, and all the steering apparatus were torn loose. The unattended sails blew out of their gaskets as the crew ran to and fro trying to protect themselves from the wreckage. The deck was a shambles. All steerageway had been lost and the ship was at the mercy of the gale. There was no purpose to the crew's actions and the skipper no longer shouted commands. The vessel broached to as the storm pushed her steadily onward.

Now three days out, at a point about fifty miles southwest of Cape Flattery, the crew was cold, hungry, and miserable. They had all but given up hope when from seemingly nowhere the barkentine *Skagit* appeared through the murk.

Though the seas had moderated somewhat, the *Skagit's* crew experienced great difficulty in getting a boat over the side. It was rowed to within hailing distance of the *Southern Chief*. Some of the haggard crewmen on the ill-fated vessel couldn't stand the torment of waiting to be rescued and plunged over the side and swam desperately to the boat. The others waited patiently and boarded the rescue craft in orderly fashion.

Bundled up in a borrowed jacket, the disconsolate master of the *Southern Chief* stood on the poop deck of the *Skagit*, as he watched his battered bark fade from sight. The *Skagit* took her load of survivors to Port Townsend, where they revealed their story of hardship and privation. Word spread rapidly and with it thought of salvage money for a derelict ship drifting about off the cape.

Within a short time, the powerful steam tugs *Sea Lion, Richard Holyoke,* and *Pioneer* were all hurrying down the strait in a race to find the *Southern Chief.* Plowing out into the stormy Pacific, the crew of the *Holyoke* finally sighted the drifting vessel forty miles west of Cape Flattery. As they drew closer they discerned the figure of a man roaming the ship's deck. It turned out that his name was Hayes, second mate of the barkentine *Retriever*—which in the interim had run across the abandoned ship. To insure a share of possible salvage money he had been placed aboard the wreck.

Dismayed by this turn of events, the skipper of the *Holyoke* nevertheless put a towline aboard, which Hayes accepted, and the tow back to the strait was begun. The seas remained high and the tug found the going difficult. About two hours later, the *Sea Lion* came alongside and with her help the unwieldy charge was taken all the way to Port Townsend.

A boarding party found that the *Southern Chief* was kept afloat only by the lumber that remained in her holds. She had, however, held together until reaching port; and in a way, one might say she had come back home to die. It was at Port Townsend almost forty years earlier that she had terminated her maiden voyage.

It was also on Puget Sound that the *Southern Chief* had gained an evil reputation that followed her throughout much of her career. Built at Bath, Maine, she had come around Cape Horn in 1857. A few years later, trouble started when she was at nearby Port Ludlow.

There had been much grumbling aboard ship, and the crew

C. E. Sherman

Old Slip Point Lighthouse inside the entrance to the Strait of Juan de Fuca in 1921.

Canadian Dept. of Transport

Left: Classic Carmanah Lighthouse boasts the most powerful marine beacon on Vancouver Island's west coast.
Right: New Cape Beale Lighthouse features an aluminum lantern house for easier maintenance, and wooden slat work surrounding the tower to make it visible from greater distances.

A study in sail—the graceful schooner *Snow & Burgess* gathers wind o Cape Flattery in the early 1900s

Bark *Colusa*, shortly after this photo was taken, was wrecked off Bonilla Point on Vancouver Island in the fall of 1899.

Norwegian freighter *Neils Nielson* drifting helplessly toward the dangerous west coast of Vancouver Island after an engine breakdown off Cape Flattery in November 1916.

Ship of death—sidewheeler *Pacific* plunged to the bottom south of Tatoosh Island after being rammed by the ship *Orpheus* on the night of November 4, 1875.

Another sailing vessel victim, the schooner *Willis A. Holden* was dismasted in a gale off Cape Flattery in February 1911. She suffered a similar experience in the same place three years later.

Tragic end of the five-masted schooner *Bianca*, lost near Clallam Bay, Washington, December 15, 1924, after a blizzard.

had left in anger. In those early years, disputes between ship's officers and crewmen frequently turned into bloody affairs when port was reached. Crews would go to saloons for the traditional grog, and when they reached a good head of steam, mayhem broke loose. The trouble usually started over pay, food, or brutality. The outcome was often adjusted in true frontier style without the interference of any legal court.

The dispute on the *Southern Chief* erupted over back wages due the men. This time, however, the seamen took a legal turn and came to Port Townsend in a body to hire a lawyer to fight their cause. The notorious attorney, Levi W. Tripp,* readily accepted the case. His nickname was "San Juan Tripp," which he earned as a wool smuggler in the San Juan Islands. He was handy with a gun and was not adverse to using it.

Tripp went to Port Ludlow and threatened to libel the *Southern Chief* unless the captain handed over the ship's money. Knowing that Tripp could enforce his boast, the captain reluctantly relinquished the cash. Tripp in turn gave a portion of the money to the sheriff to distribute among the contesting seamen. Perhaps Tripp kept the larger proportion for his services; at any rate, the seamen were highly displeased with the meager settlement and vowed to get revenge on the lawyer.

Tripp started back to Port Townsend, the long route by way of Seattle, but was unexpectedly met by five of his irate clients. They informed him that he had better take the boat all the way to Victoria and never come back if he valued his life. He partially took their advice, riding the boat to Victoria. There, however, he purchased a shotgun and returned to Port Townsend. The word got around, and when the boat tied up at the dock, some of the disgruntled seamen were waiting for him. Tripp's brother, known as "Keys," showed up in the crowd to safeguard the lawyer.

The action started fast. A bearded seaman from the *Southern Chief* approached Tripp as soon as he stepped off the gangplank.

---

*From *By Juan de Fuca's Strait* by James G. McCurdy.

"We want some words with you," he demanded.

"Very well," Tripp answered, "we'll go up to my office and talk things over."

Another of the seamen shouted from the sidelines, "Let's fix him now!"

The men closed in on the lawyer, fists clenched.

Unhesitatingly, Tripp raised his gun and fired point blank at the advancing throng. One of the sailors, James Sparrott, took the blast right in the chest and fell, blood pouring from his wound. The gun blasted a second time and seaman Alexander Clarke had part of his head blown off. Virtually crazed by what he had done, the lawyer charged wildly into the others. The butt of the weapon caught one of the men, Tom Buckley, in the head, once, twice, three times, and he fell prostrate to the board walk.

Just as the others were about to pounce on Tripp, his brother's gun began blazing over their heads, and in unorganized retreat they scattered in all directions.

The lawyer, with three dead men to account for, was immediately arrested and escorted off to the local jailhouse. In the court case that followed, he pleaded self-defense, and the witnesses backed his plea. Once acquitted, he was warned to pack up and get out of town because sailor sympathizers would be out to gain revenge. He accepted the advice, closed his affairs, left town, and was never again heard of on Puget Sound.

Tripp probably hung up his shingle in some midwestern town, well away from the little Barbary Coast known as Port Townsend.

THE JINXED CAT

For centuries black cats have been the symbol of bad luck. Not only is this true among landsmen but among seafarers as well. The late James W. Cates, Vancouver, B.C. skipper of yesteryear, has left a true and strange tale of a jet-black feline.

When he was serving as mate of the big Canadian tug *Lorne*

in the spring of 1906, the tug was dispatched to the side of a waterlogged and abandoned American schooner adrift off Cape Flattery. Only the cargo of lumber kept the derelict afloat. As the tug neared the wreck, the men made out a black cat soaked and miserable, left behind in the hasty abandonment. The feline was the only living thing aboard and the members of the *Lorne's* crew immediately went to the cat's rescue, launching a boat in pulsating seas and pulling briskly to the ship's side. One of their number scrambled aboard with great effort and managed to grab the terrified cat. As he struggled back to the boat with the cat tucked in his arms, he slipped and his foot was badly crushed between the schooner and the lifeboat.

When the *Lorne* returned to port, a misunderstood signal from the skipper caused the tug to smash part of the wharf. For this error the engineer was fired.

Captain James Cates took the cat home. As he dropped the animal in the living room, his Great Dane took up the chase, and the cat in terror jumped straight through a huge bay window. Subsequently one misfortune followed another in the Cates' household. Finally one day Captain Cates received a letter from the master of the abandoned lumber schooner. He had heard that the cat was safe. It belonged to his daughter and she was grieving for her pet. Could she have it back? The little girl lived in San Francisco.

Being a humane sort of person, Captain Cates arranged for the cat to be shipped aboard the passenger liner *Walla Walla*, then departing Victoria for San Francisco. Later the steamer was reported overdue and missing on the storm-tossed voyage south. The entire coast was apprehensive about the liner, fearing for her 280 passengers. A search was launched at sea.

Then one day the *Lorne* saw the signal flag go up at the light station on Tatoosh Island, telling her to come closer. There was news. The lighthouse keeper, using his megaphone, shouted this message:

"I thought you'd like to know: the *Walla Walla* was picked

up off Farallon Island outside of San Francisco Bay. She had broken her crankshaft and was taken in tow. All 280 passengers and the black cat got off safely."

Within a short time of the cat's delivery to its home, screaming headlines hit every newspaper across the country and around the world:

"San Francisco Destroyed by Earthquake!"

ORDERLY WRECK OF THE ALICE GERTRUDE

Skindivers have viewed the remains of many wrecks inside Juan de Fuca Strait. The wreck of the Panamanian freighter *Andalusia,* which broke in two and sank after a fire in 1949, has attracted many divers. Some years back a big bronze cannon was brought to the surface by a "hard hat" diver near Neah Bay. It bore the seal of the State of Massachusetts, and was probably from the *Ellen Foster* lost in 1867. Then there are the bones of the ancient bark *W. A. Banks,* wrecked near Clallam Bay in the fall of 1869. In the depths at the strait entrance, too deep and dangerous for divers, lie the encrusted remains of the steamer *Henry T. Scott,* lost after a collision in 1922.

One of the better remembered incidents around Clallam Bay was the loss of the *Alice Gertrude.* She was a colorful little passenger steamer which linked peninsula ports with Puget Sound in the early part of the century. This vessel, built in 1898 at Seattle, was only 130 feet in length and 413 tons. She was no charmer in appearance and certainly nothing to set one's clock by. Slowly but steadily she usually got where she was going, if the traveler had a reasonable amount of patience.

The *Alice Gertrude* flew the Black Ball houseflag of the Puget Sound Navigation Company and was the passenger, mail, and freight packer for every whistle-stop along the route. Skipper of the steamer was Captain Charles ("Charley") Kallstrom, a colorful and likable personality.

On the night of January 11, 1907, the *Alice Gertrude* pulled out of her berth at East Clallam, on the fringe of Clallam Bay. She carried a relatively small number of passengers and a few parcels of freight. It was a bitter-cold winter night, but the full sting of the weather didn't strike the vessel until out in the strait. Rolling and pitching violently she labored in the irascible seas. Ominous clouds swooped in bearing thick, wet snow.

While the passengers bundled up inside their staterooms, the battle against the elements continued. For two hours the men feeding the boiler shoveled without letup. The propeller thrashed at the water and steam pressure rose alarmingly, but the *Alice Gertrude* seemed to withstand the onslaught. Smoke poured from her tall, thin stack and quickly disintegrated.

Captain Kallstrom pondered the situation. The barometer on his cabin wall was extremely low and gave every indication that the blizzard would last through the night. For the safety of his passengers he thought it best to come about and seek shelter in Clallam Bay.

He ordered the helmsman to change course, which in itself was a "heart in the mouth" maneuver. As the steamer came broadside to the maelstrom, she heeled over so far that for a moment it appeared she might capsize. Crew and passengers alike were brought to their feet, ready to stampede the exits. But the doughty vessel recovered and was soon making good time back to the bay.

Visibility was now at zero. The steamer's quartermaster peered out the pilothouse windows into a solid wall of blowing fury. The captain ordered another lookout to join the one at the bow to listen for the fog signal at Slip Point Lighthouse. The *Alice Gertrude* came ever closer to shore, but no sound was audible save the howling of the wind.

Then the lookout shouted, "Light, dead ahead!"

It was Slip Point but the fog signal was silent—out of order. With the sighting of the light, the helm was put hard over; the steamer was now hardly a stone's throw from the shore. Captain Kallstrom stepped from the pilothouse a moment, blinking from the sting of the driving snow. He pulled his coat up around his neck and quickly stepped back inside, ringing for full astern. Grabbing the speaking tube, he whistled to the engine room.

"What is it now?" shouted the sweating chief engineer.

"We're in trouble. Give her all she'll stand." But before he had hung up the tube, the steamer was picked up by a huge wave and slammed against a fringe of rock that ripped and splintered her planking. She heaved crazily and each time she tried to recover, another sea pounded her against the rocky buttress.

For almost an hour the elements teamed up in an endeavor to add another victim to Davy Jones' Locker, but the *Alice Gertrude* remained defiant. Her whistle blasted constantly into the night, the sound wafting away on the wings of the storm. The lights of the distant town were completely obliterated. Those at the lighthouse were helpless to render aid, and it would be dawn before the lifesaving crew would arrive from Neah Bay.

The wreck fastened itself to the rocks. Everyone aboard was fearful that the steamer would break up at any moment. With water ebbing and flowing in the cabins below, the passengers dragged their bedding to the main cabin and endeavored to make themselves as comfortable as possible till morning. All prayed silently that the vessel would remain fast until dawn brought rescuers.

Captain Kallstrom instructed his crew to keep anyone from trying to escape. Despite the gyrations of the vessel the passengers maintained their composure; some even managed to catch a few winks of sleep.

The lighthouse keepers at Slip Point kept an eye on the wreck throughout the night from the occasional flare shot skyward from the deck of the steamer. By morning the wind had almost subsided, and the snow was reduced to a few flakes. Then it wasn't long before the powerful tugboats *Lorne* and *Wyadda* were standing by the stricken vessel. Their plan of pulling her off the rocky perch was soon abandoned, though, when inspection showed the hull to be badly holed. The tugs working in conjunction with the lifesaving craft moved in close and the entire company of the *Alice Gertrude* were transferred without mishap. It wasn't until the last man under his command had been evacuated and the last hope of saving his ship was gone, that Captain Kallstrom deserted his post.

Final destruction of the wreck was completed by the seas whipping in from the strait. Piece by piece the vessel was torn apart until her carcass tumbled from the rocks and slipped beneath the surface.

The court of inquiry and the steamboat inspectors were not hard on the captain. On the contrary, they praised him for the seamanlike way in which he had handled the situation. He was given command of one of the most highly regarded ships of the Black Ball fleet, the steamer *Bellingham*. Probably even today, somewhere in the depths off Clallam Bay, fish are gliding silently through the sunken remains of the proud little *Alice Gertrude*.

THE BIANCA'S LAST VOYAGE

The five-topmast schooner *Bianca,* a big, awkward sailing vessel of 2,139 tons, was battling her way into the Strait of Juan de Fuca on December 15, 1924. She was returning from Alaska with a cargo of canned salmon, and it was as if she had brought back a sample of the howling Northland weather. She was solidly engulfed in a blizzard—a driving howler of freezing snow. And the entrance to the strait was a churning mass of confused water. Visibility was zero. The cumbersome wooden craft, her sails mostly furled, was jostled about unceremoniously.

Skipper Chris Larsen was noticeably shaken. Seldom had he ever been in such a storm. The snow was driving so hard that it was thicker than fog and twice as cold.

Earlier the same year, the vessel had been purchased by the Great Northern Transportation Company, and Captain Larsen had done his best to operate a profitable vessel in a day when windships were all but finished. The *Bianca* had a jinxed sailing record when she was purchased, which accounted for her having traded hands at a rock-bottom price. Many sailing vessels similar to the *Bianca* were rotting away in Puget Sound. Completed in 1919, this 243-foot, war-born schooner was one of the few of her breed that had found steady employment in the post-war era. She had been classed A-1 with Lloyd's Register of Shipping for twelve years from the date of her delivery, but she cashed in on only five.

Her first voyage from Victoria, B. C., to Delagoa Bay, South Africa, required 176 hectic days. She proved to be a poor sailer, but demands for cargo following the armistice were heavy and she immediately departed South Africa for the Antipodes, South America, Hawaii, and then back to Puget Sound. She was several weeks overdue at each destination.

On a subsequent voyage she cleared Honolulu but was back in port four days later, having lost almost every stitch of canvas and most of her deck gear in storm-tossed seas. She was a month repairing before sale to her final owners.

Now once again she was in jeopardy—caught right in the center of a blizzard with all landmarks blotted out. Suddenly her massive wooden hull drove aground, grinding over rocks and sand. Her masts swayed like tall firs in a high wind. The navigator had completely lost his bearings and the windjammer was hard ashore somewhere between Neah Bay and Clallam Bay.

The plight of the *Bianca* was soon seen from the shore by local dwellers who alerted the lifeboat station at Neah Bay. Help arrived at once. The stranded ship was high enough on the beach to allow the successful removal of all sixteen crewmen, but she was an open target for the hostile seas and soon assumed a heavy list. Much of her salmon cargo was saved, but she worked on the rocks and within a few weeks broke up to become a total loss.

Just twenty-three years later another vessel packed with canned salmon from Alaska went to the bottom off Crescent Bay east of Port Angeles. The MS *Diamond Knot*, carrying a $3.5 million cargo, was rammed and sunk in a heavy fog by the SS *Fenn Victory*, August 13, 1947. The cargo was the target of one of the most unusual recoveries ever performed: in essence, an underwater "vacuum sweeper" sucked up thousands of cans of salmon from the holds of the ship as she lay asleep in the deep. The cargo recovery proved highly successful for the underwriters.

BURNING OF THE SKAGWAY

There was tenseness in the hearing room at the Coast Guard headquarters in Seattle. Investigating officers sat on one side of the drab edifice while crew members of the ill-fated freighter *Skagway* sat on the other. The question loomed: was Captain Eric Strandquist guilty of negligence in the loss of his fire-gutted ship on the tentacles of rock off Fuca's Pillar?

The story of the fire and the subsequent stranding had made newspaper headlines for three days. At stake were the reputation, the career, the hopes, and aspirations of a sea captain. The odds were stacked heavily against him; his officers all insisted he was guilty. It was his very first command and the ship and all its cargo were totally lost.

In the early morning of December 16, 1929, the *Skagway* was plodding along just south of Cape Flattery bound for Puget Sound. She had departed from Los Angeles and San Francisco —the latter port on Friday the thirteenth—and carried a varied assortment of highly flammable cargo, including lube oil, gas, alcohol, fish oil, and glycerine. She also had aboard one thousand tons of general cargo plus tar paper and steel.

It was cold on the Pacific but the sea was moderate as the freighter neared Tatoosh Island. Just after 4 a.m. the keepers on the island noted billows of black smoke rising from what appeared to be a ship on fire.

Aboard the vessel, Captain Strandquist had been informed of a stubborn boiler-room fire. Aware of the explosive danger of the cargo he carried, and of the responsibility for his twenty-eight-man crew, he immediately sprang into action. The flames were already licking their way through the recesses of the vessel. Hoses were rolled out, axes passed about, and extinguishers exhausted. Despite their efforts, the fire spread rapidly. Strandquist and his men soon learned that they were no match for the raging blaze. The ship's master accordingly set a course for the nearest shore, hoping to put his ship aground.

The decks grew hotter and hotter as the flames ate through the cargo. The steering became somewhat erratic, the freighter failing to answer her helm properly.

There was a wireless set but no wireless operator. The smoke and fire, however, had already conveyed the message to the lighthouse keepers at Tatoosh, and the Coast Guard had been notified accordingly.

As the order to abandon ship was given, two boats were hastily lowered and the fire-smudged crewmen tumbled in. The captain and some of the ship's officers remained behind in the vain hope of saving the vessel, even though the chance of explosion threatened. The decks were now so hot that the men could smell rubber burning on their shoes.

The frustrated skipper heard his officers mumbling something behind his back which made little sense to him—something about taking the ship inside the strait and beaching her near Neah Bay. But this was the farthest thing from his mind. Though the terror of losing his first command weighed heavily on him, he was using his best judgment gained from years of experience.

The *Skagway* was now almost dead in the water. In a dangerous manipulation, the chief engineer got the engine into reverse, and the vessel, at the captain's direction, made her way astern into the treacherous area known as the Devil's Playground, a spot under the shadow of Fuca's Pillar. Shortly afterwards the freighter, now almost an inferno, crunched aground on a jagged reef of solid rock. When the breakers plunged at their prey, giant geysers of white steam scudded skyward as the cold sea water inundated the hot steel decks.

Shortly after midday, lifesaving crews in two open craft stood off the burning ship while the Coast Guard cutters *Snohomish* and *CG-207* circled the area.

The *Skagway* was blazing furiously but the captain and his officers could still be seen aboard. The coastguardmen finally persuaded them to quit the ship for fear of explosion. One of the last to leave was the first assistant engineer, W. A. Martin. Just as he was entering the boat he jumped back to the deck to find the ship's mascot, a black kitten which had almost been forgotten. Some of the more superstitious crew members would have just as soon left the cat to die, inasmuch as the *Skagway* had sailed from San Francisco on Friday the thirteenth, with the black feline aboard. The terrified cat eagerly quit the ship, the pads of its paws all but scorched. It was later given to the helpful surfmen at the Neah Bay station and survived to become a salty member of their lifesaving unit.

The Coast Guard picked up all the survivors, took them to Neah Bay, and then transferred them to Seattle to await the hearing.

The *Skagway*, built in 1908, was under charter to McCormick Steamship Company and was to have berthed at Pier 6 in Seattle on the day of her loss. The ensuing days were hard on Captain Strandquist and there was an obvious undercurrent among his shipmates, who were blaming him for the loss of the ship. The insurance people were active and the news hawks were hounding him constantly. Charges of cowardice, drunkenness, negligence, and conspiracy were being made unjustifiably.

Finally came the day of the hearing. Odds were running heavy along the waterfront that Captain Strandquist would not only lose his license but would be fined and sent to jail. U. S.

Steamboat Inspectors Donald Ames and Thomas Short were in charge of the hearing. They were men of high repute and well versed in their profession. Involved was a ship insured for $100,-000 and a cargo valued at $150,000.

Testimony made headlines. First officer Peter Strom, second officer Raymond E. Cook, and third officer Peter Toft all openly charged that the captain had mishandled the freighter in running her aground on the rocks. Strom testified that he had urged the skipper to go to Neah Bay and run the ship onto a protected beach so she could be salvaged. Under oath the ship's cook stated, "In my opinion he deliberately ran the vessel on the rocks."

It was as if the cards were all stacked against the *Skagway's* master. Testimony ran heavily against him for two days. Only a few of the members of the engine-room gang joined his cause to attest that he had done the best possible under the circumstances. Despite the testimony of the ship's officers, Captain Strandquist firmly denied that any of them had insisted that he ground the *Skagway* on a beach from which salvage would have been possible.

Finally came the day of the decision. The eyes and ears of the maritime world were on the outcome of the hearing. It was a cold and miserable December 21, when Captain Strandquist rose to hear the findings. His face was drawn and he was obviously nervous.

The wise inspectors had not been swayed by the adverse testimony. They announced that the *Skagway's* master had used wise judgment and had done all he could do to save the ship; that he had considered the danger to his crew in putting his ship aground; and that if he had endeavored to run the ship aground elsewhere, the peril would have been too great from wasted time.

Even as the captain was exonerated of all blame, the Indians from the Makah Reservation were reaping a harvest from the wreck. They were out in their canoes or combing the beaches to pick up vegetables, fruit, tires, tar paper, lumber, and drums of oil. The Pacific Salvage Company sent its tug *Salvage King* down from British Columbia waters, with an eye toward recovery, but what the fire had not consumed, the thundering breakers had torn asunder.

Today Skagway Rocks mark the grave of the freighter, but none come to mourn. Those who frequent the area—and then only during the best days of summer—are far more interested in catching big salmon that sometimes frequent the surrounding sea acres.

TWIN BARGE TROUBLE

Though ships are inanimate they often seem to possess human qualities. Back in the year 1929, the same year the *Skagway* was lost, two medium-sized, shallow-draft oil tankers began life together in the same shipyard at Belfast, Ireland. They were typical workhorses—325 feet long and designed for the haulage of petroleum on Lake Maracaibo, Venezuela.

After a few decades of employment they became surplus to the needs of their owner and were placed on the auction block. Some representatives of Island Tug & Barge Limited, headquartered in Victoria, B. C., traveled thousands of miles to look over the dingy old ships and two similar tankers, with an eye toward converting them to barges. Even through their smut and grime the men saw possibilities and accordingly tendered an offer. The deal was accepted and towing arrangements consummated. This was the only tow of its kind in marine history: four tankers in tandem behind the powerful Canadian tugs *Sudbury* and *Island Sovereign*, on a 5,000-mile voyage via the Panama Canal from Venezuela to Victoria, B. C.

The unusual tow was a success, and once the tankers were safe in Canadian waters, a local shipyard was designated to cut away their superstructures and surplus deck gear until all that remained were the bare hulls. Several weeks later the four vessels emerged from the yard, scraped, painted, thoroughly overhauled, and looking like brand new barges. Of the twins, one was named *Island Cypress,* the other, *Island Maple.* They were similar in every detail, as they had been from the beginning.

The first of the barges, the *Cypress,* put to sea from Wood-fibre, B. C., in mid-October 1963, in tow of the powerful company tug *Sudbury II.* Laboring under a capacity cargo of waste pulp liquor destined for a mill on Grays Harbor, the barge rounded Cape Flattery right in the teeth of a gale. As the tow continued southward the barge began to behave strangely. Concern was expressed by those on the tug. The barge was not recovering from the heavy seas; instead, she was settling lower and lower. Finally her decks were awash and the towline was taut as a fiddle string.

"Cut the hawser!" the tug's skipper shouted frantically. Oil-skinned figures darted about the tug's fantail and suddenly the laboring vessel jerked free of its burden.

As if trying for a last breath, the barge broke the surface for a brief moment, then settled beneath the turbulence. Massive convulsions of foam and bubbles erupted. The liquid cavern that had opened now sealed quickly and it was all over. Fortunately nobody was aboard—but gone was a barge valued at a quarter of a million dollars, plus a full cargo of pulp liquor.

Exactly one week later, October 22, 1963, the ill-fated barge's sister, the *Island Maple,* in tow of another company tug, the *Sudbury* (1), was plowing through storm-tossed seas south of Cape Flattery. As if the same scene were being re-enacted, giant waves rose to great peaks, their summits nipped off by driving winds. The barge carried an identical cargo and was headed for the same port as was her sister. Suddenly, under similar circumstances she showed signs of breaking up. With little warning, her back suddenly snapped and her cargo cascaded into the sea. For a short while the *Island Maple* tried to recover. Then, almost like her sister barge, she broke in two and sank rapidly. The crew of the *Sudbury* stood by, watching helplessly as they reeled in the cut towing hawser. Another $250,000 barge and her cargo were gone.

Truth is sometimes stranger than fiction: there they were, two ships built at the same yard to identical specifications, operated together in similar trades, sold at the same time, purchased by the same new owner, converted to barges at the same time, and lost under exact circumstances in the same vicinity, with the same cargo destined for the same port.

COLOSSAL COLLISION—MARIE SKOU AND CHITOSE MARU

Just four years after the loss of the *Island Cypress* and *Island Maple*, in the fog-filled entrance to the Strait of Juan de Fuca—where the imaginary boundary divides Canada and the United States—a devastating collision occurred in the dark hours of September 20, 1967. Due north from Neah Bay, the stillness was shattered in a quick exchange of whistles followed by an ear-rending crash. The pert little all-white Danish freighter *Marie Skou* and the big 40,000-deadweight-ton bulk carrier *Chitose Maru*—on her maiden voyage from Japan—were locked in a fearful grinding of torn plate and twisted fittings.

The *Skou* rammed her bow into the side of the towering Japanese ship with such force that she obliterated her own name by pushing her stem back more than fifty feet. So sudden was the crash that the crews of both vessels stood shocked and rigid, waiting for their ships to go to the bottom. As they pulled apart from the reverse action of their engines, the Danish ship left her ripped-out windlass, chain, and other forward deck fittings dangling precariously from jagged edges of steel inside the *Chitose Maru*.

The Japanese vessel had a great, gaping 40-by-20-foot hole opened up in her forward section. Fortunately this opening was just above the water line and her hold was empty; she rode light, seeking a full cargo of Canadian coal for her homeland. Had she been loaded, water would have gushed into the opening and perhaps have taken the brand-new ship to Davy Jones' Locker.

As the Japanese crewmen scurried over the *Chitose Maru's* decks amid eerie lights, searching the extent of the damage, those aboard the 416-foot *Marie Skou* were startled to find that their ship had shrunk considerably in size from the impact.

Distress messages filled the night, but both vessels soon discovered that they were in no danger of sinking, and miraculously there were no major personal injuries on either ship. From a monetary point of view, it was one of the worst ship collisions ever to occur at the entrance to the strait; yet despite the severity of the damage, both vessels and crews were spared.

Ironically, within a few hours of the *Marie Skou-Chitose Maru* encounter, another major ship collision of about the same proportions occurred on Puget Sound between Point Wells and President Point. The Liberian log ship *Silver Shelton* and the Sea-Land Service's American-flag van ship *Fairland* locked horns, the former sustaining such a gigantic slice out of her side that she had to be beached near Point Wells to keep from sinking. The *Fairland* had her nose badly bent out of shape. Again fog was the culprit and again the amount of damage was to reach astronomical figures.

As rescue vessels rushed to the strait entrance, the badly gouged *Chitose Maru,* all 650 feet of her, limped off under a slow bell toward Victoria, like a great monster wounded in combat. Tugs stood by as she proceeded. Meanwhile her attacker —which probably took the greater beating—was surrounded by rescue and tow craft as she also took off for Victoria. Several hours later—news of the disaster having reached the Canadian port—newsmen, photographers, and radiomen, as well as a generous sprinkling of local citizenry, came down to watch the two cargo ships limp into port.

Both vessels were taken immediately to the Victoria Machinery Depot for inspection of damage. The survey showed that the *Marie Skou* would need an entire new bow section and that the *Chitose Maru* would require numerous plates and structural repairs where her skin had been ripped wide open. Repairs would run well over the million-dollar figure and cost of repairs in British Columbia would be higher than elsewhere. There was talk of towing the ships to Japan for overhaul, but B. C. authorities refused clearance because of the unseaworthy condition of the ships. They made it mandatory that repairs be handled by the Canadian yard.

The Japanese owners of the *Chitose Maru* were losing money hourly on their cargoless ship; she had yet to pack a payload. It was quickly decided to work on her twenty-four hours a day around the clock until she was ready to go back to sea.

In an outstanding piece of emergency work, the shipyard had the vessel completely repaired in three weeks. Then she was ushered off to Vancouver, B. C., to take on a full load of coal for the land of Nippon. The 8,750-ton *Marie Skou* did not receive similar fast repair action, but eventually she got a brand-new bow section—to the satisfaction of her owner, Ove Skou of Copenhagen, but to the dismay of those who carried the insurance.

That both ships were able to return to sea was in itself a small miracle. The graveyard of ships at the entrance to Juan de Fuca's Strait was robbed of two choice victims.

PART 4

RAIDERS OF THE DEEP

Including the feared arrival of the confederate raider
Shenandoah . . . *the disputed submarine attack and
subsequent sinking of the freighter* Coast Trader . . .
and the defiant escapades of the SS Fort Camosun,
*which refused to sink after a torpedo almost severed her
hull.*

THE RAIDER SHENANDOAH

The Confederate raider *Shenandoah,* a feared naval vessel of
the Civil War era, did most of her foul deeds in the North
Pacific. As if there were not enough dangers a hundred years
ago, sailors of old found this added man-made feature something
that struck fear in their hearts. The *Shenandoah* embarked on a
wild escapade in the Pacific which continued even after the Civil
War had ended.

The intrepid Captain James I. Waddell, master of the raider,
sought and destroyed Union merchantmen, mainly whalers, in an
effort to spread the war to remote sectors of supply far from the
bloody American battlefields. He brought his *Shenandoah* to the
North Pacific for just one reason—to plunder. The waters from
California to Alaska were frequented by numerous unarmed
merchant vessels which were like sitting ducks for this formidable warship, with both steam and sail potential.

So, added to the hostile shores, the storms, fog, currents,
shoals, reefs, and rocks was a new terror.

The crafty master of the *Shenandoah* was a native of North Carolina. Appointed midshipman in the United States Navy, he had variable traits of kindness, daring, stubbornness, and temper. Once he engaged in a duel with another midshipman which cost him eleven months of active duty and a limp from which he never fully recovered.

Waddell had served with honor on the naval vessels *Somers* and *Release* during the Mexican War and once sailed a ship single-handed in the Panama area when his entire crew was stricken with yellow fever. A splendid navigator, he was later assigned to teach for a short time at the United States Naval Academy. When the Civil War broke out, he was quick to join the Southern cause. Resigning his lieutenant's commission, he joined the Confederacy as a naval officer.

A British subject who acted as a private agent for Captain James D. Bulloch, of the Confederate States Navy, purchased the *Sea King*, which had been built in England for the Bombay trade. The papers were signed after the ship had made but one commercial voyage. She was purchased in September 1864 and, according to the departure notices, was to sail from London for Bombay on October 8 carrying coal as ballast. Instead, on leaving London as scheduled, she fell into company with the steamer *Laurel*, out of Liverpool and carrying a cargo of six guns with appurtenances and nineteen passengers—Captain Waddell and eighteen Confederate officers. This ship had been purchased for a blockade runner, without any subterfuge. Meanwhile Lieutenant Whittle of the Confederate Navy had booked passage on the *Sea King*.

The two ships sailed to the Madeira Islands and then shifted to the Desertas, uninhabited islets of the group. Out of the eye of local authority, the passengers and cargo were transferred to the *Sea King*, which was then commissioned the CSS *Shenandoah* under command of Captain Waddell. All did not come off smoothly, however, as most of the crew refused to join when they learned the true object of the voyage. The *Shenandoah* left her anchorage with only twenty-three seamen instead of the 120 which were planned as her complement.

The course was to Melbourne, Australia—and nine American vessels were captured en route, of which seven were sunk and two ransomed. From the ill-fated vessels, twenty-four crewmen were recruited. The *Shenandoah* arrived at Melbourne on January 25, 1865 and was admitted into a shipyard for repairs. During the next four weeks her machinery was overhauled and three hundred tons of coal taken aboard. Meanwhile there were some desertions and several recruits added until the complement was built up to seventy-two, still far short of the intended crew. The recruiting went on in spite of the strenuous protests of the United States Consul.

The *Shenandoah* sailed from Melbourne on February 18 and set a northerly course. She captured three Union ships in April and one in May, arriving in the Bering Sea in June. There, between June 20 and 28, a total of twenty vessels was destroyed. This was two months after the Confederacy had ceased to exist, thereby creating one of the most useless acts of hostility in naval annals. The *Shenandoah* fired her last shot in defense of the South on June 22, 1865.

Rumor persisted that the *Shenandoah* was planning a landing inside the Strait of Juan de Fuca and the destruction of Yankee ships in the area. A famous Northwest pioneer, James G. Swan, tells in his journals of the apprehension at Neah Bay over the reputed coming of the warship. All vessels entering the strait were eyed with suspicion and talk ran rampant that local villages might be destroyed by cannon fire.

Swan, then teaching at the Neah Bay Indian Village, had celebrated the news of Robert E. Lee's surrender in early April 1865 by placing a new flagstaff atop the school belfry, the highest spot in the settlement. Intelligence had earlier reached Neah Bay that the Confederate raider was continuing the war. According to Swan, one typical, rainy afternoon a large steam vessel was sighted off the strait. She was observed from the tower of the little school. When it became obvious that she was headed for the village, George Jones, an Indian reservation farmer, conferred with Swan. It was suggested that Jones climb the school's new flagstaff and nail the flag to it. "I'll never haul it down to a rebel," Swan vowed.

Jones carried out the order and the Indians and whites waited in anticipation. The vessel was sighted anchored off Waada Island taking on some sand ballast, but nothing more happened that night. The next day it was learned that the vessel was not the *Shenandoah* at all but the HMS *Clio*, a Britisher bound for the West Coast of Vancouver Island to check out Indian troubles at Clayoquot Sound. On learning of the fear that had struck the village, her captain came ashore and congratulated Swan and Jones on their brave defiance in keeping the flag flying.

The *Shenandoah* never did enter the Strait of Juan de Fuca and shipping soon returned to normal. In August, the defiant Captain Waddell was informed by the British Ship *Barracouta*, off the coast of Mexico, that the war was officially over.

It was learned, however, that Waddell and some of his officers were already aware of the surrender and had aboard a newspaper telling of the South's cessation many weeks earlier. To continue raiding after the armistice would make the *Shenandoah* a pirate ship. To avoid capture they sailed to England by way of Cape Horn and by superb navigation avoided detection. Waddell surrendered his command to the British warship *Donegal* at Liverpool. The crew was released and the raider turned over to the American consul.

Fears that the *Shenandoah* might enter the strait and prey on shipping were not totally unfounded. In June of 1865, the raider destroyed an American vessel several miles north northwest of Cape Flattery. She was the brig *Susan Abigail*, which had departed San Francisco April 19. The sailing vessel was captured and burned and the crew taken captive. It was the *Abigail's* master who gave Waddell the newspapers telling of the South's surrender.

News of the *Abigail's* loss struck a blow to the local maritime world for the brig had operated from Pacific ports since 1851, after coming around the Horn from the East Coast. Fortunately she was the only war casualty near Fuca's graveyard—but had the war been prolonged, the *Shenandoah* might have been as feared as Captain Nemo's fictional submarine *Nautilus* in *Twenty Thousand Leagues Under the Sea.*

COAST TRADER—TORPEDOED

Raiders of another kind appeared along the fringes of the graveyard of ships a century later, during another conflict—World War II. This time the raiders were submarines. Though not equal to the Nazi U-boat menace in the North Atlantic, Japanese submarines torpedoed several Allied ships in the Pacific. Some of these were attacked off the northwest Washington Coast. Perhaps the best remembered was the American freighter *Coast Trader*, sunk June 7, 1942, just six months after Pearl Harbor. The vessel went to her doom forty-three miles west of Cape Flattery.

A neophyte group of naval reservists later pronounced the sinking was caused by an internal explosion rather than a torpedo, despite the fact that a ship's officer and three other crew members testified they had sighted a submarine's conning tower following the blast.

Under jurisdiction of the Army, the *Coast Trader*, a unit of Coastwise Line, put out to sea from Port Angeles bound for San Francisco with 1,250 tons of newsprint and some miscellaneous freight. In command of Captain Lyle G. Havens, the vessel moved out through the strait and took a southwesterly course. The weather was relatively calm and neither Captain Havens nor his chief officer E. W. Nystrom had any inkling of enemy submarine activity so near the coast. The freighter carried an Army gunnery crew in case of attack, but the voyage appeared routine on this oft-traveled sealane. The *Coast Trader* carried fifty-six men including her twenty-man gunnery crew.

It was nearing midday and the sea had moderated. The ship moved along methodically at a comfortable ten knots, lookouts posted forward and aft. Just before noon, the course was altered to 180° south. A pall of smoke draped a faint trail aft. Then the peaceful scene was suddenly shattered by a dull, reverberating explosion—a direct hit that buckled the ship as if it were a child's toy. The blow just abaft the engine room bulkhead was fatal. The vessel began to settle by the stern. Shocked, Captain Havens rushed to his cabin to destroy all confidential codes that could be of assistance to the enemy. At the same time the crew hurried to their lifeboat stations with the order to abandon ship.

The projectile had torn into the engine room and exploded, leaving several of the black gang injured and dazed. Water poured in unchecked, turning the deep recesses of the vessel into a shambles. In their haste to struggle topside, the men did not even look back on the scene of devastation. Their efforts were hampered by ammonia fumes escaping from the reefer plant. Meanwhile the inexperienced gunnery crew, already lowering one of the lifeboats, let it drop in the falls and two men inside were spilled into the water. After they were rescued, the evacuation came off with reasonable dispatch. One lifeboat and two rafts were successfully set adrift.

The torpedo had struck the freighter with such precision that it knocked out all communications. Even the antenna was destroyed, preventing the sending of a distress message.

The three small craft pulled slowly away from the sinking cargo ship. They watched in silence as she lifted her bow, dropped her stern, and in a gripping moment disappeared in ninety-three fathoms. The entire drama had been enacted in forty minutes.

Just before the *Coast Trader* sank, some of the survivors reported what they thought to be the conning tower of a submarine in the distance but it soon disappeared, much to their relief.

The seas then began to grow rougher and the chilling wind set the men to grumbling and complaining of their misery.

Dazed, the ship's cook, Stephen Chance, went out of his head and slumped over in the thwart, dead. Shortly after, the lifeboat drifted away from the two rafts. Finally a fishboat spotted the lifeboat and took aboard the suffering men. Searching Coast Guard planes located the two rafts and directed a Canadian corvette to their rescue. All of the survivors were taken to Neah Bay and deployed at the Naval Section Base there. The injured were immediately transferred to the hospital at Port Angeles, where all recovered.

The sinking of the *Coast Trader* was unofficially credited to the Japanese submarine *I-25*. Through Naval Intelligence it was established that the *I-25* and the *I-26* were assigned to positions off the Washington Coast on reconnaissance missions, but records do not officially credit the loss of the *Coast Trader* to any submarine. Retained as confidential information during World War II were the findings of the hearing over the vessel's loss, signed by Lieutenant A. J. Powers, USNR. It read:

> "It is the consensus of interviewing officers that the ship was sunk by an internal explosion, and not by torpedo or mine, for the following reasons: (1) The explosion took place amidships under No. 4 hatch in the after part of the ship; (2) There was no loud noise, smoke or flame; (3) There was no submarine, no wake of a torpedo; (4) A jagged six-foot hole, with rough edges bent inboard, was on the starboard side at the waterline. If a delayed-action torpedo had been used, the plates would have been blown outboard; (5) The ship at no time listed; (6) If it had been a floating mine, it would have struck the forward part of the ship."

At the conclusion of the hearing, one of *Coast Trader's* officers commented that such a conclusion was only wishful thinking on the part of some reserve officers with no seafaring experience.

The case was officially closed without further delay in order to get back to the more pressing business of war. Unfortunately the men who heard the testimony were unable to imagine that Japanese submarines could be marauding so close to the mainland.

Uncovered in Japanese naval files after the war was a record of events from the commander of the *I-26*. He reported having made a torpedo attack on an unidentified merchant ship on the date and location where the *Coast Trader* went to her doom, according to Captain Grahame F. Shrader of Seattle, who has researched the subject thoroughly.

Experts outside the hearing room reasoned that the *Coast Trader* probably was struck by a well-aimed but malfunctioning torpedo which crashed through the ship's aging sides and exploded an instant later—igniting one thousand pounds of devastation. Japanese torpedoes were among the poorest made but the most deadly on explosion

Undaunted by his experience as master of the *Coast Trader*, Captain Havens continued his sea career, finally meeting his doom as a pilot on the Hospital Ship *Benevolence*, which foundered August 26, 1950, after a collision with the freighter *Mary Luckenbach* at the entrance to the Golden Gate.

THE DEFIANT SS FORT CAMOSUN

Within twelve days of the sinking of the SS *Coast Trader*, a Japanese submarine struck again off the Northwest Washington Coast. This time the target was a brand-new, Canadian-built Liberty ship fresh out of the builder's yard and on her maiden voyage. The SS *Fort Camosun* had steamed out of Victoria, B. C. flying the British flag. She was carrying lumber, plywood, zinc, lead, and general cargo, and her destination was the British Isles.

The *Fort Camosun* was the first of nearly two hundred freighters built in Canadian shipyards during the World War II period. They were actually constructed for the United States Maritime Commission for operation under the British flag and were similar in many respects to the American Liberty ships—but they were coal rather than oil burners.

The *Fort Camosun* was built by the Victoria Machinery Depot at Victoria, B. C. and completed in the late spring of 1942. Well built and engineered, the vessel received much attention at her launching ceremony. Following successful completion of her trials, she was delivered in top-flight condition, but in a cloak of drab gray paint, from stem to stern. Her operator was T. & J. Brocklebank Ltd., of Liverpool, England.

Under the command of Captain T. S. Eggleston, the vessel steamed out of Victoria Harbor and passed Ogden Point at 8:30 a.m. on June 19. Before heading for the Pacific, the vessel's gunnery crew conducted gun trials in the strait. The ship then put out to sea, black smoke belching from her stack. At 2:30 p.m. she was abeam of Cape Flattery.

As the vessel headed down coast, all went well until 10:45 p.m. when the night air was shattered by a violent explosion.

The ship's company was stunned by the suddenness of it all. Within minutes the ship was down by the head, a massive hole in her port side. The ship's wireless operator immediately sent out a distress message and within fifteen minutes Captain Eggleston had all hands at their boat stations. Fortunately only two of the engine-room gang had been injured by the blast.

At ten minutes before midnight the crew were in the boats and the command was given to lower away.

It was a pleasant night on the Pacific and the men suffered little hardship in the open boats. But fear struck them when suddenly under the night's dark veil the attacking submarine rose momentarily to the surface and began pumping shells into the wounded freighter, which had refused to take her final plunge. The boats kept their distance from the floundering freighter.

At five in the morning, an American plane flew over the *Fort Camosun*, much to the joy of the survivors. Four hours later, two Canadian Naval vessels, the *Quensel* and *Edmondson*, arrived on the scene. Captain Eggleston and all of his crew were soon rescued and the two warships endeavored to put towlines on the defiant *Fort Camosun*, which was still afloat. The posture of the wounded ship, however, made her virtually unmanageable and the towlines snapped.

Toward evening, the Grays Harbor tug *Dauntless* arrived on the scene, placed a line aboard the abandoned ship, and commenced towing her at a speed of about two knots. Captain Hill Hubble, master of the tug, had earlier received a request from the duty officer of the Thirteenth Naval District to go to the assistance of the *Fort Camosun*. His tug had been en route from Tillamook Bay to Grays Harbor with a log raft when he received the order. He left his tow with a fishboat and informed its operator that he would be well compensated for his efforts.

When the *Dauntless* arrived to assist the freighter, there was no other vessel in sight. Appearing like a ghost ship, the derelict was rolling gently on the ocean swell.

Hubble put his engineer Neil Logue aboard the wreck to make fast a towline. The *Fort Camosun,* held afloat by the buoyancy of her lumber cargo, was well down by the head and her rudder was hard over. Logue made the line fast at the stern and the tow was soon begun toward Cape Flattery. Shortly after, the powerful Navy tug *Tatnuck* arrived and ordered Hubble to relinquish the tow. The master of the *Dauntless* finally made the Navy skipper understand that it was an extremely difficult towing effort and the two tugs should join forces.

Within twenty-four hours, during which time the tugs made steady progress in a calm sea, the *Edmundson* and *Quensel* returned to check the progress and to offer protection. The strange armada became kin to a marine parade when the tug *Henry Foss* arrived from Port Townsend, followed by the Canadian salvage tug *Salvage Queen* from Victoria. The tow meanwhile was making a steady four knots and was abeam of Cape Flattery at 6 p.m. on June 22. All the time a steady eye was kept on the freighter should she start to go down. But all went well and a little over seven hours later the *Fort Camosun,* virtually submerged forward, was at anchor in the protected calm waters of Neah Bay.

Here, salvage men swarmed all over the ship, inspecting damage and preparing to make her sufficiently seaworthy for return to dry dock in Victoria. Examination revealed that the engine room stokehold and holds Nos. 1, 2, and 3 were flooded. From amidships forward, the main deck was awash. Divers inspected the 30x12-foot hole in the ship's side and set up big pumps to help reduce the vessel's draft. A temporary timber and canvas patch was placed over the hole. The following morning at 6 a.m. the freighter was moved into the strait, yawing badly.

The handsome, gleaming ship of one week earlier was soon back home, a deplorable sight. Her stern was high in the air, she listed sharply to port, and great streams of water issued from her confines as pumps worked steadily to keep her afloat. But, jinx ship or no jinx ship, she had proved that she was a gallant ship and built well enough to survive a submarine attack. On the morning of June 27, she was hoisted up on dry dock.

Following temporary repairs, the vessel was towed to the Todd dry-dock facility in Seattle for final repairs, which could not be completed in Victoria because of the Canadian steel shortage brought on by the large shipbuilding program. The *Fort Camosun* was on the dry dock from August 1 till August 29 and remained at the yard until September 7. The hole in her side had gone completely through No. 3 hold, almost severing her. She received new hull plates, framing, decking, 'tween decks, and double bottom, as well as new wiring, piping, and engine realignment.

By early fall, the rebuilt *Fort Camosun* put out to sea once more. The jinx, however, remained. British Ministry of Transport records show her to have been torpedoed again in December of 1943, less than eighteen months after her first fatality, but she reached the Port of Aden in the Middle East unassisted, thus surviving a second submarine attack.

On September 18, 1947, the *Fort Camosun* made her final voyage under the British flag, after which she was returned to the United States government. She was placed in the reserve fleet and swung at anchor with scores of other war-built ships. Then, without fanfare on October 5, 1959, she was declared surplus to government needs and sold for dismantling. Apparently no sentimental tear was shed at the passing of this noble freighter, survivor of two torpedoings.

Grahame F. Shrader's research on Japanese submarine operations in the North Pacific asserts that the *Fort Camosun* was torpedoed by the Japanese submarine *I-25*, which in company with the *I-26* was lurking off the Washington Coast. The *I-25* was commanded by Captain S. Tagami. The *I-26*, as mentioned earlier, was unofficially credited with the sinking of the *Coast Trader*, which went to the bottom only a few days before the *Fort Camosun* was attacked.

PART 5

SOMBRIO POINT-PORT SAN JUAN AREA

Including the loss of the schooner D. L. *Clinch and its impact on British Columbia . . . the ordeal of the swift brig* Cyrus *. . . the fate of the clipper ship* Gem of the Ocean *which started her life on one coast and ended it on another . . . and the last ride of the American bark* Revere.

WRECK OF THE D. L. CLINCH

The loss on November 10, 1860 of the schooner *D. L. Clinch* was a blow to the entire Pacific Northwest but especially to British Columbians. Within days of the tragedy the news reached Victoria by Indian canoe that the wreck had been cast up near Sombrio Point on Vancouver Island.

Only a year earlier the schooner had distinguished herself under command of Captain L. Bunker when she sailed from New Westminster, B. C., with the first commercial cargo to be consigned to a foreign port from the Canadian West Coast. Till that time, cargo had come into the area but none had gone out unless one counted the pelts collected by the early fur-trading ships. The *Clinch* opened an era in trade that progressed steadily through the years. Today the Vancouver-New Westminster port complexes are among the largest exporters of cargo in the Pacific.

On her celebrated voyage, the *D. L. Clinch* departed the British Columbia port in December 1859 with sixty thousand feet of cabinet wood and fifty barrels of cranberries consigned to the booming city of San Francisco. The cargo arrived in good condition and prompted orders for more of the same. Extreme disappointment was evident eleven months later on news of the vessel's loss.

Sombrio, the scene of the wreck—where a small river empties into the Strait of Juan de Fuca—is about twelve miles east of Port San Juan and is not a prominent landmark on the charts. In fact, when the Spanish Lieutenant Manuel Quimper named it in 1792, he was so little impressed by "its dark and shady appearance" that he named it Sombrio, which in Spanish means "shady place." While Quimper was exploring the strait and applying names to its geographical features, there were nine English and seven American vessels trading with the Indians along this section of the coast.

Circumstances involving the loss of the *D. L. Clinch* are vague but records show that another small schooner, the *Dance*, was lost on the same day, November 10, 1860, a few miles southeast of Sombrio Point toward the Jordan River. Fragmentary information claimed the crews of both vessels reached shore safely.

From Sombrio Point to Barkley Sound, a distance of some forty isolated miles, almost fifty known wrecks have been recorded down through the years. Countless other ships were lost without trace in the area.

A few miles west of Sombrio Point lies Port San Juan Harbor, the only deepwater bay of any real importance until Barkley Sound. The port is conspicuous from seaward, appearing as a deep gap between two mountain ranges, the entrance being two miles wide and situated thirteen miles northeastward of Cape Flattery Light. The port is open to southeasterly winds, and a heavy sea rolls in when a moderate gale is blowing from that direction.

Port Renfrew is a quaint little settlement on the southeastern side of the harbor. There a wharf, a few stores, and a post office are scattered about, and the year-round population is about four hundred hardy souls, mostly fishermen and loggers. Almost one hundred seine and gillnet fishboats gather at Port San Juan annually.

The harbor is remembered as a rendezvous center for the Canadian and American rum-running vessels during prohibition days. It was surveyed in 1847 by the HMS *Pandora*, under Lieutenant Commander James Wood. With establishment of a post office there in 1896, Port Renfrew was named in honor of Baron Renfrew, Earl of Selkirk.

Since man first came by water to the Strait of Juan de Fuca, Neah Bay and Port San Juan have been the harbors of refuge for tempest-tossed seafarers—but Neah Bay, because of its location and protection, is more often used. Residents of Port San Juan have been pressing for a protective breakwater like the one at Neah Bay. As late as January 22, 1949, the Vancouver B. C. tugboat *St. Clair* came to grief at Port San Juan with the loss of two lives; and seldom a year passes without at least one fishboat encountering trouble in this area.

A sizable fleet of small commercial fiishing vessels has been lost, mostly around Port Renfrew. During the stormy years of 1947 and 1948, five such craft were destroyed and several others damaged. On January 24, 1947, the *Ray Roberts* stranded; on October 31, the *Cape Wolf* was driven ashore; and on November 3 of the same year, the *Fisher Boy* burned to the waterline. The fishboat *Waterwing* stranded on December 2, 1948, and the *Phyllis G. 118* foundered eleven days later. Another fishing craft, the *Newcastle*, was lost just east of Sombrio Point on December 11, 1953. Small wonder that local residents have long been demanding a breakwater within their sometimes dangerous harbor.

THE CYRUS—1858

One of the first of many victims of Port San Juan was the 213-ton American brig *Cyrus*, wrecked at the harbor entrance, December 23, 1858. The *Cyrus* was one of the finest and fastest of the early sailing vessels on Puget Sound. She was owned by

Losing part of her rigging, the American ship *William H. Smith* was towed to Seattle in 1910 after being whipped into subjection off Cape Flattery.

'Port of no return''—the Russian freighter *Uzbekistan* off Darling Creek, not far from Pachena Point, after grounding April 30, 1943.

Old *Umatilla Lightship No. 67*, the first lightship assigned to the Umatilla Reef station. This wooden-hulled vessel did yeoman duty from 1898 until 1930.

In May 1948, the fishboat *Pennsylvania* piled up on the rocks off Carroll Island and later sank.

SS *Umatilla* was the vessel for which treacherous Umatilla Reef was named. This vessel struck the then uncharted reef in 1884 and was saved by the famous Captain Johnny "Dynamite" O'Brien.

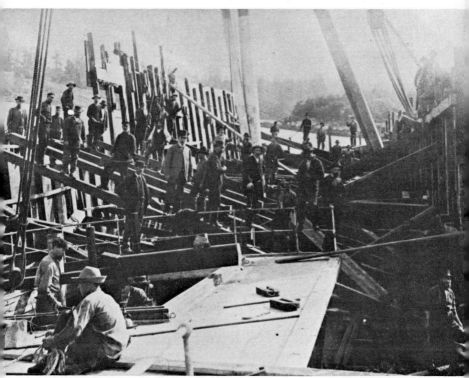

Salvage is underway for the SS *Umatilla*, which sank at Esquimalt, B.C., after being towed in from Umatilla Reef. A cradle was built around the vessel to act as a cofferdam.

Victoria, B.C., Provincial Archives

Tangled mass of wreckage below the precipitous walls of Vancouver Island near Pachena Point marked the grave of the SS *Valencia* and the 117 persons who perished with her.

SS *Valencia*, coastwise passenger vessel, was a favorite with tourists until her tragic loss on Vancouver Island's rugged west coast in 1906.

the prominent Captain Lafayette Balch, former master of the schooner *Damariscove*, and San Francisco shipowners Curtis & Farwell. The vessel was one of the regulars in the Portland-San Francisco trade and later was diverted to Puget Sound, where she ran in Balch & Weber's packet line.

The *Cyrus's* most famous master was Captain William Biggs, but he was not in command on the vessel's final voyage. Instead, she was skippered by Captain S. C. Mitchell, a native of Maine and a resident of the Grays Harbor area.

Like those in other walks of life, seafaring men have long had a superstition that tragedies occur in series of three. Captain Mitchell subscribed to this belief. He had been shipwrecked three times since making the sea his career, and he figured himself immune from further mishap. After ten years on the Atlantic and in the West Indies, he took leave of the sea and returned to New England. There he constructed his own brig, the *W. D. Rice*, at Lubeck, Maine, and in 1857 piloted her around Cape Horn with general cargo for San Francisco and Puget Sound ports. Despite a strenuous voyage plagued with constant storms, Captain Mitchell was confident, for he had experienced his full share of shipwreck. After a few months of enjoying Puget Sound country, he accepted command of the brig *Cyrus*. Though small, this vessel could out-sail just about anything under canvas in the North Pacific.

Rain pelted down in torrents the morning of December 11, 1858, as the *Cyrus* pulled away from the dock at Steilacoom. She was heavily laden with several thousand board feet of lumber. Spreading her sodden sails, she glided through Puget Sound and Admiralty Inlet and dropped her hook at Port Townsend, as adverse winds were reported in the Strait of Juan de Fuca.

Anchor was weighed again on December 15, but no sooner was the brig out in the strait than troublesome winds thwarted her progress. She beat against them for six days before the captain was finally able to gain the open Pacific. A tremendous sea was running, whipped into a foamy froth by a full gale. Because the windjammer was no match for the storm, the captain elected to come about and seek temporary shelter inside the strait. Turning before the storm, the *Cyrus* heeled over almost to her beam ends. There was a terrible rumble below as the cargo shifted. Then the lashings snapped and the deckload of lumber spilled overboard, splintering and grinding. The listing vessel was unable to recover and was shipping so much water she could not be properly steered.

Captain Mitchell tried to set his course for Port San Juan Harbor but the *Cyrus* labored awkwardly and refused to answer the helm. After he had jettisoned additional lumber, the vessel gained some stability and moved toward her goal by taking advantage of the wind. The craft finally reached the harbor with half of her sails blown to rags. She was nosed inside the entrance but the persistent southwest winds offered little succor and all hands were employed throughout the night trying to keep the vessel from going aground on shoals inside the harbor. The captain and crew spent a sleepless night as the vessel pitched and tossed, dragging both anchors.

The following day, the hooks were lifted but the driving wind and running seas prevented the vessel's return to the strait. The situation grew more frustrating when, on December 23, a flash squall struck, again necessitating the dropping of both anchors. This time the strain was too great—the chains parted and the vessel was carried onto the outer spit of Port San Juan. There she was an open target for the watery onslaught.

Captain Mitchell was now forced to accept the fact that he was not immune to shipwreck. Before long, the brig broke its back almost amidships and the crew was forced to struggle through the surf to the safety of the beach. Though surviving his fourth calamity, the skipper refused to call it quits and returned to the sea to round out a long and successful career both as master and shipbuilder.

LAST VOYAGE OF THE GEM OF THE OCEAN

The first white settlers arrived at Seattle's Alki Point in the early fall of 1851, aboard the schooner *Exact*. Two years later, a plat was filed and Seattle became the seat of King County, Oregon Territory. Later the same year the region became part of the newly proclaimed Washington Territory. Meanwhile, on the eastern coast, the clipper ship *Gem of the Ocean* was completed at the shipyard of Hayden & Cudworth in Medford, Massachusetts, for William Lincoln of Boston. At the time, none guessed this vessel would one day operate out of the struggling little port of Seattle.

The *Gem of the Ocean* had beautiful lines and was built with the skill of master craftsmen. She was 152 feet long with a beam of 32 feet and registered at 702 tons. Her initial master was Captain Freeman Crosby, who brought his ship from Boston around Cape Horn to San Francisco in 121 days. The American clipper, the *Gem of the Ocean*, more than lived up to her name.

In 1867, she was sold to McPherson & Witherbee, San Francisco, and found a new homeport at the city by the Golden Gate. There she was assigned to the Seattle-San Francisco run as a coal carrier. In command of Captain Hawse, the clipper put to sea from Seattle in August of 1879, overloaded with coal and bound for the Bay City. A heavy fog hung over the entrance to the strait and the vessel had a difficult time filling her canvas.

Feeling her way about and hampered by the prevailing current, the craft got in too close to shore. Then the breeze completely died, causing her to strike the rocky outcroppings eight miles southeast of Port San Juan Harbor. The sharp fangs pierced her hull in several places. Captain Hawse hastily ordered his crew to abandon ship. Rather than run the surf or cross the strait, they remained just outside the breakers, rowing along the Vancouver Island shore in an easterly direction. A course was then set for Port Townsend. By relieving each other at the oars and utilizing a small sail, they continued for a hundred miles until they reached their destination.

Once safely in the American port, Captain Hawse alerted the authorities of the wreck, but by the time a salvage vessel had arrived at the scene, the *Gem of the Ocean* was totally destroyed.

LAST RIDE OF THE REVERE

Port San Juan Harbor failed to provide sufficient refuge for the American bark *Revere*, Captain J. F. Hinds; it was wrecked there, September 9, 1883. Like the *Gem of the Ocean*—lost in the same month and almost the same day four years earlier—the *Revere* was engulfed in a thick fog off the entrance to the Strait of Juan de Fuca. Unable to secure cargo at Honolulu, the vessel had sailed for Port Townsend in ballast on August 22 and had had a trouble-free voyage until the pea-soup fog enclosed her in the graveyard of ships. Moving slowly through the shrouded sea, the persistent currents went unnoticed by Captain Hinds until the vessel was carried to within hearing distance of the breakers. The skipper then realized that he had not made proper allowance for the northerly drift. Aware of his predicament, he frantically ordered a sharp lookout in the hope that through the murk the entrance to Port San Juan Harbor might be sighted. Before he could find a landfall, the watch sang out, "Breakers! Breakers!"

The drone of the surf grew ever louder. Anchors were dropped, sails put aback. A treacherous barrier of rock suddenly drove its fangs into the wooden hull, ripping the timbers. Voluminous combers then turned the ship broadside as succeeding breakers inundated the deck with rivers of water. As the bark worked on the reef, another massive hole opened alongside the keel.

Nearby Indians who spotted the wreck hastened to assist the crew and the terrified handful of passengers. With little thought for their own lives, the valiant natives formed a human chain in the surf. After frantic struggles in the frigid waters, all of the survivors found themselves on the beach suffering terribly from exposure and hunger. The very next day, the Indians willingly took them to Victoria, B. C. in their canoes, thus completing an unrewarded act of mercy.

Tugs were dispatched to the wreck scene but the ship had been leveled. The *Revere* had ended her last ride.

PART 6

THE BONILLA-CARMANAH AREA

Including the 1884 wreck of the Lizzie Marshall *and the demise of the ship* Belvidere *two years later . . . the escapades of the Indian-manned sealer* Dart *. . . unwilling victims of Nitinat Bar . . . Pope &* Talbot's *unfortunate schooner* Skagit *. . . wrecks in Vancouver Island's paradise . . . the great real estate scheme that failed . . . and the breeches buoy rescue of the* Santa Rita's *crew.*

Bonilla Point lies twelve miles west of Port Renfrew. It was named by Lieutenant Manuel Quimper, master of the sloop *Princessa Real,* who titled it Bonilla because the word in Spanish means high or bold. Bonilla Point marks the western boundary on the Vancouver Island side of the Strait of Juan de Fuca. Carmanah Point is about two miles westward from Bonilla.

The name Carmanah was unofficially bequeathed to the point by navigators of old and officially adopted by the Admiralty surveyors in 1860. It came into general use because of the white man's difficulty in pronouncing the name of the Indian village Qua-ma-doa. The native settlement there was located under the eastern bluff of the point and was inhabited by members of the Nitinat tribe. As the crow flies, it is some fifty-five miles from Victoria. Since 1891, a navigation light originally intended for Bonilla has shined out over the Pacific from Carmanah.

About five and a half miles westward from Carmanah is Clooose, a small village and mission lying in a narrow cove at the mouth of the Chuckwear River. The tiny village is populated mostly by Indians. There are no roads leading to it and much of the supply has to be packed in, or brought in by water. Small vessels sometimes land their cargo right on the beach. Indian-canoe transportation is still not uncommon here and Indian-owned fishboats occasionally bring in supplies from Port Renfrew.

Just a hop, skip, and jump from Clo-oose is Nitinat Lake, a long, narrow body of water twelve miles long and half a mile wide. The lake is connected to the ocean by a narrow entrance with depths ranging from one to two fathoms. Nitinat Bar is not recommended for anything larger than a yacht, fishboat, or medium-sized tug, and only then with the aid of an experienced pilot. Many who have tried to enter the lake by vessel—seeking shelter from a storm—have met with disaster.

At one time, Clo-oose and its neighboring lake boasted a population of nearly two hundred and fifty, but since the cannery of Nitinat Lake ceased full operation some forty years ago, the population has dwindled to a handful of stalwart holdouts.

At the seaward entrance to the lake there was once the village headquarters of the powerful Nitinats (Nittin-ahts), who were among the finest hunters, whalers, and fishermen on the British Columbia Coast. They were also excellent warriors and frequently did battle with the Ohiats from Barkley Sound, or the Makahs from Neah Bay. Like the Nootkas to the north, the Nitinats most feared the Haidas, who conducted frequent raids in their great war canoes. For such surprise attacks the Nitinats fortified their village stronghold, and traces of those fortifications still exist.

One of the most unusual attractions along the entire Vancouver Island Coast is just about three miles west of Nitinat Lake. This is Tsusiat, a magnificent waterfall visible for many miles at sea. Often used as a landmark, veil-like Tsusiat is the only waterfall on this part of the coast. One hundred feet wide, the falls drop over an eighty-foot precipitous rock wall in a perfect harmony of nature. The beautiful cascading water comes by way of a stream supplied from a small lake also known as Tsusiat. Behind the lake, mountains rise to more than two thousand feet.

In the immediate area along the rugged shoreline are interesting ocean caves, an occasional blowhole, tidal pools, strange rock formations, and glistening sand. For many years the skipper of the Canadian Pacific passenger liner *Princess Maquinna*—which served Vancouver Island ports—brought his ship in close to the beach so that tourists could get a better look at the falls of Tsusiat.

The Bonilla-Carmanah area today is planned as the eventual site of a great natural park under jurisdiction of the Canadian government; an area that has been the scene of scores of wrecked ships and sacrificed lives down through the years.

LIZZIE MARSHALL

Pilot books warn of the danger of loss of wind near the shore in the vicinity of Bonilla Point. It is a precipitous, rocky bluff, and the hills behind it rise gently in elevation to 3,500 feet. Rain, wind, and fog in extremes are common off Bonilla, elements which have contributed to the rash of shipwrecks in the area.

On February 22, 1884, the American bark *Lizzie Marshall*, a fine-lined three-master of 434 tons was a victim of Bonilla Point. Built on the Sacramento River in 1876 for Prescott & Marshall, the *Lizzie*, as she was affectionately known to her crew, had been a highly successful coaster. She made many profitable passages along the Pacific Coast, packing lumber south and returning with general merchandise.

On her final voyage, she was fourteen days out from San Francisco when she gained the latitudes of Cape Flattery. Sailing in close to Tatoosh Island, her signal flags were run up and acknowledged, but shortly after, adverse winds forced her to move farther offshore. She later worked her way back, but again was driven out to sea. A third attempt brought her within the shadow of Cape Flattery but this time the wind died altogether and fog set in. Without steerageway, and sails hanging almost limp, the *Lizzie* ghosted along with the northerly drift.

Captain Adolph Bergman had been in such situations many times before but heretofore had been able to count on enough breeze to get him out of trouble. This time, however, the sea was little more than a mill pond and the vessel drifted out of one fog bank into another. There was no fog signal audible on Tatoosh and the craft seemed to float in a white shroud. When the incoming tide joined forces with the northerly current, the vessel drifted toward Vancouver Island's coast of lost ships.

On the morning of February 21, the bark was off dreaded Bonilla Point. The lead was dropped constantly. When the leadsman shouted, "Twenty Fathoms!" the order was given to drop both anchors. Soon the vessel was shackled to the bottom. Fearing that they might drive ashore with the rising seas, Captain Bergman ordered a boat lowered and manned by four volunteers who would go to Neah Bay for assistance. The boat got away safely but was gone only a few hours when a southwest gale struck with great suddenness. The *Lizzie Marshall's* anchors began dragging, sweeping her dangerously close to the hostile coastal ramparts. Frantically, Captain Bergman ordered the masts cut away to give the vessel more buoyancy. Like giant trees the masts crashed into the surf in a wild tangle of rigging.

The velocity of the wind continued to grow and the seas mounted. The strain was so great on the anchor chains that one finally parted; the added stress on the other soon caused it to snap. The vessel was now at the mercy of the seething breakers. Then one huge swell erupted, lifting the bark mightily and slamming her broadside against a rocky barrier, splitting her hull wide open. The captain, his wife, and the crew crouched in fear. Miraculously the stern of the vessel from the mizzenmast aft held together and jammed tightly between two pyramid-shaped rocks inside the reef. From it the survivors were able to reach the adjoining rocks and make their way to the beach.

Captain Bergman tried to help his wife across the rocky obstacles that separated them from the shore but she did not have sufficient strength to hold her footing. Several times she was knocked against the rocks and badly bruised. Meanwhile, one of the crew, a German sailor named Hibler, made a hasty decision to return to the wreck for his personal belongings. A giant breaker struck him as he boarded, sucking him into the vortex and sudden death.

The volunteers who had taken off for Neah Bay in the ship's boat arrived safely and revealed the plight of the *Lizzie Marshall*. Rescue vessels came none too soon, for the survivors would surely have perished in short order on that inhospitable shore, without sufficient clothing and food in the dead of winter. All were brought to safety except the German sailor who had put too high a premium on a few personal belongings.

THE BELVIDERE—1886

Less than three years after the loss of the *Lizzie Marshall*, the American ship *Belvidere* came to grief in almost the same place. The vessel was under the command of Captain J. S. Gibson, one of the most popular master mariners on the West Coast.

According to the late Carl C. Cutler's *Greyhounds of the Sea*, the *Belvidere* was built as a true clipper by Paul Curtis at Boston, Massachusetts, in 1857, for Richard Baker, Jr. and William F. Weld of Boston. The vessel was initially commanded by Captain Isaac N. Jackson, who skippered her on two commendable voyages from Boston to San Francisco, one in 127 days and the other in 157 days. Though these passages were not records for the clipper era, they were considered superior voyages inasmuch as the *Belvidere* was a large ship in her day, packing a good payload. She was registered at 1,321 tons and measured 189 feet in length. With a fine spread of canvas the vessel sailed well in fair weather and foul.

When Captain Gibson became her master three decades later, the clipper had lost much of her luster but she still rendered superb service and had been remarkably free of accidents. Her

owners were listed as Captain Nelson, and Goodall, Perkins &
Company of San Francisco—who in turn had chartered her to
Canadian industrialist R. Dunsmuir.

We thus find the *Belvidere* in ballast en route to Departure
Bay (Nanaimo, B. C.), from Wilmington, California, in the fall
of 1886. She was slated to take on a full cargo of coal at the
British Columbia port. After a fair passage up the coast under
the watchful eye of her master, the world closed in about her
in thick fog at the entrance to the Strait of Juan de Fuca. The
sea was rough; and under a partial load of ballast, the *Belvidere*
was somewhat cranky. When the fog persisted, Captain Gibson
lost his bearings.

On the morning of November 29, the groping craft got in too
close to dreaded Bonilla Point. Unable to garner sufficient wind
to claw away, she struck a barrier of rock and became immobile,
holding fast in an upright position. It was hard to ascertain the
full extent of damage but there appeared no immediate danger.
The captain kept his nineteen-man crew under subjection. The
boat was provisioned but no immediate plans were made for
abandoning ship. Before nightfall a sailing vessel passed offshore within signalling distance. Distress flags were run up on
the *Belvidere* and were promptly answered by the passing vessel. The bad news was carried to port and the tug *Tyee* was
immediately dispatched to the aid of the stranded *Belvidere*.

The tug arrived in time and quickly set to work. Anchors were
dropped, lines rigged, and the tug placed in proper position to
give its full muscle on the flood tide. The sea remained moderate as the tide surged in—nature appeared to be cooperating. As
the snorting tug went into action, her triple-expansion steam
engine purred at full bore. The boilers were fired and the steam
pressure rose. Slowly, ever so slowly, the *Belvidere* grated over
the craggy reef in a screaching crescendo. Then suddenly she
was afloat, free of the barrier at last.

The victory over the elements seemed assured, but the hull
damage was far greater than had been estimated. Despite a

flurry of action at the pumps, water roared in rapidly. The tug dropped the hawser and hastily maneuvered to the ship's side in a desperate effort to push her to a nearby beach. The water level rose so rapidly that the *Belvidere's* exhausted crew leaped aboard the tug, just at the nick of time. For fear that the *Tyee* would be pulled down, lines were cut. In a matter of minutes it was all over; the ship plummeted to the bottom, irretrievably lost.

Though despondent over the loss of his ship, Captain Gibson continued his career at sea, commanding many other coasters in the lumber and coal trades. No episode in his many years of seafaring, however, weighed so heavily upon him as the loss of the *Belvidere*, which he had considered his finest command.

LOSS OF THE SEALER DART

The Indian-owned and -manned sealing schooner *Dart* was the pride of the Neah Bay Indians. Built at Lummi, Washington, in 1890, she was perhaps the smallest unit of the Northwest sealing fleet, which flourished prior to the turn of the century. The *Dart* was just slightly over thirty-seven feet in length, and she often had more Indians aboard than she did seals. The only official record kept of her activities shows her to have taken twenty-nine seals off the Washington coast in 1894.

The pelagic sealing business, which for a time was one of the major maritime industries of the North Pacific, started in a small way in the early 1870s, reached its peak about 1894, and rapidly declined by 1900. An Act of December 29, 1897, made it illegal for American citizens or their vessels to be employed in such practices. A treaty between the United States, Great Britain, Japan, and Russia in 1911 outlawed the commercial killing of seals at sea in the North Pacific. Prior to this, small schooners, generally between thirty and one hundred gross tons, were used in the business and a sealing voyage was, in many respects, much like a whaling voyage.

The season began in January or February and lasted until

about the middle of September. There were, and are, two main seal herds in the North Pacific: one of them follows the American Coast and goes to the Pribilof Islands to bear their young and breed; the other follows the Asiatic Coast and makes its summer home on the Commander Islands, owned by Russia.

Because of these two main herds, the sealing fleet was split into two groups. One of them started off the coast of California and followed the American herd northward, while the other crossed the Pacific and started hunting southeast of Japan. Both ended the season in the Bering Sea. On several occasions an effort was made to follow the herds southward at the end of the breeding season, but this was unsuccessful as the herds scattered much more widely during the southward migration than they did during the northward.

This thriving industry, which involved a fleet of almost three hundred small sailing vessels, owed much of its success to the Northwest coastal Indians. It was their seal-hunting methods that were copied by the Caucasians. Many Indians were carried aboard the "pale face" schooners as hunters, and their dugout canoes were frequently taken along on the voyage with two men assigned to a canoe, one to paddle and the other to throw the spear or harpoon.

The sealing or "killer" boat used by the white hunters was modeled after the whaleboat but was somewhat smaller. According to marine historian R. N. "Bob" De Armond of Ketchikan, Alaska, three men comprised a killer-boat crew: a boat-puller, a boat-steerer, and a hunter who usually used both a shotgun and a rifle.

Dead seals were taken aboard the schooner to be skinned and the raw skins were salted in the hold of the vessel until the end of the season, or until they could be shipped to the home port by another vessel. The owner of the craft usually provided all supplies and ammunition for the voyage and the captain and crew members, except the hunters, received wages. The hunters were paid on a "piece basis" and a good hunter could demand as much as $2.50 or $3.00 for each skin he turned in. On some vessels, the boat-puller and boat-steerer also received a "piece" payment in addition to wages.

Most of the schooners in the sealing fleet were constructed in the three coast states and British Columbia. Others were built in Alaska or came around Cape Horn from the East Coast, where they had previously engaged in cod and mackerel fishery. It was from the North Pacific sealing fleet that Jack London found inspiration for his famous novel, *The Sea-Wolf*.

The Indians possessed great skill for killing seals and whales, but they lacked knowledge of navigation, once away from their shores with their familiar landmarks. For the most part, they had little money to purchase the white men's sailing vessels. However, some of the native hunters were so expert that they struck it rich on long voyages and came home with considerable money. The *Dart* was one of the sealers both owned and manned by Neah Bay Indians.

The mortality rate among the sealing fleet was high. Scores of craft were lost or wrecked along many sectors of the Pacific rim, both on the Asiatic and American side. And death was frequent during the long, rugged voyages; at least nineteen of these schooners are known to have been lost with all hands.

Branching out from their traditional hunting grounds off the Washington Coast in April 1895, the Indians had taken the *Dart* northward to seek prey off the West Coast of Vancouver Island. While hunting seals, the vessel piled up on the outer fangs of Carmanah Point. The company of men made it safely to shore but their beloved vessel was quickly destroyed by the breakers.

The Makah Indians, once the greatest of seal hunters, have long since given up such practices. The last Indian sealerman of the area, Chief Maquinna Jongie Claplanhoo, eighty-one, died at Neah Bay on July 10, 1957. He was laid to rest in the local happy hunting ground, ending a life that had begun in that same village on June 15, 1876, as the son of chieftain Captain John. The latter was among the forty-one chiefs and sub-chiefs of the

Makah tribe who signed a peace treaty with the United States government, January 31, 1855. Governor Isaac I. Stevens, first governor of the Territory of Washington, sailed to Neah Bay aboard a sloop to negotiate that treaty.

As a youth, young Claplanhoo went to sea as a seal and whale hunter, and after making considerable money for his efforts, later became the owner of three schooners, one of which was the ill-fated *Dart*. But the Indians had to give up their "winged" sealing ships when the federal government outlawed unrestricted seal hunting. Shortly before his death, Claplanhoo said that the Naval officer who had brought word about regulations outlawing pelagic sealing had promised him compensation for his schooners. For a half century the chief had tried to get that promised compensation, but it was never paid.

Under terms of the treaty, the Makahs were still allowed to take seals in their "accustomed manner" in hand-paddled canoes, though sealing schooners were outlawed. The Indians obeyed, but American and Canadian counterparts did considerable poaching even after the law was enforced.

CHAMPION AND RUSTLER

Two well-known units of the Pacific Northwest sealing fleet were claimed the same year, 1887, in almost the same place. Both tried to seek shelter by crossing the Nitinat Bar and both came to grief after capsizing.

The *Champion* was a trim little schooner built by Captain E. H. McAlmond, at Port Townsend in 1880, for Captain Henry McAlmond, a native of Port Angeles. The vessel was a small two-master, built strong and stout, and her master was willing to sail her anywhere an honest dollar was to be made. He first took her sealing, and when catches were poor he traded anywhere he could find cargo.

Captain Henry McAlmond eventually sailed the *Champion* to Alaska. This was to be a combination trading and sea-otter hunting expedition and aboard the schooner was the first crew of

Indian hunters to commercially engage in the sea-otter business. The expedition proved reasonably successful but not up to expectations. On his return to Puget Sound, the Captain had the small schooner *Ariel* fitted out as a pilot vessel and personally assumed command. He retained ownership of the *Champion* until 1886, when he sold her to Chief Peter of the Makah tribe. Chief Peter was one of the few Indians to own commercial sealers, but as already mentioned, their seal-hunting techniques were far superior to their knowledge of navigation.

In 1887, just a few months after the Indians had purchased the *Champion*, she was taken out on the sealing grounds off the West Coast of Vancouver Island. Working near the shore, the vessel managed to get a fair number of seals when a sudden gale came up and caught Chief Peter and his men with their sails down. A mad scramble was made to hoist the canvas and stand out to sea.

The howler was so severe that they were forced to run before the wind in an endeavor to cross nearby Nitinat Bar and gain protected waters inside the lake. Scudding through the swell at the narrow opening, a tail wind caught the *Champion's* stern and swung her broadside. In the twinkling of an eye the vessel flipped over and threw her company into the churning waters. The terrified Indians swam desperately for the shore, but one of their number, hunter Cultus George, was drowned. The others were helped to safety by the natives of Clo-oose—an Indian name which means "safe landing."

These circumstances were almost duplicated when the Canadian sealing schooner *Rustler* met a similar fate in December of the same year. Built on Orcas Island in 1883, the fifty-footer was registered out of Victoria, B. C. and owned by J. D. Warren, one of the pioneers in the sealing industry of British Columbia. The *Rustler* went in search of seals each year from 1884 until 1887.

On Christmas Day of 1887, the vessel—in command of Captain James W. Dodd—was working off Vancouver Island, while the crew enjoyed a feast of seal meat. On the following day, they awakened to a leaden sky and a severe southerly gale. The seas were whipped into frightening white-lipped fury and the schooner's mainsail was soon blown to ribbons. A desperate run was made for Nitinat Bar but it, too, was a solid mass of white foam. While negotiating the shallow bar entrance, the vessel missed stays and was brought down hard on the sea floor. Broaching to, she was forced over on her beam ends. Gasping and struggling as they were cast into the turbulent waters the survivors fought their way toward the shore, where landsmen rushed to their rescue and pulled all to safety.

The loss of the vessel came as a severe blow to her owner, Captain Warren, but he took it in stride. He was born on Prince Edward Island in 1837 and came to British Columbia while still young; he spent virtually his entire career as a master mariner and owner of both sail and powered vessels. He commenced trading along the Vancouver and Queen Charlotte Islands in 1864 with the *Thornton* and participated in some wild skirmishes with unfriendly Indians. In one incident, some Northern British Columbia Indians concealed weapons under blankets as they allegedly came out to trade in their canoes. When the nefarious scheme to capture the schooner was uncovered, a melee broke out. The ship's crew forced the natives to retreat by killing twenty of their number.

Warren later became the first man in the sealing business to send out steam vessels, and he once owned and operated eight sail and powered vessels.

Government seizures of sealing ships for poaching in 1886 and 1887 were particularly hard on Captain Warren, and the loss of the *Rustler* had compounded his losses. The accumulated profits of his many years of hard work in maritime trades were quickly lost. His indomitable spirit, however, prevailed and he engaged in a more stable ship-owning venture in freight and passenger services out of Victoria.

The year 1887 was especially hard on the sealing fleet in

Fuca's graveyard of ships. In addition to the *Champion* and *Rustler*, a third sealer was lost—the 42-ton schooner *Active*, owned by both Canadian and Indian interests. Under the command of Captain J. Gutterman, she foundered in a gale thirty miles west of Cape Flattery, April 1, 1887, with the loss of all hands. Besides Captain Gutterman, the vessel carried a 28-man crew of Makah Indians. The *Active* was built at Mayne Island, B. C., in 1885.

THE SKAGIT TRAGEDY

In the early 1880s, the Puget Sound Commercial Company—as legal owners of Pope & Talbot's Puget Mill Company—embarked on a shipbuilding program. They elected to have constructed a fleet of sailing vessels especially adapted for carrying lumber from its own Puget Sound mills. Prior to this, the fleet had consisted of ships, barks, and barkentines, all square-riggers built on the American East Coast between the years 1847 and 1874.

The new ships designed and built in the Pacific Northwest included the sister barkentines *Skagit* and *Klikitat*, which were exclusively for the Puget Sound-Hawaiian Islands trade. They homeported at Port Gamble and both could carry about 500,000 board feet of lumber. The *Skagit*, of 506 tons, was built at Port Ludlow, Washington, in 1883, by master builder Hiram Doncaster. She was 156 feet in length and highly pleasing to the eye. The *Skagit* and *Klikitat* were among the most popular ships serving the islands, though the *Klikitat* was faster and more publicized. The *Skagit* was a workaday vessel seldom in print except for her 1894 rescue of the crew of the ill-fated *Southern Chief* off Cape Flattery. She never set any records, and never had serious crew troubles or ill-starred voyages; she was always a dependable windjammer and a constant money maker.

The year 1906 was disastrous for Pacific Coast shipping. Many fine craft were wrecked and among them was the *Skagit*. After twenty-three years of uninterrupted service to the paradise isles, the vessel became ensnared in fog, October 25, 1906, and drove aground almost directly in front of Vancouver Island's Clo-oose village. She shared headlines with the big British bark *Peter Iredale*, lost on the same day just south of the Columbia River entrance.

The *Skagit*, inbound from San Francisco, struck the beach hard and was turned broadside to the booming breakers. While boarding the boat, Captain Rose was swept into the sea. The cook leaped into the water to save him but he also was drowned. After futile efforts to recover the bodies, the mate and seven crewmen pulled for the shore and ran the wild surf. The residents of the village came quickly to their aid. The survivors were cared for by Mr. and Mrs. Dave Logan—white settlers in the predominantly Indian settlement—until they could get passage back to Puget Sound.

WRECKS IN PARADISE

The beautiful Tsusiat Falls area, a natural paradise, was the scene of the loss of two familiar windships just before the turn of the century. Shipwreck is never pleasant, but at least it can occur at a scenic spot such as Tsusiat.

A wreck there on December 10, 1897, involved the three-masted schooner *Vesta*, owned by Albert Rowe of San Francisco. The *Vesta* was carried into the breakers with her sails still set, as if lured by a mermaid's lyre. The crew abandoned in orderly fashion and reached shore safely, setting up a comfortable camp near Tsusiat Falls with material recovered from the wreck. Rescue soon came for the survivors, but the *Vesta*, a fifteen-year-old vessel, lay in a precarious spot which defied salvage. She remained erect for several days before succumbing to the elements.

Much more complex was the loss of the barkentine *Uncle John*. A severe gale was lashing the North Pacific on October 7, 1899. The horizons closed down and the blur of Vancouver Island was but a black suggestion to starboard. The ship's master, Captain Carl Henningsen, took frequent glances at the compass. The helmsman struggled to maintain the course. The morning seas came up from the stern, borne in by a strong southwester. Nearby in the sea mist, the violent surf broke against the ragged coastal cliffs, exploding into wild, white spume.

The skipper peered over the taffrail and watched the deep-gullied waves run by. Gulls were flung in all directions by the air currents; wheeling and screeching, they seemed to warn of a greater storm to come.

Since 1881, the *Uncle John* had been engaged in the coastwise trade flying the banner of the John Vance Mill & Lumber Company of Eureka, California. The unusual name was attributed to the pride of the owner in that his nephews and nieces called him Uncle John. This so pleased him that he applied the name to his ship.

Never before, in her many years of operation, had the vessel been in such a precarious position as she was that October day of 1899. Though Captain Henningsen knew this coast very well, his superior knowledge was no match for the full gale. Oilskins glistened with rain as the crew shortened sail. The men had gone for hours without warm food. All night the skipper had feared the coast and had twice reset his course to pull away; now he had lost all touch with it. Westward was only the gray, ominous gloom.

Altering course a few degrees, the vessel fell into a deep trough. While green avalanches inundated her deck, the vessel labored to recover from the tons of water. Gradually she rose and swung into the seas. Henningsen shouted to the helmsman, "Point West!" and cupped his hand to his ear for the possible rumble of distant surf. The ship's master well knew he was in the dreaded graveyard of ships.

"Get that lead to work!" he called to the mate. "Don't let up till you can't touch bottom."

Before the lead had been tossed for the second time, the vessel struck. The impact threw the men to the deck. An underwater reef cut deeply along the keel, causing the ship to lose all freedom of motion. She trembled violently, grinding herself deeper upon the obstruction. Seas boarded in rapid succession, leaving the deck a shambles. The masts were canted at strange angles and the fear-stricken crewmen dodged free-swinging rigging.

As the vessel showed every sign of breaking up, the order to abandon was given. When a hole in the haze opened for a moment, the shore loomed ominously. The *Uncle John* was in jeopardy seven miles north of Carmanah Light, between Tsusiat and Nitinat. The surf was mighty, the wind howling. The crew could not get the boat into the surf. To stay aboard was to perish; to evacuate was suicide.

The situation grew tense—while the eight-man crew clung to the swaying masts. At long last, the wreck was seen by some natives along the shore and after a frantic struggle a surf line was rigged. Soaked to the skin, the crew managed to reach shore just before their vessel broke up.

THE INLET QUEEN

Nitinat, though beautiful, is not on the most hospitable coastline in the world. Back in 1912, a Canadian real estate firm was taken by the natural beauty of this last frontier and endeavored to promote its merits. They visualized a great seaside resort where the wealthy would gather each summer, away from the cares of the outside world—a bit of paradise tucked far away from civilization. Their enthusiasm caught fire and the high price asked for the properties attracted the well-to-do. Much of the property was purchased unseen.

To give the new investors and prospective buyers their first glimpse of the area, a fifty-foot cabin cruiser named *Inlet Queen* was chartered on April 12, 1912, for the cruise from Victoria. There was considerable fanfare surrounding the voyage and the local papers played it up to the hilt.

All went well till the *Inlet Queen* left dockside. Nasty winds were fanning the Strait of Juan de Fuca, and all the way to the Nitinat Coast the craft took a terrible pounding. The passengers became violently seasick. In crossing the Nitinat Bar, the craft ran hard aground and the passengers were forced to struggle ashore, sick, wet, and discouraged.

Despite the setback, including the total loss of the *Inlet Queen,* the real estate firm was persistent. They still planned a resort similar to those on the coast of southern England. Before the scheme could gain impetus, however, World War I broke out; this, coupled with stories of great amounts of rainfall in the area, defeated the plan once and for all.

The sinister reputation of the Nitinat Bar has continued down through the years. In November 1918, the Canadian cannery tender *Renfrew* left the cannery on Nitinat Lake and crossed the bar outbound. In the trough of a bar swell, the vessel struck bottom and capsized, drowning thirteen persons, most of them cannery employees homeward bound. Thirteen other persons aboard were rescued through the efforts of the citizens of nearby Clooose. One of the few white residents of the area, Dave Logan, spent the next two days picking up the dead bodies that washed ashore.

The tugboat *Beryl* was lost on the Nitinat Bar in 1920, and many other small craft have been seriously damaged there.

STRANDING OF THE SANTA RITA

At the Union Iron Works in San Francisco in the year 1913, the steel steam schooner *William Chatham,* of 1,600 tons, was delivered to her owners, the Loop Lumber Company of San Francisco. The vessel had a capacity of 1.5 million board feet of lumber and was powered by a triple-expansion engine. In 1915 she was purchased by Grace Steamship Company, renamed *Santa Rita,* and placed in intercoastal service until 1922, when A. F. Mahoney of San Francisco assumed ownership.

The *Santa Rita* had traveled to many parts of the world and had come through the war years unscathed, but when she ran ashore on Clo-oose Beach, February 14, 1923, fate had determined that she would no longer sail the seas . . .

A blinding snowstorm was blowing off Vancouver Island and all landmarks were blotted out. The SS *Santa Rita*, with her crew of thirty-two, was feeling her way offshore when she crunched over the barnacle-infested boulders and came to a grinding halt directly adjacent to Clo-oose Village. She immediately took a starboard list.

Residents of the settlement were quick to respond as the word spread from house to house. While the seas hammered the steamer, the rescue party assembled. Aboard the ship, a Lyle gun was fired, carrying a line to the beach; natives lost little time making it fast. A breeches buoy was rigged, and as the snow pelted down, the survivors made their orderly exit over crashing surf, one after another, until all had been rescued.

The *Santa Rita* remained on the beach, beyond salvage, and for years thereafter her steel ribs and rusting boiler gave grim testimony to the incident.

Again among the rescue party was Dave Logan, store operator, postmaster, and justice of the peace. Hired originally by a Victoria, B. C. man, Logan had come to the area in 1899 to care for a herd of cattle. The livestock soon died off because the climate and surroundings were not conducive to their welfare, but Logan stayed on. During almost four decades at Clo-oose, he probably witnessed more shipwrecks firsthand than any other white man along the West Coast of the island. He and his wife cared for scores of castaways at their modest home during those years. Though Logan died in 1938, his name is still remembered because of his many humane acts as a linesman patrolling a twenty-five-mile section (Carmanah to Pachena), where a single wire, tree-to-tree telephone line was the lone means of contact with the outside world.

PART 7

PACHENA POINT-CAPE BEALE AREA

Including the pioneer wreck of the brig William . . .
the ghostly meanderings of the Maria J. Smith . . . *the
sentimental loss of the steamer* Woodside . . . *the quick
death of the Nova Scotian bark* Sarah . . . *the steam
schooner that bequeathed her name to a creek . . . suffering and privation of the crew of the* Janet Cowan
. . . *how Grace Darling of Vancouver Island earned her
title . . . the tragic* Soquel *incident . . . barratry hinted at
in the* Lewers *wreck . . . and the grisly loss of the
passenger liner* Valencia.

Mariners describe the coastline between Pachena Point and
Cape Beale on Vancouver Island's West Coast as one of the most
rugged in the world. Here rock-studded beaches, formidable
headlands, and wool-thick forests abound. The only shelter for
ships, if indeed it could be termed as such, is deceptive Pachena
Bay. Lighthouses mark both Pachena Point and Cape Beale,
warning navigators to remain well to seaward of the many outlying protuberances that regularly sink their teeth into unsuspect-
ing ships. Danger lurks all along this forsaken area, especially in
thick weather when vessels hug the shoreline endeavoring to
round Cape Beale and enter Barkley Sound.

FIRST RECORDED LOSS

Numerous unrecorded wrecks undoubtedly lie along Vancouver Island's West Coast. The first recorded tragedy was that of

the British brig *William*, well over a century ago, near Pachena Point.

This vessel was northbound from San Francisco en route to Victoria. On New Year's Day 1854, she fell victim to inclement weather and drove ashore about five miles east southeast of Pachena Point. In the seething surf, while trying to escape the wreck, the captain and the cook were drowned. Fourteen others —cold, hungry, and miserable—struggled ashore and were found by friendly Indians. The natives cared for them, offering crude shelter and a scanty diet of dried fish. Though suffering terribly from exposure, the Indians kept them alive and then transported them by canoe to the primitive logging town of Sooke, west of Victoria, where they recovered from their ordeal.

THE WANDERING MARIA J. SMITH

One vessel that flirted with every danger along Vancouver Island's West Coast, but finally escaped, was the American bark *Maria J. Smith*. Skippered by Captain David Smith, she departed Port Townsend on November 6, 1869, laden with lumber. The vessel passed Cape Flattery Light on November 8 at 2 a.m. Four hours later she was struck by a gale which created insurmountable seas from the south southeast. The onslaught loosened the fastenings on the bark's deckload and great stacks of lumber were carried over the side. The howling wind blew out several of the sails and water filled the bilge.

A temporary lull near the eye of the storm prompted the captain to break out the topsails in order to work the vessel offshore. Land was faintly visible to leeward and every endeavor was made to gain deeper water. But the wind and the currents seemed to draw them landward. Closer and closer the shore loomed. With his ship virtually unmanageable, Captain Smith decided on abandonment in the boats before they were locked in the grip of the breakers. Added to his decision was the fact that his wife and children were aboard. He knew the sinister reputation of these shores.

The boats were lowered away, but remained offshore until a sandy beach was located. Then they ran the breakers and made a safe landing. The survivors lived in the bush three days, suffering much privation until they were able to signal the schooner *Surprise*, Captain Francis, which transported them to Victoria.

By the morning of November 9, the derelict *Maria J. Smith* was hard aground on a reef about five miles east of Pachena Point. Salvagers had ruled out refloating her as virtually impossible and the wreck was sold in a hasty transaction—"as is where is," at Port Townsend. A self-styled salvage expert named Broderick purchased the bark for $950, the lumber for $750, and the gear for $300. Immediately he rounded up a green crew and hastened to the wreck in a small boat. The men worked around the clock to get the impaled derelict free of the reef. Pumped out and temporarily patched by early January 1870, she was towed to Port Madison by the tug *Politkofsky*—former gunboat acquired from the Russians in the 1867 purchase of Alaska.

Salvage expert Broderick stood to make a handsome profit and might have done so except that another gale erupted just as the *Politkofsky* was towing her charge into the Strait of Juan de Fuca. Aboard the wreck was Captain Smith (who had returned at the request of the new owner), and a skeleton crew. The mounting seas made it mandatory that the tug cut the towing line, and the *Maria J. Smith* once again was carried out to sea, masts and rigging badly damaged. She drifted for more than twelve days at the mercy of the winds and current. Finally, when no towing vessel came to their assistance, Captain Smith and his men were once again forced to abandon. Fortunately the bark *Sampson* inbound for Port Townsend had sighted their distress signals and stood by to make the rescue.

The abandoned vessel then set her own course, drifting in an erratic pattern. Later sighted off Cape Flattery, tugs were dispatched to tow her in. By the time they arrived she again had vanished. Two months later and five hundred miles from where she had previously been sighted, the Indians at Bella Bella, B. C., reported seeing the weather-beaten derelict still afloat. Late in March, the *Maria J. Smith,* guided by invisible hands, drove ashore and broke up on a small island north of Millbank Sound.

STEAMER WOODSIDE

In 1878, in the little British Columbia logging town of Sooke, B. C., west of Victoria, there was great fanfare with the launching of the small steamer *Woodside.* The handsome craft was designed as an all-purpose carrier for connecting Sooke with Victoria and other villages along the west coast of Vancouver Island. The vessel served as an all-purpose freight, passenger, mail, and towboat. She was the lifeline for the people of Sooke; their link with the outside world. Though only eighty feet long and slightly over fifteen feet wide, the *Woodside* was highly dependable and was operated with reasonable punctuality by her owner. Thus it can be readily understood why there was great sadness among the residents of Sooke when, a decade later, they received the terse news of the loss of the little steamer.

While en route to Alberni from Sooke, under Captain Colin Cluness, the *Woodside* lost her propeller and became unmanageable, off Pachena Point. The crew and four passengers were forced to take to the boats at 11 a.m., March 12, 1888. They made a landing three miles from Pachena Point and were cared for by the Nitinat Indians who eventually took them by canoe to Victoria. During that night the *Woodside* drifted ashore and broke up.

THE SARAH SUCCUMBS

Swift and sudden was the loss of the Nova Scotian bark *Sarah.* Lewis & Dryden's *Marine History of the Pacific Northwest* records that this sailing vessel, in command of Captain Greenhalgh, was bound for Port Blakely from Manila in ballast, and was to have picked up a load of lumber on Puget Sound. Off the West Coast of Vancouver Island, she encountered a gale accompanied by a wraith-like surface fog.

Losing sight of land, the vessel missed the entrance to the strait and crashed ashore about three miles from Pachena Point. The surf was running high on that eighth day of November 1891, and much difficulty was experienced in getting the two boats over the side. One boat contained the captain, his wife and child, plus a few crew members. The other boat carried a mixture of officers and seamen. While trying to run the breakers to the beach, the second boat overturned and two were drowned in the surf. Through the captain's skillful guidance, the other boat landed safely with its passengers.

The wreck itself was pulverized by the surf. Because the seventeen-year-old, 1,142-ton vessel was only partly insured, the owners were left with a considerable financial loss.

THE MICHIGAN

Time erases the memory of most common shipwrecks, but one that is still recalled is that of the steamer *Michigan*—because the vessel's name was given to the creek where she stranded in 1893.

The *Michigan* was one of the early coastal steam schooners. These schooners were a West Coast innovation designed to replace the windjammers. Built somewhat on the lines of a sailing schooner, the steam schooners carried sail for use in emergency only. Their steam engines ended the long delays suffered by windships at bar entrances.

According to John Lyman, maritime history authority, the first wooden steam schooners were built in 1884 but it took a couple of years for mill operators to discover that this type of vessel offered considerable improvement over windjammers. If a sailing schooner was caught by a storm at an unprotected Pacific coastal "chute" landing, she might be either blown ashore or driven far out to sea and waste days getting back. The steam schooner, being more independent of wind, had less to fear from bad weather at the loading ports. Likewise, although there was usually a fair wind on the run down to San Francisco, the return trip northward was made against the prevailing Northwest trades, and here again the steam schooner was at an advantage.

The L. E. White Lumber Company of San Francisco is credited with being the first firm to successfully operate steam schooners in the lumber trade. In 1886 they commissioned the *Whiteboro* and *Greenwood* and these were followed by larger vessels. The only steam schooners to antedate the *Whiteboro* and *Greenwood* were the *C. G. White, Julia H. Ray, Celia,* and *Surprise,* which were actually in the experimental stages of development.

The earliest steam schooners were purely schooners in design, having two or three-masted rigs, the engine amidships, a bowsprit with headsails, and an overhanging counter stern. Builders, however, quickly improved on the design and began to produce a more suitable type. The bowsprit was the first thing to go; it was always a nuisance when handling a powered vessel alongside a dock. At the same time the engine was moved aft, in order to permit the weight of engine and boilers to keep the propeller under water even when the vessel was without cargo. The two-masted rig was settled on as being most suitable. The masts became more and more for supporting the cargo gear and less for sails, although not until 1910 was sail eliminated.

This unusual fleet of wooden steam schooners, from their inception in 1884 until the last one was built in 1924, numbered almost 250 vessels. They carried on a remarkable trade coastwise and became affectionately known as the "Scandinavian Navy," inasmuch as they were almost completely manned by Scandinavians. The fleet developed many colorful characters with comical names, but there were no more capable master mariners in the world than those who ran these unique vessels. They operated dangerously close to shore, loaded in areas where no other ships would venture, and continuously ran the treacherous bar entrances. As a result, the mortality rate among them and their crews was extremely high. There wasn't a single shoreline from Vancouver Island to the Mexican border that did not claim the bones of at least one of these stout little vessels, but not until the advanced steel steam schooner was developed during World War I were they phased out.

The third wooden steam schooner built in the Pacific Northwest and the thirty-first built on the Pacific Coast was the *Michigan*. She was a stout vessel of 566 tons, constructed at Skamokawa, Washington, on the Columbia River, by Ludwig Mortensen for William M. and George L. Colwell. She had a lumber capacity of 400,000 board feet and was slightly in excess of 158 feet in length with a 34-foot beam. Her steam plant and boilers were cumbersome but she was considered the finest steam schooner built up to that year—1888. Her career was somewhat disappointing, however, and she soon acquired a bad name.

In command of Captain C. H. Lewis, the *Michigan* caught fire off the Washington Coast in November of 1890, while steaming from Puget Sound to Portland. The crew valiantly fought the blaze but barely held their own. In a daring gamble, Captain Lewis refused to abandon ship, electing to run full-bore down the coast and cross the Columbia River Bar to Astoria. With the vessel blazing like a torch and her company gathered aft fighting flames by bucket brigade, the drama continued for several anguishing hours. Finally the *Michigan* crossed the bar and, blazing furiously, neared port.

As a great crowd gathered, the Astoria Fire Department's pumper—pulled by a spirited team of horses—waited at dockside. They pumped the *Michigan* so full of water that she partially rested on the river bottom. The fire was squelched and the vessel saved. After extensive repairs the steamer went back to work only slightly worse for the experience.

Though strongly built, the *Michigan* was no match for her next tragic episode, which became the final entry in her logbook. She was bound for Puget Sound from San Francisco, in command of Captain Graves, and was heavily laden with general cargo. She was near the entrance of the Strait of Juan de Fuca, four days out of the Golden Gate, when she encountered thick weather and a heavy westerly sea. This, together with a strong wind and the persistent northerly current, carried the vessel to a spot well to the north of her intended position. As night came on, visibility was reduced to zero. Groping blindly about, the *Michigan*, at 10:50 p.m. on the night of January 21, 1893, struck the outlying rocks at what was to be later known as Michigan Creek, near Pachena Point. The first impact did severe structural damage to the vessel.

Her precarious position, fully exposed to the hammering seas, gave Captain Graves no choice but to quit his ship. After allowing his men a few minutes to gather their personal effects, the boats, in the darkness, were lowered away on the lee side and managed to clear the wreck without accident.

The survivors looked sadly back at the faint outline of the *Michigan*: she was working hard on the reef under the extreme weight of her cargo and relentless breakers were taking their toll. Meanwhile the survivors concentrated on the best place to make a landing. The boats parted company, one coming ashore not far from the wreck and the other, the captain's craft, moving southward to the vicinity of Carmanah Light. There by daylight the latter found a place to make a safe landing and came in through the breakers. At the light station, however, they were unable to communicate with Victoria, so Captain Graves and his men sailed the small boat on a hazardous voyage to Neah Bay, where they telegraphed for assistance.

Three powerful American tugs, the *Discovery, Tacoma,* and *Sea Lion,* hastened to the wreck scene while the revenue cutter *Oliver Wolcott* was dispatched to pick up the survivors. At Victoria, the Canadian wrecking steamer *Mascotte* was readied for salvage work. The dangerous position of the wreck prevented attempts to refloat her, but the tugs and the salvage ship recovered most of the cargo and fittings.

The *Michigan* had carried a crew of twenty-one plus four passengers. All suffered much from exposure during the escape in the boats. After the first lifeboat landed, one German crewman became delirious and wandered off into the bush, where he later died from exposure. The ship's purser, F. M. Bucklin, also suffered delirium from exposure and was many weeks recovering. The *Michigan,* which to all intents and purposes should have experienced at least forty years of active service, failed to complete five and was dropped from registry as an unfortunate victim of the graveyard of ships.

THE JANET COWAN

A tragic wreck before the turn of the century was that of the four-masted iron bark *Janet Cowan,* one of the finest ships of her day. Hailing from Greenock, Scotland, and registering 2,500 tons, she met her demise on December 31, 1895, four miles east of Pachena Point. The vessel was 108 days out of Cape Town inbound for Royal Roads, B. C. She was to have taken on a full load of lumber at British Columbia ports for South Africa, but her destination was never reached.

A gale was lashing the North Pacific when the tall square-rigger arrived off the entrance to the strait, December 28. For two days she was obliged to stand out to sea, waiting for the blow to abate and for the opportune time to enter the strait and enlist the aid of a tug. But there was no letup in the storm and the weather obliterated all sight of shore. The vessel was being carried toward Vancouver Island's dreaded graveyard.

There was no opportunity to get a boat over the side, and within a short time the big ship was scraping along the shoals, refusing to mind the helm. Captain Thompson mustered his crew aft to discuss chances of their survival. A seaman volunteered to swim ashore with a line, and the captain accepted his offer. With little hesitation the seaman tied a light line to his belt and leaped overboard amid the feeble cheers of his shipmates. With arms and legs flailing the foamy seas, he managed to make his way to shore and struggle up on the beach. Though numb from the cold, he reeled in the line, to which had been attached a heavier line. Without ceasing, the work continued at both ends until a breeches buoy had been rigged. Throughout

U. S. Revenue Cutter Service

U. S. Lifesaving Station on Waada Island, in 1909, prior to the completion of a new station at Neah Bay the following year.

Surfboat crew at U. S. Lifesaving Station, Neah Bay, shortly after its opening in 1910. From left, Pickles, the mascot; George Hiesie, on the sweep; Rube Rogers, Charles Miller, Ray Northrup, Pete Hewitt, Earl Nielson, and Orval Baughn.

U. S. Coast Guard

Neah Bay Lifeboat Station is an important segment of the U. S. Coast Guard. Here motor lifeboats and other Coast Guard craft are kept in readiness to aid any vessel in need.

Ancient photo believed to be the now non-existent Indian village at Ozette, Cape Alava, Washington. The ship in the foreground is the wreck of the bark *Austria*, destroyed on Flattery Rocks in 1887. Inset, top left, shows the *Austria's* three-ton anchor.

Great cliffs hammered by restless seas for countless centuries form bastion for the light station atop Tatoosh Island.

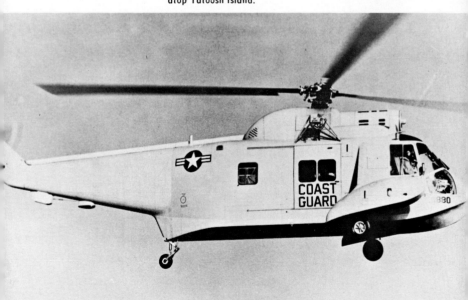

"The modern touch"—a Coast Guard helicopter based at Port Angeles is always ready to aid distressed seafarers in Juan de Fuca's graveyard of ships.

SS *Coast Trader* was reputedly the victim of a Japanese submarine torpedo, northwest of Cape Flattery during World War II.

SS *Richard Harding Davis,* aground between Carmanah and Cape Beale, B.C., June 22, 1944— during the hectic years of World War II.

the day, one at a time, the twenty-nine-man crew of the *Cowan* was ferried ashore, each getting a salty bath when the line sagged.

Once on the cold, forbidding beach, it was agreed that seven of their number would follow a downed telephone wire, draped from tree to tree above the beach, to the nearest shipwreck cabin. (These survival cabins were located at intervals, placed there by the Canadian government for such emergencies.) The small party finally arrived at one which was fortunately only a mile west of their stranded ship. Since the cabin was stocked with provisions, it was decided that the party should remain there in the hope that the telephone wire might eventually be repaired, permitting them to call for assistance.

The rest of the crew had stayed on the beach opposite the wreck, improvising shelter from bits of wreckage. The weather was so cold and miserable that they suffered greatly from exposure. Finally, after ten days of no relief, Captain Thompson, the ship's cook, and two seamen succumbed; another seaman committed suicide. The others endeavored to get back out to the wreck for blankets, supplies, and medicine, but in the attempt, two apprentices were drowned and the second mate broke his leg.

When hope of survival was all but abandoned, the passing American tug *Tyee*, Captain William Gove, out of Port Townsend, sighted the wreck. She came in near to shore and sent in a boat to pick up the fifteen exhausted survivors. The seven others, at the survival station, were rescued the following day by a Canadian vessel and taken to Victoria. Bodies of two of the dead were later recovered and given proper burial, and thus ended another tragic tale of shipwreck and privation on Vancouver Island's notorious west coast.

THE COLOMA

On a clear day one can easily look from one promontory to the other and catch a glimpse of the churning water dividing

Pachena Point and Cape Beale. The rugged character of the latter headland is made friendly only by its crowning lighthouse. In 1787, the cape was named for John Beale, purser of Barkley's *Imperial Eagle*.

It was here that the bark *Coloma* went to a watery grave on December 6, 1906, the same year as the tragic *Valencia* disaster. The old trader, built at Warren, Rhode Island, in 1869, was of 850 tons and could be classed as little more than a floating coffin. Obviously her owners had planned to run her until she fell apart.

The *Coloma* sailed out of Puget Sound, a faded American ensign waving from her shroud. Her principals had managed to get a cargo of lumber for Australia. After passing Tatoosh Island, the bark ran into a driving southeast gale. With but little freeboard under a heavy deckload of lumber, she labored violently. The pumps were taxed to the limit and finally became clogged with debris. Captain J. Allison and his nine crew members tried to repair the rusty mechanism but failed. The vessel yawed as thundering walls of water slopped over the deckload. Soon rigging pulled loose, the yardarms crashed to the deck, and the masts swayed precariously. The skipper ordered the wreckage over the side to afford more buoyancy.

The *Coloma* now drifted helpless, carried ever closer to the perilous reefs of Vancouver Island. The vigilant lighthouse keeper at Cape Beale, Thomas Paterson, saw the dim outline of the stricken ship, her ensign inverted at the stump of her mizzenmast. He could do nothing by himself, but the lighthouse tender *Quadra* lay at anchor at Bamfield six miles away, if only there were some way to deliver the message. The storm had blown down the telephone lines to Bamfield and Victoria.

George Nicholson, in his book, *Vancouver Island's West Coast* relates that the light keeper had to keep steam up in the boiler for the station fog signal and was unable to leave his post. His stalwart wife, Minnie, aware of the problem that confronted her husband, insisted on making the rugged overland trek to Bamfield, despite the driving gale.

Darkness was coming on. Even by daylight, the path was a challenge to the hardiest individual. Donning heavy storm gear, Minnie Paterson took her dog and a lantern and started off on the six-mile junket. She didn't turn back once, but just kept pushing ahead along the rugged stretches of beach, through forest and bush and gullies. Danger lurked everywhere, especially from the scores of tall trees that had been blown down by the driving winds.

Exhausted, she finally reached the home of an old friend, Mrs. Annie McKay, daughter of a former lighthouse keeper at Cape Beale. Mrs. McKay's husband was away, but without hesitation the two women ran down to the shore and rowed the family boat out to the *Quadra*, which was at anchor in the bay. On hearing their story, Captain Hackett prepared for immediate departure. The *Quadra* moved out in the storm-lashed waters bucking furious seas. Somewhat later, the drone of a fog signal was heard, and this was followed by a faint shaft of light filtering through the haze of an otherwise somber night. Then the wreck was outlined, diving, rolling, and straining at her anchor cables.

By now the storm had somewhat subsided but the sea had yet to moderate and the *Quadra* was forced to stand well off the troubled ship. Volunteers were requested by Captain Hackett. Under second mate McDonald, they took to the ship's boat and rowed through the pulsating sea to where they could heave a line aboard the *Coloma*. In a fine display of seamanship the small boat jockeyed in and out, rising on the swell and dropping in the trough until, one by one, all of the crew members of the wreck were removed.

Within a few hours of the evacuation, the wreck was smashed against the outer reef. So thick was the weather that light keeper Paterson was unable to observe the rescue operation from the station. In fact, it was not until a week later, after the telephone line had been repaired, that he learned that his wife's mission had succeeded. When finally Minnie Paterson, the mother of five children, returned to her husband at Cape Beale, there was great rejoicing in the family. Her effort had earned for her the title of "British Columbia's Grace Darling." She, however, never fully recovered from that strenuous ordeal and, with great sadness, the Paterson family laid her to rest just five years later.

THE SOQUEL SAGA

It was a case of a mistaken light that caused the loss of the four-masted schooner *Soquel,* January 22, 1909. The 767-ton vessel—bound for Port Townsend from Callao and San Francisco with a small cargo of general freight—approached the entrance to the Strait of Juan de Fuca on a tempestuous winter night. The prevailing winds and currents carried her past the obscured entrance.

All eyes strained into the eerie pall, trying to catch a glimpse of Cape Flattery Light. Suddenly a dim glow broke through the gloom, and the watch sang out the glad news. The order was immediately given to change course, and the schooner slowly came about, pursuing an easterly bearing. Gathering headway, her sheets had begun to fill when there came the chill cry, "Breakers Ahead!" Massive sea-washed rocks appeared on all sides. The vessel sideswiped one and reeled crazily. Captain Henningson rushed to his cabin, stumbling as he hurried through the midnight gloom. Rousing his wife and small child, he herded them—clad only in their night clothes—in the direction of the deck. Just as they came out of the hatchway door, one of the masts thundered down on top of them, killing Mrs. Henningson and her child outright, breaking the skipper's arm, and the leg of a seaman.

By now the *Soquel* was impaled on the rocks and her decks were in sad disarray. The first mate took charge and immediately ordered the boat provisioned and lowered. As they struggled to get it into the churning waters the other masts threatened to let go. Working frantically against time, they got the boat afloat on the lee side, and all twelve survivors, with the bodies of the dead, broke away from the wreck just before it started to break up. The seamen pulled at the oars, and with the mate as the steersman, they made a daring run through the breakers to land safely on the beach.

It was not until the following day that they learned the schooner had struck the Seabird Rock outcroppings, after having mistaken Pachena Light for Flattery. That fatal mistake cost the lives of two and the total loss of the *Soquel,* which was valued at $60,000 and owned by J. R. Hanify, San Francisco merchant.

STRANDING OF THE ROBERT LEWERS

Barratry is a nasty word in marine insurance circles. Webster describes it as fraud or gross negligence of a ship's officer or seaman against owners, insurers, and so forth. In most cases barratry is difficult to prove. The word is often freely flaunted about simply because intervening circumstances suggest such an act. Many navigators guilty of casting a ship away have gone unpunished for lack of evidence, while others have suffered for something that was unavoidable.

In the following story, the navigator's name won't be mentioned, nor was he held liable for the loss of his ship. Nevertheless, the word barratry was on many tongues. The vessel was lost at a time when the windjammer had reached the end of its usefulness in an era of steam.

Collection of insurance on an aging wooden hull that has little market value usually opens the door to behind-the-scenes investigation. Nevertheless, insurance must be paid on a wrecked ship, regardless of type, age, or condition, unless there is overwhelming evidence of malicious intent to purposely destroy the vessel. In question was the four-masted schooner *Robert Lewers.* Named for one of the owning partners, Lewers & Cooke, of Honolulu—for whom she was built at Port Blakely, Washington, in 1889—she was one of the finest windjammers of her day. She was a money-maker too, running almost constantly, carrying lumber from Puget Sound to the Hawaiian Islands. Under the management of Higgins & Collins of San Francisco, the 732-ton vessel was profitably operated from 1889 until 1917—twenty-eight years on the same run;

perhaps a record. Throughout much of her active life she was skippered by Captain William G. Goodman. During World War I, the *Lewers'* area of trade was expanded somewhat but later she was returned to her familiar sea road between Puget Sound and Hawaii.

In April of 1923, the schooner was on her way back from Honolulu. The brisk trade immediately after the war had dwindled and steamers were finding it hard to secure cargo. Windjammers were riding aimlessly at anchor in backwater moorages or being burned to recover what scrap they would render. But not the *Robert Lewers;* she kept on winging her way in such grand style that she caused many to ponder. After thirty-four hard-working years, the veteran lumber schooner was still at it. No wonder suspicious minds issued accusations on the morning of April 11, when the *Lewers* was reported by the Coast Guard to be hard aground near Pachena Point.

The big tug *Humaconna* was dispatched to sea to assist the schooner, but when she arrived salvage was found impossible and the best the tug could do was to remove the crew. The *Lewers* had to be abandoned to the elements. In the hearing that followed, there was behind-the-scenes talk about barratry, but being without proof this was not brought up as testimony. Without proof, accusations are cheap. The official findings of the hearing were that the wreck was a result of adverse weather and currents. No charges were filed against the captain or officers. The case was officially closed.

In defense of the *Robert Lewers* it should also be a matter of public record that Lewers & Cooke, Ltd., Honolulu, were among the most highly regarded in Pacific trade and all credit is due them and their operating managers and crews for keeping the schooner running successfully for so many years with nothing to guide her but the wind that billowed her canvas.

VALENCIA DISASTER

Following the loss of the steamer *Pacific* in 1875, steamboat inspection laws were stiffened; ships were built stronger and fitted with better lifesaving devices for emergencies. Passenger steam-ship operators vowed there would never be another tragedy on the North Pacific like that of the steamer *Pacific*. But, another grisly ship disaster did occur in the winter of 1906, with the loss of the SS *Valencia* and 117 lives.

The ships' graveyard off Vancouver Island's West Coast ac-quired its most valuable prize on the bleak night of January 22, 1906. Freezing sleet borne on the wings of gale-like winds put the *Valencia* on the rocks three miles east of Pachena Point, ironically close to the site of a proposed lighthouse.

The SS *Valencia* was a staunch, iron-hulled passenger vessel, owned by the Pacific Coast Steamship Company. In compari-son with the *Pacific*, she was much more strongly built—turned out in 1882 by the reputable W. Cramp & Sons yard at Phila-delphia. She measured 252 feet in length, was propeller driven, and fitted with four separate bulkheads. Popular with tourists, she had long been one of the vital links in coastwise passenger travel.

In command of Captain O. M. Johnson, the *Valencia* departed San Francisco on her final voyage with ninety-four passengers and sixty crewmen. Her destination was Seattle via Victoria, B. C. The voyage north was a routine winter passage and all went well till reaching the forty-eighth parallel. The entrance to the Strait of Juan de Fuca was heavily shrouded by fog, and squalls were frequent.

Forlorn blasts of the ship's whistle pierced the night air; lights along the shore were completely obliterated. Navigation was by dead reckoning, and the strong northerly pull of the current was not fully taken into consideration. The ship's officers reasoned the ship to be in the vicinity of *Umatilla Reef Lightship*.

Captain Johnson had been in the service of the Pacific Coast Steamship Company for more than twelve years and was one of their most trusted servants. He was not overly concerned about the weather as it was typical of that encountered on numerous other voyages on the coastwise run. This time, however, he had miscalculated and his ship was nineteen miles off course.

As a precaution on the evening of January 22, the chief officer ordered the boatswain to have two leads ready. The Thompson sounding machine was inoperative and in need of repair. The ship carried no wireless and had no contact with the shore. As midnight approached, the lead began touching the bottom and depths varied. Most of the passengers had retired for the night —their sleep made uneasy by the ship's rolling and the continuous blasting of the whistle which reverberated along the passageways.

Steadfast on the bridge, Captain Johnson was becoming more concerned. He did not realize his navigational error until, without forewarning, the liner sideswiped an unseen obstruction and shuddered from stem to stern. Listing to one side, the vessel broke free momentarily. Bells clanged, the whistle blew, and passengers were aroused from their sleep. The quartermaster was ordered to put the wheel hard over, and the ship swung abruptly about in search of deeper water. Her propeller beat the sea into a creamy froth. Lights all over the ship blinked off and on. For a moment it appeared that the danger was over, but the swinging bow struck another sharp pinnacle which gouged deeply into the iron hull plates.

Captain Johnson grabbed the speaking tube and shouted to Chief Engineer E. W. Downing for more steam. The pressure rose; the maximum horsepower was exerted, and the ship vibrated as terrified passengers, clad in night clothes, demanded reassurance from the ship's officers.

The *Valencia* again freed herself, but only briefly. Captain Johnson sighed with momentary relief until he looked aft from the bridge and saw the engine-room crew emerging. The ship had been holed below the waterline and the sea was rushing in. The engine and boiler rooms were flooding and the pumps were unable to function properly.

Knowing that Chief Engineer Downing must still be standing

by, the captain rang for full astern to get the ship back on the reef. Then he picked up the speaking tube and shouted to Downing, "Get topside quick!"

The chief engineer narrowly escaped with his life as he waded through water waist-high to an escape ladder deep in the recesses of the ship. As he ascended, the ship plowed back onto the reef, the momentum causing massive punctures all along the waterline. This time there was no restitution for the *Valencia*. She was aground between Cape Beale and Clo-oose on a fringe of Walla Walla Reef. It was almost midnight and the seas were bearing down relentlessly. There was utter confusion aboard. Men, women, and children ran about the decks. The driving wind and a chilling drizzle soaked them to the skin.

The ship's boatswain, T. J. McCarthy, afterwards related before a coroner's jury at Victoria, B. C., his version of the wreck scene:

> I was in my bunk asleep. I got up at once and went on deck. It was thick dark, sleeting and blowing a stiff breeze. I could not see any light. I went back and got my clothes. By that time the passengers were getting out of their rooms and most of them had life preservers on. At the time the engines were working, but I don't know which way. The chief officer told me to clear away the boats, which I did. The deck was crowded and it was so dark I could not tell the crew from passengers. We only carried eight sailors and four quartermasters. We had seven boats and three rafts. The davits were drop davits.
>
> The captain shouted from the bridge to lower all boats to the saloon rail and keep them there, but the four forward boats were lowered all the way; most of them were full of passengers and there was a strain on the tackles. Of those four boats, only one, No. 2, got away from the ship's side. There was a heavy sea running, breaking almost to the bridge, and I am doubtful if those boats could have got away even in daylight. The captain turned the searchlight

all around. I saw No. 2 boat off at some little distance; then someone pulled the whistle and the electric lights went out.

I saw No. 1 boat smash alongside. There would be 15 or 20 people in her. I had a ladder thrown over, also some ropes, and I saw one man climb aboard.

At that time the *Valencia* took a heavy list to port and No. 7 boat was lowered. I saw the firemen's mess boy in No. 6 boat. She got away from the ship's side. One raft was also put overboard. There were at that time several people in the rigging and the rest on the hurricane deck. Some rockets were fired and we could see the beach. The officers were then assuring the passengers that they would be all right. At the same time the social hall and the weather side of the saloon were the only dry places on the ship.

Almost at once the ship began to break up and seas combed the decks carrying some overboard. Husbands tied their wives and children to stanchions and davits to keep them from being swept away.

Captain Johnson courageously set about to save what lives he could. Shouting commands, he finally got a lifeboat swung clear on the port side. A huge, lunging sea caught the one craft and—with part of the crew still clinging—demolished it.

The frustrated captain next attempted to get the port quarter boat lowered. Doggedly the men worked the ropes while passengers leaped into the craft. The command was to lower only part way, but while the captain was busy attending to the needs of others, the boat was lowered all the way and it splintered against the side of the *Valencia*. The roar of the onrushing water drowned out the agonizing cries.

Passengers now cowered back, fearing to take their chances in the lifeboats. Captain Johnson rushed to the starboard side where he was joined by a volunteer crew as he attempted to clear another boat. But mild panic had taken over. There weren't sufficient life preservers to go around. Families were embracing one another as the captain and officers insisted that women and children go first. A few had to be almost thrown into the lifeboat. Wives clung desperately to their husbands, some refusing to go. Several of the unattached men had to be restrained from boarding. Finally the boat was filled and the order given to lower away. It struck the water awkwardly but those clinging tenaciously to it managed to get free of the ship.

Through the terrible hours of that night, while flares were shot into the inky sky, chilling scenes were being enacted aboard the ship. A little boy was running about the decks, crying for his mother who had drowned. A woman dropped her baby into the sea while trying to hand it to her husband in one of the boats.

Still another attempt was made to get a boat over the side. Filled with passengers and with a few skilled crewmen at the oars, the craft hit the water with a splash. Backs and arms straining, the men pulled away from the liner. Feeble sounds of cheering from those still aboard the *Valencia* were soon carried away by the icy wind. The test of endurance continued. Then, suddenly, from out of nowhere came a sea much greater than the others. It swung the boat broadside and flipped it over, throwing all into the sea to fend for themselves. Their struggle for survival soon ended.

Captain Johnson felt personally responsible. As master of the ship, he was doing all that was humanly possible but with no wireless his only hope of help lay in the arching flares that pierced the sky at intervals throughout the night. The *Valencia,* however, had wandered well out of the steamer lanes and time was running out.

After consulting with his officers, the captain decided to await daylight before gambling with the last lifeboats. It was a difficult decision to make, for the ship gave every indication of breaking up. The deck was buckling, cracks had opened in the hull, and water poured in unchecked.

The minutes and hours before daybreak dragged slowly by. Above the howling wind were heard the moans and cries of troubled souls. The engine room was flooded, the fires out, all steam was gone, and the electrical facilities were inoperable. Except for a few kerosene lamps salvaged from the debris, the ship lay in total darkness.

A short time later, the *Valencia* assumed a heavy list to port and No. 7 boat had to be lowered, followed by No. 6. Then a single raft was floated. But in the growing half-light nobody could see much of anything. At least one of the boats got away.

The boatswain McCarthy, continuing his eye-witness account, said:

> . . . at daylight we could see the people on the beach right under the cliff at almost low water. They would be a hundred yards or more away. Captain Johnson ordered me to get a five-inch line to shore. I sent a man aloft and rigged the blocks and got the Lyle gun aft on the hurricane deck. The tide was coming in and the seas were getting stronger and Captain Johnson asked me if I would go in the remaining boat and try and make a landing, in order to take a line.
>
> I finally got a crew and got away with No. 5 boat; Captain Johnson was in charge of lowering it. We got away with considerable difficulty; the bow oar broke. They cheered us from the ship but it was so thick we could not see her. We kept outside the breakers but at times could not see shore; it was so thick that we could not find a place to land. I came to some rocks which I took to be the Durken [Duncan] Rocks off Tatooche [Tatoosh] and finally a heavy sea hit us. Two of the men lost their oars and we had only two left. We pulled a little farther and one of the men said he thought it was the Vancouver Island shore. Finally we made a landing in a place I afterwards found to be between Pachena Bay and Cape Beale.

After an eight-mile row, the boatswain and his companions struggled to the beach through the breakers and trudged along the rugged shoreline until they reached Cape Beale Lighthouse, three miles from where they had landed. Here they told their harrowing tale of shipwreck to keeper Patterson, who wired the tragic news to Victoria.

Meanwhile back on the *Valencia*, the gray dawn grew to full light. The liner was reduced to a near-total wreck but still balanced uneasily on the reef. Those aboard were sickened by the sight of dead bodies floating around with the debris. There was one cheerful moment, though, when they saw the figures of three survivors in a sea cave under the precipitous cliff inshore. Their cheer, however, quickly turned to sorrow as they watched the men fall to their deaths while endeavoring to scale the cliff.

The last boats had been cleared away just at daybreak; one, as mentioned, going toward Cape Beale and the other, containing five crewmen, endeavoring to land on some nearby beach. Without the added weight of passengers, both boats were given a good chance of making a safe landing and getting assistance. The second boat landed at a spot where a telephone line was located, fifteen miles from Cape Beale.

A rescue party was eventually summoned and traveled on foot to the cliff above the wreck, but once there they were unable to fire a line over the wide abyss separating them from the *Valencia*.

The city of Victoria was shocked by the news of the *Valencia* disaster. The liner, *Queen*, just in from California, discharged her passengers and made full steam toward the wreck scene. The salvage tug *Salvor* moved out of the harbor immediately. Small craft of many descriptions took off on the mercy mission. As far south as Seattle, the SS *City of Topeka* steamed out of the harbor to join the rescue fleet. However, the U. S. Revenue Cutter *Grant*, in port for boiler repairs, did not go; her skipper had received no word from Washington, D. C., to aid the *Valencia*. This incident caused much public agitation, but certainly there was no lack of vessels ready to render every possible assistance.

In a matter of hours a flotilla stood off the grim wreck scene, but the waters were so treacherous and shallow that they were unable to perfect a rescue. By the morning of January 24, only the *Valencia's* funnel and masts broke the surface. Some thirty human forms still clung to them . . . hoping and praying. The ship still could not be approached from seaward and none could get to it from the landward side. She was in a veritable trap.

On January 25, heavy seas forced some of the rescue craft to abandon their offshore vigil. Meanwhile the survivors still clinging to the *Valencia's* rigging had thinned out considerably. When the shallow-draft steam whaler *Orion* appeared on the scene, she was able to get closer to the reef than any of her counterparts, but by that time all signs of life on the ship had vanished. Later that same day the *City of Topeka* picked up a life raft that had managed to get clear of the wreck. It contained eighteen half-starved survivors.

Second officer P. E. Petterson, who was aboard that raft, told of his harrowing experience:

> I was in the main rigging on the port side. We launched the starboard raft. Captain Johnson wanted the women to go on it. We then launched the port raft with much difficulty. Six or seven men got on it and the women refused to go. Some of the men also refused to leave the ship. There were 17 men on it and Captain Johnson told me that I had better go on it. I jumped overboard and got on the raft. We got cleared away and later, about 12 a.m., some of the men wanted to beach it; just as we started to do this we saw some smoke, and shortly after the SS *Topeka* came and picked us up. We saw nothing of the raft that left the *Valencia* 15 minutes before us.

Petterson praised Captain Johnson for staying bravely with his ship, and noted that the skipper had burned off two of his fingers in a mishap while firing distress rockets.

Aboard the other raft was chief cook Sam Hancock who told of the terrible frustration he and those with him went through trying to gain the attention of the liners *Queen* and *City of*

Topeka. They went unseen because of the high seas and heavy drizzle, gradually drifting toward the shore.

Hancock later recounted:

> We struck the beach about midnight and three more went insane and died on the raft. The remaining four went into the bush until daylight, and then we walked about on the island all day Thursday. Toward evening three of us got to the beach and saw an Indian settlement about a mile away. Some Indians came and afterwards a cannery steamer took us to Toquart on Barkley Sound. In the morning the SS *Salvor* came and took us off. They went to the island and got the raft and afterwards found Connors (the man who had wandered off).

On the *Valencia*, shortly after daylight, efforts were made to shoot a line ashore. They bridged the gap to the beach but nobody was there to make the line fast. Watching the unsuccessful endeavor was mustachioed Joe Cigalos (Segalos), a Greek fireman. Though slight of build he had a stout heart. In a sudden maneuver he made one end of a line fast to the vessel and tied the other about his waist and plunged into the icy waters. While those aboard stood gaping at him from the railing, he fought his way through the water with remarkable agility.

His shipmates forgot their misery as they watched the contest develop and the line pay out. The seas would sometimes bury him and the undertow pulled at him, but he kept on thrashing at the water. For twenty long minutes he pursued his task, fighting the seething breakers like one possessed. Then suddenly the strength ebbed from his tensed body, and the men on the *Valencia* knew the struggle was over. They started reeling in the line but one of the life rafts that had been launched earlier managed to maneuver to the exhausted swimmer and pull him aboard. His selfless endeavor encouraged those still aboard the wreck.

Eventually the raft containing the Greek hero was recovered by the *City of Topeka*. When the rescuers attempted to give

Cigalos a glass of brandy, he murmured, "Give it to them," nodding toward the others picked up from the raft. They had been rescued six miles from Cape Beale; all were nearly frozen and suffering greatly from exposure. This was the same raft that carried second mate Petterson and quartermaster Martin Tarpey. Tarpey later became a well-known master mariner.

When Cigalos finally got back to Seattle, he received a hero's welcome and was presented a medal for his brave act. Alexander Pantages, well-known Seattle theater owner, had the Greek appear on his stage. Cigalos carried an American and Greek flag and answered questions from the audience concerning the tragedy.

Also accorded much praise was Captain Thomas H. Cann, master of the rescue ship SS *City of Topeka*. It was just seven years after the *Valencia* disaster that, as master of the SS *State of California*, he suffered through that tragic shipwreck (August 17, 1913), at Gambier Bay, Alaska, which claimed thirty-four lives.

Still another raft that had managed to get away from the *Valencia* washed ashore on Turtle Island in Barkley Sound. The Indians dwelling nearby came out in the surf to pull them to safety. Four were rescued but the remaining six had gone mad; they flung themselves into the sea and were drowned.

When all the mercy ships had reported in, the grim statistics were compiled: passengers originally aboard 94; lost 80, saved 14. Officers and crewmen 60; lost 37, saved 23. Total aboard the ship 154; total rescued 37; total lost 117.

At the subsequent hearing, many harrowing experiences were brought to light, such as the account given by Frank Lehm, ship's clerk:

> Screams of men, women, and children mingled in awful chorus with the shriek of the wind, the dash of the rain, and the roar of the breakers. As the passengers rushed on deck they were carried away in bunches by the huge waves that seemed as high as the ship's mastheads. The ship be-

Modern *Umatilla Lightship* stands guard to warn ships of treacherous Umatilla Reef.

Coast Guard motor lifeboat noses into giant Pacific swell as spray goes scudding.

Danish MS *Marie Skou*—her bow a twisted mass of steel following collision with the Japanese cargo ship *Chitose Maru* at the entrance to the strait in September 1967.

Jim Ryan

Jim Ryan

Here is the monstrous hole gouged in the bow of the 40,000-ton *Chitose Maru* when she was rammed by the *Marie Skou*.

British freighter *Darton*, off Cape Flattery, lost her propeller in March 1952. She was aided by the Coast Guard cutter *Winona*, out of Port Angeles.

Derelict Japanese motor fishing vessel *Ryo Yei Maru*, with a crew of dead men, was taken in tow off Cape Flattery by the SS *Margaret Dollar*, October 31, 1927.

Mystery surrounds the freighter *Haida*, which vanished with all hands in October 1937, somewhere off Cape Flattery. She was bound for the Orient via Hawaii, with her cargo of sulphur camouflaged by coal.

Canadian lighthouse tender *Quadra* in February 1917, after being sunk in a collision with the liner *Charmer* near Nanaimo.

gan to break up almost at once and the women and children were lashed to the rigging above the reach of the sea. It was a pitiful sight to see frail women, wearing only night dresses, with bare feet on the frozen ratlines, trying to shield children in their arms from the icy wind and rain.

Lehm recalled a vivid picture of the evacuation, of the hollow-eyed, terrified passengers being put to sea in frail lifeboats:

Again we heard the strong voice of the captain, touched with tears, "Get out the amidships boat!"

The boat was filled with more women and children and safely launched. Oarsmen's faces were contorted as they strove to pull away from the ship's side in the boil of surf and the undertow from the cliffs. At last they started to forge ahead. A great cheer for those who were to be saved went up from the hundred left on board. Even the faces of the terrified women in the little boat looked more hopeful as they began to clear the wreck.

We all thought them saved when suddenly a great breaker, larger than any I had ever seen, aided by a terrible gust of wind, struck the boat, slewing her around in spite of all that the man at the steering oar and sailors could do. The next moment she was overturned.

What a sight! The searchlight showed every detail of the terrible tragedy—the men and women struggling in the water, their faces ghastly in the glare; eyes that stared at us unseeingly, already glazed with the touch of death; the bodies of children swept toward the terrible rocks, in a wild chaos of boiling surf. Suddenly all of this vanished, the searchlight revealing only a tossing, rolling, terrifying rush of water.

At Victoria, another account was given by the three would-be rescuers who had hiked to the scene in response to survivor McCarthy's plea at Cape Beale Lighthouse. These men—Joe

Martin, Phil Daykin, and Dave Logan, all of Clo-oose—arrived with ropes and provisions. They reached the cliff and reported seeing twenty-five persons in the *Valencia's* port rigging and thirty more on the poop. When these perishing people saw the rescuers on top of the high cliff they sent up a feeble cheer.

The rescuers picked up the line that still hung over the edge of the cliff and gave it a pull—but it quickly parted in the surf. The extreme distance and lack of cartridges on the ship ended further attempts to utilize the Lyle gun.

At the order of Mayor Morley of Victoria, the last vessel to go to the wreck scene was the Canadian tug *Lorne*, most powerful towing craft in British Columbia waters. In charge of Captain Butler and a hand-picked Navy crew, they steamed out of port but on arrival off Pachena Point it was obvious that all hope was gone. The sea had completed its conquest.

No one actually witnessed the death of the *Valencia's* Captain Johnson but all survivors were high in their praise of him. According to those questioned at subsequent hearings, he had done everything humanly possible to save all under his command. Up till this time, Johnson had held an unblemished record. At least death did save him from the haunting memory of the disaster; there was not a woman or child among the survivors.

Even out of this great tragedy came some good, for at Pachena Point, three miles east of the *Valencia* wreck scene, an urgently needed lighthouse was established the following year. Its blazing beam and blaring foghorn have stood as a symbol of hope down through the years that such a catastrophe will never be repeated.

PART 8

THE VANISHING FLEET

Including the disappearance of the overloaded Ivanhoe . . . *the two double tragedies of the* Keeweenah *and*
Montserrat *and* Matteawan *and* HMS Condor . . . *the
unsolved mystery of the vanishing tramp ship* Haida . . .
the terrible ordeal of the Jane Gray's *survivors . . . and
the burning fishboat caper.*

The account of a vanishing ship always smacks of mystery.
Marine history records a long list of such vessels that have passed
out through the Strait of Juan de Fuca and into oblivion. Particularly around the turn of the century did a series of such
unexplained events take place.

THE OVERLOADED IVANHOE

On September 27, 1894, the coal-laden 1,600-ton sailing vessel
Ivanhoe left her Seattle dock in tow of the tug *Tyee*. Riding low
in the water—much lower than the load-limit laws allowed—there
was but little freeboard. Captain Edward Griffin was master of
this ship, which was as well known in Pacific Coast shipping as
her namesake in the literary world.

There was nothing unusual about the *Ivanhoe's* departure, for
throughout much of the vessel's thirty years, she had filled her
hungry holds with coal for San Francisco and towed out to Cape
Flattery to spread her canvas. Aboard were twenty-three persons, including two women and two male passengers. One of

the latter was Frederick J. Grant, prominent editor and part owner of the Seattle *Post-Intelligencer*.

Just off Cape Flattery, the towing hawser was dropped, and with a blast of her whistle the tug steamed away. Ironically, the ship *Yosemite*, owned by the same company, cast off from another tug at almost the same time. The two sailing vessels were within hailing distance of each other, and inasmuch as both were bound for San Francisco, a race to the Golden Gate appeared in the making.

Captain Griffin never turned down a challenge. The sea was his life and like all downeast skippers he was proud of his ship. At thirty-eight years of age, he was well seasoned in the ways of the sea, having been sailing almost constantly from the tender age of thirteen. He was once one of only eight survivors out of a company of fifty, when the ship *Stewart Henneman* capsized near the Equator. The ordeal had not dulled his love of the sea. Acquiring his master's papers while still a young man, he had earned a fine reputation as a navigator. The *Ivanhoe's* owners, Black Diamond Coal Company, had the highest praise for Captain Griffin's services.

The race started almost evenly, but as dusk came on, the *Ivanhoe* lost sight of the *Yosemite* and fell in company with the barkentine *Robert Sudden*. The two ships remained together throughout the night and into the next day, unable to make headway against the strong southerly winds. Rain and hail slanted down with cutting force. Visibility was reduced to less than two hundred feet as the storm developed into a full gale.

When a pallid dawn broke over the ocean, the men of the *Robert Sudden* searched the horizon but could find no trace of the *Ivanhoe*. All through the day the hunt continued. Other ships returning to the strait were asked about it in vain. The revenue cutter *Grant* sailed a few days later with orders to keep on the alert for the *Ivanhoe*. But the sea guarded its secret well; the vessel could not be found, nor any trace of her.

Weeks passed. Then reports began to come in of wreckage

found along coastal beaches. The first wreckage identified as being from the *Ivanhoe* was one of her life rings picked up far to the north at Christie Island in Barkley Sound. Then the ship's quarterboard was found by the lighthouse keeper's wife at the north entrance to Willapa Bay. The two pieces of wreckage had come ashore more than 150 miles apart and both had been found in December less than three months after the *Ivanhoe* went missing.

Perhaps the most generally accepted theory as to the loss of the vessel was that she was grossly overloaded and heavy head seas swamped her, causing her to plummet to her grave with all hands.

KEWEENAH AND MONTSERRAT

Just two months after the *Ivanhoe* vanished, two big steam colliers were loading coal at British Columbia ports—the SS *Keweenah* at Comox and the SS *Montserrat* at Nanaimo. Both were scheduled to depart for San Francisco.

The *Montserrat*, a stout iron steamer, 221 feet in length, was one of the finest ships in the trade. She was built in England in 1881 for the International Company of Lower California, to carry copper ore between Ensenada and San Francisco. Later she was sold to John Rosenfeld and J. L. Howard of the Bay City, who in turn chartered her to Captain David O. Blackburn for operation as a collier.

Now, Captain Blackburn was affectionately named "Lucky Blackburn," and for good reason. Though daring and sometimes reckless, he had never lost a ship and had never run one that was unprofitable. A Nova Scotian by birth, he arrived on the Columbia River while young and became a commercial fisherman. Later he quit the fishing industry, got his third mate's ticket, and worked his way quickly up to master mariner. Though jovial by nature, Blackburn had his enemies, many of whom were highly envious of him. On many occasions he had collected handsome salvage fees for towing disabled ships to port. Needless to say, he always had his eye open for a fast dollar.

When the *Montserrat* was purchased for the coal trade, Blackburn not only became her skipper but shortly managed to get a small piece of the ownership. By taking the steamer to the Gilbert Islands on a "blackbirding" expedition—which resulted in a very profitable venture—he soon held the controlling interest.

When the *Montserrat* departed the coal dock at Nanaimo on the evening of December 6, 1894, she carried a qualified crew. Seamen often stood in line for a berth on Captain Blackburn's ship. His officers included some of the best available—John Brewer, first mate; M. Carroll, second mate, and capable Thomas Brennan, chief engineer. In all, the crew numbered twenty-six, but as was his practice, Lucky Blackburn gave passage to three money-short passengers headed back to San Francisco.

The lighthouse keepers at Tatoosh Island saw the *Montserrat* round their rocky abode and head south into the teeth of a howling southerly gale. Her progress was so slight that the SS *Keweenah*, which left Comox the morning of December 7, fell in company with her on the outbound trek. Concerned with the rising tempest, the lookouts at the lighthouse kept a tight watch on both ships throughout the day. At dusk on the evening of December 7, the two ships could still be faintly observed about ten miles out, doggedly fighting to hold their own against the howling southwester. Carrying overloads of coal, both steamers rode low in the water, the *Montserrat* about a mile ahead of the *Keweenah*. As darkness came on, both were shipping immense seas.

The *Keweenah*, commanded by Captain W. H. Jenkins, was carrying a crew of thirty-one. Virtually a new ship, she had been built at West Bay City, Michigan, just three years earlier. Constructed of iron and measuring 271 feet in length, she was designed to trade between New York and the Pacific Coast. To win the contract for construction of the ship, the builders had to agree to some unusual requirements. The vessel had to be built with several watertight compartments designed to keep her afloat in case of collision or stranding; also with a reinforced double bottom divided into sections by the keel and bulkheads.

The spaces between the bulkheads were arranged to act as tanks so that in the event of a mishap the sea cocks on the weather side could be opened to allow a steadying flow of water. Further, the *Keweenah* was too large to pass through the Welland Locks so she had to be cut in half. This the builders had provided for, and when the fore and after sections had passed through the locks, they were riveted back together in a Montreal shipyard.

On her maiden voyage from New York, the *Keweenah* became disabled near the Straits of Magellan and had to be repaired at Valparaiso. On reaching San Francisco, the Black Diamond Coal Company, owners of the ill-fated *Ivanhoe,* signed to charter the ship. Thus it was that two of the most seaworthy ships on the Pacific Coast, in company, were battling a driving hurricane off Cape Flattery on the bleak night of December 7 and the morning of December 8, 1894. Like the *Ivanhoe,* both vanished from the face of the sea sometime during that period of time. The fierce storm that apparently claimed the two ships grew to such proportions that it continued unabated for an entire week, spreading devastation from Alaska to California.

That such seaworthy vessels could both have fallen victim to the elements was hardly believable. Daily, news of their whereabouts was awaited, but the days turned into weeks and the weeks to months. Grim reminders began drifting up on the coastal beaches. On February 28 of the following year, the medicine chest of the *Montserrat* was found at the southeast end of Etalin Island, B. C., having drifted northward for many weeks after the disaster. In May, the trading schooner *Maude S* called at Rose Harbor in the Queen Charlotte Islands. While there, the crew visited the nearby Indian village where they saw some wreckage imprinted with the names *Montserrat* and *Keweenah.*

Speculation followed. It was surmised that the ships had unsuccessfully turned before the gale and sought refuge at some northerly anchorage. Newspapers played up the story of one of the two ships having broken down and the other having collided with it while attempting to take a towline. This theory was given

impetus from the fact that Captain Blackburn was noted for sal-
vaging disabled ships and was once quoted as having said that
his ship could even "climb a tree." The most widely accepted
theory, however, was that both ships were grossly overloaded
and foundered when great head seas tore off their hatch covers.

The mystery remains unsolved to this day.

SS MATTEAWAN AND HMS CONDOR

A near repetition of the *Montserrat-Keweenah* mystery was
enacted just six years later. On December 2, 1901, the sizable
steam colliers *Matteawan* and *San Mateo* were loading coal at
Comox, B. C., for San Francisco. At the same time at the nearby
Canadian naval port of Esquimalt, the British Navy's new steam-
powered sloop-of-war *Condor* was preparing to depart for Honolulu.

The *Matteawan* was a steel steamship of 3,300 tons, built at
South Shields, England, in 1893, as the *Asturian Prince.* Measuring 336 feet in length, she was elegantly fitted throughout and
one of the few ships of her day fully equipped with electric
lights. In command of Captain H. B. Crosscup, the vessel put to
sea, holds bulging with five thousand tons of coal and flying the
house flag of J. Jerome & Company.

Within a few hours of the departure of the *Matteawan,* two
other big coal carriers also departed British Columbia waters,
the *Wellington* and the *San Mateo.* On word of an approaching
gale, the master of the *Wellington* wisely took temporary refuge
at Neah Bay.

Meanwhile, the HMS *Condor* was scheduled to depart Esquimalt for Honolulu, in company with the HMS *Warspite,* but instead remained in the Strait of Juan de Fuca for additional gunnery practice. The 180-foot *Condor,* built at Sheerness, England,
in 1898, was heavily armed with ten four-inch quick-fire guns
and four three pounders, plus smaller auxiliary fire power. She
was commissioned at Chatham, November 1, 1900, and was virtually a new fighting ship.

Under the command of Commander Clinton Sclater, the *Condor* saluted Tatoosh Island and pursued her southwesterly course into harassing winds and heavy seas. Her standard complement was 130 but ten additional men were reported to have boarded the sloop-of-war at the naval base.

There is little else to tell, for neither the *Matteawan* nor the *Condor* was ever seen or heard of again. They completely vanished, leaving only tragic memories behind. Thus, somewhere out on the irascible Pacific, two great ships underwent a terrifying drama, with death as the leading character. There were no witnesses to either tragedy. For a time it was feared that the SS *San Mateo,* a ship built in the same English shipyard as the *Matteawan,* was also a victim of that fatal gale. She went unreported for several days, having ridden out the storm by altering her course to the path of least resistance. One thing is sure though—death must have come swiftly to the thirty-three persons aboard the *Matteawan* and the 140 aboard the *Condor.*

Wreckage thought to be from the *Condor,* including a damaged work boat, drifted ashore at Ahousat, B. C., several days later. Other unidentified wreckage was found at Clayoquot; and at Wreck Bay, several months later, a sailor's cap and a broom marked *Condor* were found. The HMS *Warspite,* which was to have accompanied the *Condor,* reported on reaching Honolulu that she had encountered gigantic seas after leaving Juan de Fuca Strait, seas that inflicted much damage on deck.

The loss of the *Condor* was one of the British Admiralty's greatest peace-time losses, from the standpoint of both personnel and property. Nor was the loss of the *Matteawan* dismissed lightly. Replacement value of the ship and her cargo was set at $250,000; the insurance carried was $175,000 on the hull and $15,000 on the cargo of coal. The full coverage was paid by the insurance company after the steamer was officially listed as lost with all hands.

At the height of the gale which reputedly claimed the *Matteawan* and *Condor,* the *Umatilla Reef Lightship* was blown from her anchorage and for several hours was off station. Some mariners expressed the thought that the lightship missing from station may have had a bearing on the loss of the ships—either from striking unguarded and treacherous Umatilla Reef or from being unable to get a fix on the lightship.

In the spring of 1949, the fishboat *Blanco*, out of Seattle, skippered by Ole Stokke, made an unusual haul. While fishing for petrole sole forty miles northwest of Cape Flattery, the nets were reeled in and there entwined were the remains of an old clinker-built lifeboat and a binnacle. The lifeboat was so heavy that it had to be cut loose without identification, but the fishermen landed the binnacle along with the haul of fish. The instrument was riddled with teredo holes and its brass top badly mangled. The compass was missing, but the maker's brass name plate was still legible. It read:

Lord Kelvin's Patents

(Sir William Thomson)

sole makers

No. 9011

Kelvin and James White Ltd.

16 Cambridge St., Glasgow

This writer was contacted to see if he could shed any light on the identity of the binnacle. A check with the British Admiralty indicated through the serial number that it was of the same series ordered for British warships of that period and was also under the same patent as the instrument supplied during the construction of the *Matteawan*. It could well have belonged to either ship. Had only the nets been able to hold the lifeboat, positive identification would undoubtedly have been made. Perhaps it is well that the wreck remains undisturbed, for it must be the crypt of the scores who perished with it.

MYSTERY OF THE HAIDA

On October 24, 1937, the British-registered, Chinese-owned freighter *Haida* departed Bell Street Terminal on the Seattle waterfront. Destination of the dingy old tramp was Shanghai and Hong Kong via Kahului, Hawaii. She cleared Puget Sound, dropped her pilot at Port Angeles, and headed down the strait, out into the Pacific and oblivion.

Her story began on the Atlantic seaboard a few months earlier. The 3,800-ton *Haida* was purchased there by British-Chinese interests, registered at Shanghai, and then transferred to the Chinese flag. The ship was well up in years at the time, dating from 1909, when built at Sunderland, England as the *Vogesen*. Under her new owners, she sailed for gulf ports to refuel and take on a cargo of sulphur. Later, passing through the Panama Canal, the *Haida* proceeded up the Pacific Coast to Vancouver, B. C. Refueling once again, she prepared for her transpacific crossing. With the advent of the Sino-Japanese war, the owners postponed the ship's departure and steamed instead to Seattle.

For weeks the freighter was idle on the waterfront. Questions were asked but no answers were forthcoming. Then one gray autumn day, the decks seemed to spring into action. On the sides of her superstructure were painted massive British flags, depicting signs of neutrality. At last the freighter's long delay at Seattle was explained. She was undergoing secret changes from Chinese to British registry to avoid running afoul of the Japanese sea blockade.

The bulk of her cargo consisted of sulphur, but to hide this fact, a thin layer of coal was spread over the tops of her hatches to mislead suspicious Japanese war vessels. Sulphur was urgently needed in China for the war effort and it was hoped that the new registry and the sight of coal would keep Japanese agents from boarding for inspection. To further safeguard the vessel, a new wireless apparatus was installed while she lay at her Seattle pier.

The *Haida's* crew consisted of twenty-six Chinese, all reputedly in sympathy with the Chiang Kai-shek government, and a Norwegian ship master, Captain F. C. Norvick, the lone Caucasian. On the day she put to sea, there was no one to see her off but those who cast off the lines: a representative of the agency and a few pier employees.

The *Haida* had begun her voyage into oblivion, and the mystery of her disappearance became one of the most baffling in modern maritime annals. When she failed to arrive in Hawaii, or at any Chinese or British port, all merchant vessels plying the North Pacific were asked to be on the lookout for the ship or any survivors. All reports were negative, and after several months, the freighter had to be marked by Lloyd's Register as lost at sea with all hands.

Most of the theories concerning the fate of the *Haida* were hardly plausible. It was suggested, for instance, that one of her crew was a spy—that he had blown the ship up at sea. Another theory was that a Japanese submarine operating close to the Pacific Coast fired a torpedo at the sulphur-laden ship and triggered a devastating explosion. Other theories were that the ship broke up in a severe gale and foundered in minutes—or suffered a flash explosion when her cargo caught on fire. The explosion, if such occurred, must have been sudden or the wireless operator should have had sufficient time to get out at least one call for assistance. There was, however, no signal of any kind, nor did any other ship report receiving an SOS. It is surmised that she must have gone down southwest of Cape Flattery. Wind and currents finally deposited a badly mauled life ring and an oar blade, believed from the *Haida,* on the beach near Carmanah Point; but these small pieces of wreckage were almost the only clues as to the fate of the freighter.

A careful check was later made of the background of each crew member and officer. Starting with first officer K. F. Yank, a Cantonese, they sought some link with the disappearance of the ship, but to no avail. It was said that Captain Norvick gave a letter to a friend on the Seattle waterfront before the ship sailed, asking that it be sent to his wife back in Norway. It is told that the man forgot to mail the letter until after the ship was reported missing. It was later revealed that the letter contained a photo of the ship's master and words to the effect that this might be his last voyage to sea.

THE JANE GRAY ORDEAL

In the year 1887, a spritely 112-ton, two-masted schooner slid down the ways of a Bath, Maine, shipyard. Shortly after, she came around Cape Horn to serve as a whaler out of San Francisco. In August of the same year, along with four other whaling vessels, she was caught in a severe gale between the ice and the lee shore, and was cast onto the beach at Point Barrow, Alaska. The revenue cutter *Bear* rushed to the scene in time to rescue the skipper, Captain W. H. Kelly, and his twenty-one-man crew. The *Jane Gray* was abandoned, but later salvaged, temporarily refitted, and returned to San Francisco for overhaul. The following year she was back in search of whales.

In 1892, the schooner was sent out to catch seals, but bad luck persisted; and under Captain Edward Kelly, she was seized for poaching and escorted to Sitka by a government vessel. Fined and released by the court, the *Jane Gray* promptly returned to the Bering Sea to complete the season. In 1893 and 1894, she did her sealing off the Japanese Coast, bringing home some good catches, one of which totaled 1,300 skins. The following year she took the same number of skins off the Russian and Siberian coasts, and again in 1896 and 1897. At last the jinx that had earlier plagued the schooner appeared to have ended.

Then came news of the great gold strike in the Far North. Virtually overnight Seattle became the gateway to Alaska and the Yukon Territory. The struggling little port city mushroomed into a beehive of activity with ships of every size and description arriving. All were filled to capacity and even overflowing with men from every walk of life who had one common goal—to find gold.

Ironically, the *Jane Gray* was about the only vessel in port not headed for the gold fields. A scientific expedition had paid a high charter fee to secure the vessel for a special mission. She was to take an exploring party to the Kotzebue, Alaska, area under direction of Major E. S. Ingraham, formerly superintendent of Seattle Public Schools. On a May morning in 1898, the *Jane Gray*, Captain Crockett, left the bustling port for sea. She carried a total of sixty-four persons, thirty-two of whom were members of Ingraham's party. Among the other passengers were Mr. and Mrs V. C. Gambell, missionary teachers who had taken passage for remote St. Lawrence Island. Most of the passengers had berths in the fo'c'sle, usually occupied by sealer crewmen.

As night came on off Cape Flattery, the winds gained in velocity and the schooner had rough going as she headed north. The skipper ordered her hove to, headed into the wind, and had all sails except the foresail taken in. After giving the order, he retired. At midnight the mate also turned in, leaving only two seamen on deck. The weather appeared to be moderating when suddenly a flash squall struck, rolling the schooner almost onto her beam ends. Seawater rushed along her decks on the starboard side and down the hatch into the cabin.

The captain was rudely aroused from his slumber. Struggling topside, he rallied his crew and endeavored to get the vessel back on an even keel. Sea after sea boarded in rapid succession. The pumps were useless. So suddenly had everything happened that there wasn't even time to think clearly. The passengers were in near panic—the schooner was sinking beneath their feet and land was miles away. The night was shockingly dark and the wind cut to the marrow.

Major Ingraham had lashed to the deck a small steam launch which was to have been used for their scientific work. Amid the confusion he had the foresight to cut the lashings. Meanwhile the captain and his men worked ceaselessly using buckets to curb the inflow of water. Their efforts went for nought. The schooner settled lower and lower until the waves were making a clean sweep of the deck. It became every man for himself. Only the cabin top and masts were above the sloshing water. The frantic passengers, along with some of the crew, fought for a place in the ship's boat. In a desperate effort to get it cleared, a huge wave upended it, dumping all inside into the sea. A few minutes later the *Jane Gray* sank in a convulsive upheaval of water. She quickly disappeared into the vortex, leaving only struggling humanity and bits of wreckage.

The steam launch floated free and with it the last hope of survival. It was so dark and stormy that even the sounds of voices were carried away with the wind. Several victims were sucked down into the watery vacuum; others clung to anything that floated in an effort to reach the launch. Those who managed to get aboard aided others until twenty-seven survivors were packed in the craft. The survivors searched further, but as near as they could tell thirty-four passengers and three crew members were missing.

Except for the foresight of Major Ingraham in cutting the launch free, all hands would have perished. The boat's propelling machinery was inoperative and no oars were available. Out of boards picked up from the wreckage, paddles were fashioned, and an old piece of canvas proved of some use as a sail. By hard and painful toil, the frail little craft moved ever so slowly toward land for five days and five nights. From sheer fortitude, the survivors pushed on in utter misery, clothes soaked and without food. The voyage finally ended when the boat, caught up in the surf, was dashed rudely ashore in the desolate Kyuquot area of Vancouver Island.

The wretched company found little succor and suffered endless hardship before being found by the crew of the trading schooner *Favourite*, who cared for them and took them to Victoria. Among the missing were the missionary couple and the master of the schooner.

Had the little launch foundered at sea, which only a miracle prevented, the *Jane Gray* would also have been listed among the vanishing fleet.

MYSTERY OF THE BURNING VESSEL

The unsolved mysteries of the sea are legion. In days of old when no form of communication existed, it was commonplace for a ship and its crew to vanish without trace. In our decade of miracle communications, even the smallest of craft is usually in constant touch with shore installations, and it is indeed the exception when a vessel disappears.

On November 2, 1957, the Japanese freighter *Meitetsu Maru*, of the Mitsui Line, was nearing the end of a transpacific crossing from Japan. At one o'clock in the morning, when about forty miles northwest of Cape Flattery, the lookout reported a strange sight off the starboard bow. The ship's captain, R. Ouchi, was notified. He took the glasses and scanned the object, at the same time ordering the helmsman to alter course to head directly for it.

The ship knifed through the gentle swell at a fast clip. A short time later the shrouded glow grew in size and it became apparent it was a burning vessel. The orange flames played weird patterns on the dark waters.

The captain ordered all hands to stand by to lower a boat. The freighter drew to within a hundred yards. Fire had licked at the craft for hours, as was evidenced by the cabin having been burned away completely. The white paint on the hull was scorched black and the only indentifying marks were the partial letters on the bow—K13AC. Captain Ouchi reasoned the craft to be approximately seventy feet in length and similar to a purse-seine type fishing boat.

At 3:55 a.m., the freighter's radio crackled the news of the mysterious fire to American and Canadian shore stations. Meanwhile the *Meitetsu Maru* continued circling the inferno in search of any possible survivors. It was certain that no live thing could

The SS *Walla Walla*, of the Pacific Coast Steamship Co., once carried the famous jinxed black cat to San Francisco.

The 7,200-ton SS *George Walton* caught fire south of Cape Flattery in November of 1951. Tugs tried to pull her to shore, but off the entrance to the Strait of Juan de Fuca she opened up and sank.

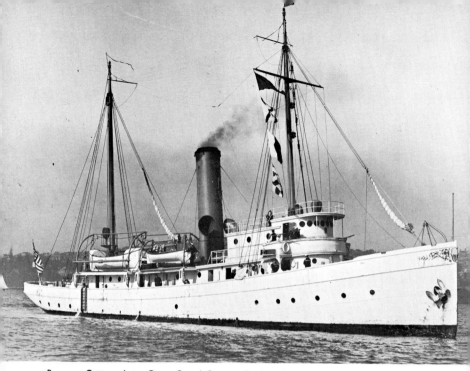

Revenue Cutter—later Coast Guard Cutter—*Snohomish* played an outstanding role in Juan de Fuca's graveyard during her long tenure of duty.

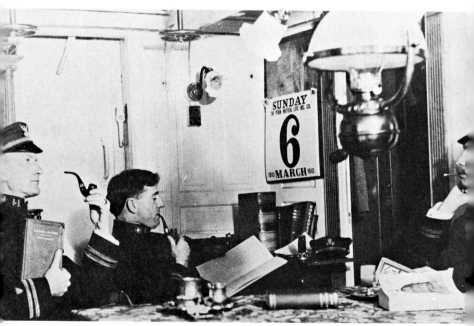

Wardroom of the *Snohomish* on a quiet day in 1910. The vessel berthed at both Port Angeles and Neah Bay.

The steamer *Alice Gertrude* as she appeared a short time before making her fatal voyage out of Clallam Bay. Her passengers and crew miraculously escaped after she struck a reef inside the bay.

The HMS *Condor* vanished with all hands, in December 1901, off Cape Flattery in a full gale, and was never seen again after leaving the strait.

Victoria, B.C., Provincial Archives

Steam Tug *Alexander*—shown here in Victoria Harbor in the early days—brought the first keeper to Cape Beale Lighthouse in 1874.

Ex-Russian gunboat *Politkofsky* was towing the *Maria J. Smith* to safety in 1869 off Vancouver Island, when the towline broke.

be on the derelict. Anyone aboard would either have been burned to death or would have taken the quickest means of escape. The mystery craft blazed furiously, right down to the waterline, sending ominous clouds of dense smoke billowing into the crisp morning air.

As his ship left the scene, Captain Ouchi reconstructed the circumstances in his mind's eye. He recalled seeing a white light near the burning craft while his ship was still a good distance away. He could not tell what it was or if it had any connection with possible survivors from the burning vessel. Whatever the light, it too was to become part of the tangled mystery.

The U. S. Coast Guard and the Royal Canadian Air Force launched an immediate and intensive search for possible survivors. With the break of day, surface craft and planes scoured the entire area. After some 16,000 miles had been covered in the air and on the sea, nothing more was sighted of the burning vessel or its crew.

The Coast Guard cutter *Winona* later picked up a small metal gas tank with bits of charred wood attached, and a chopping block bearing fish scales, in the reported vicinity of the fire. These and these alone were the few shreds of evidence. The vessel had evidently gone down just before dawn.

Dispatches were sent out from Canadian and American sources seeking information on a missing fishing vessel of the type. Days slipped by but no vessels were reported missing or in trouble. The partial letters and numbers sighted by the Japanese on the side of the mystery craft were checked and rechecked in registers and by official sources. Though similar sequences of lettering were sometimes used in Canadian vessel registration, no vessel of any type registered in Canada was reported missing. A similar check of all American-registered craft was made with negative results.

A week passed, then two weeks, and the Coast Guard admitted that it was completely baffled in its efforts to learn the identity of the vessel. Nor did it know whence the craft came, where it was going, or how many were aboard.

Photos of the gas tank and chopping block were circulated to fishermen from Alaska to Mexico and displayed in prominent places. The 18x24x40-inch tank bore a strong odor of naphtha, which was often used in galleys on foreign vessels.

Despite the all-out effort, no clue or identity was forthcoming. When the case was thrown open to speculation, rumors poured in. Even the most fantastic of these could not be overlooked in the face of the circumstances. Most frequent rumors were of Russian spy activity: the vessel had been set on fire by Soviet agents to destroy certain evidence. It was also surmised that the craft, posing as a fishboat, was used to take spies off Russian submarines, or to bring fuel from the mainland. Many believed that something had gone wrong while the vessel was operating in some illicit trade, and was disposed of to destroy incriminating evidence.

Another theory advanced was that the vessel was of Oriental origin, having broken down off Japan and drifted across the Pacific with the Japanese Current—as so many other craft had done through the years. The incident was listed as one of the unsolved mysteries of the sea.

To those who thought that the crew of the *Meitetsu Maru* had seen an apparition, it was pointed out that another fishing vessel, the *Kodiak*, also reported seeing a mysterious fire at sea on the morning of November 2. She, however, was at a much greater distance, too far away to investigate.

Several months later a possible solution was forthcoming. The gas tank that was picked up near the scene of the sinking had been passed among fishermen up and down the Pacific Coast. In British Columbia it also went the rounds. Somebody reasoned it to be similar to one used by the small troller *Jo-Joe*, a veteran fishing boat operated out of Vancouver, B. C.

John Ochs—her owner-skipper and a "loner"—was overdue from the fishing banks. From the existing evidence it was surmised he must have fallen overboard or perished in some other way after his vessel caught fire. Ochs has never been found, and the possibility remains that the seventy-foot vessel sighted by the Japanese freighter may have actually been the small thirty-two-foot *Jo-Joe*. The simple but sad tale of the loss of the man and his fishboat seems an anticlimax to what had the earmarks of a genuine mystery of the sea. Some of the eyewitnesses insisted that the burning vessel could not have been the *Jo-Joe*—the latter was much too small. For many, the mystery remains unsolved.

PART 9

FOR THOSE IN PERIL ON THE SEAS

Including the stories of the lifesaving stations serving Juan de Fuca's portals . . . the strange Indian town of Neah Bay . . . the Baada crew to the rescue . . . ups and downs of the cutter Snohomish *. . . the tragic loss of the W. J. Pirrie . . . how the* CG-52300 *performs yeoman service . . . and the mysterious disappearance of the* Jessie Island's *crew.*

Only those who go down to the sea in ships can fully appreciate those who stand ever ready to render aid in time of peril. The serenity of a lifesaving station on a fair day would tend to make one think they are places of inactivity and a life of ease. But those on duty are constantly alert to spring into action any time and in any weather. They are well drilled and equipped for emergencies at sea. Certainly modern methods of safeguarding seafarers are far advanced from those of yesteryear, but the purpose is still the same.

In addition to the ships lost at Juan de Fuca's entrance, there are countless others that have been seriously damaged. Numerous sailing ships have been partially or totally dismasted, steamers have limped in with damaged housing, lifeboats have been smashed, and deckloads of lumber lost. The Coast Guard and its predecessor, the old U. S. Lifesaving Service, have treated every distress call with the same efficiency; a small fishing craft in trouble gets the same immediate attention as an ocean liner in peril. Both the Neah Bay and La Push Coast Guard Lifeboat stations are attached to the Coast Guard's Grays Harbor group.

The Neah Bay station, for the most part, covers the area between Pillar Point on the Strait of Juan de Fuca and the *Umatilla Lightship*. The small cutters attached to the station sometimes range up to sixty miles due west of the strait entrance when the situation demands; and often it does, because on an average week-end more than three hundred small boats fish in the vast area. This involves both sports and commercial fishermen. Many neophytes among the former go well out into the Pacific with insufficient gasoline, no compasses, no lights, inadequate lifesaving gear, and little knowledge of the elements.

The station is manned by sixteen regular Coastguardmen and seven reserves in training. A constant watch is kept on the many boats in the area by men from the station who go to the highest elevation near the establishment and climb to a little watch room in a mounted steel structure. This chore was formerly done from the cupola of the original station at Baada Point.

Beach patrols are no longer maintained but a radioman is on constant duty for calls, or to get a "fix" on the location of the craft or person in need of assistance.

There are five small craft attached to the station, and aside from search and rescue operations, the boats supply Cape Flattery Lighthouse on Tatoosh Island with food, mail, and change of personnel frequently. The vessels are also assigned to federal fisheries patrol duty in the area during the gillnet season in the summer months.

The station also has a unique claim to goat-keeping. The animals hold sway on nearby Waada Island to help keep down the undergrowth on the thorny path between the two aids to navigation at either end of the island. These two lights demand frequent attention because of vandals who seem to delight in defacing them. Sometimes the goats discourage this practice with a little persuasion from the hind side. In times past, watch dogs have also been considered as a deterrent to trespassers.

If one digs deep enough into the earth on Waada Island, he may find some of the old foundation timbers of the lifeboat station located there from 1908 to 1910. The station was moved to the mainland not only because of easier access but also because winter storms washed out the marine railway for launching the motor lifeboats and surfboats. It is said that long before a station was built at Waada, volunteers were frequently called to the aid of distressed vessels in the area.

The present station is a far cry from the original. It has several outbuildings, in addition to the boathouse for the crew and the commanding officer's home.

NEAH BAY

Once remote and desolate, the village of Neah Bay traces its origin as an Indian gathering place to many years before the era of Northwest exploration. Well over half of the town's present population of approximately a thousand is Indian. This number is swelled, however, during the sports fishing season from May until October, when scores of fishermen come to the Neah Bay resorts to catch the "big ones."

Neah Bay is far from attractive, but it is located in a beautiful natural setting. It is a two-hour drive from Port Angeles; a village of boats and fishnets, stripped cars and many mongrel dogs. The principal commerce of the area is fishing and logging, although no deep-sea commercial cargo ships ever enter the harbor. In recent years, disabled Russian fishing vessels have been permitted entrance into the harbor for repairs.

The western shore of Neah Bay is high, precipitous, and bordered by craggy outcroppings. The shoreline drops to a low, sandy beach continuing eastward to Baada Point, where the Coast Guard maintains its station. Waada Island, in the center of Neah Bay, is joined to the mainland by an 8,000-foot breakwater which provides necessary docking facilities and protection for a large fishing fleet.

The Coast Guard also maintains an air-sea rescue unit at Port Angeles, where planes, helicopters, and a deep-sea cutter stand ready.

OLD BAADA LIFESAVING STATION

A telegram arrived at the Baada Point Lifesaving Station (on Neah Bay), November 26, 1913. The keeper of the station, a ruddy-appearing individual with sharp features, ripped open the envelope and read:

> A man attached to a Coast Survey party is reported marooned on Carroll Island thirty-five or forty miles to the southward. Your job—locate and rescue him.

With one strident command, the station master had his small band of skilled men at work readying their Beebe-McLellan surfboat for the mission. The doors of the boathouse were flung open and the craft slid down the ways into the bay. Instructions were to fall in with the revenue cutter *Manning*, which would pick up the surfboat and take it to a spot off the island.

The surfboat crew were veterans and had performed many thrilling and courageous rescues. The fact that only one man's life was at stake this time did not make the mission less important, and the surfmen as always were willing to face any obstacles.

The man in peril had become marooned on uninhabited Carroll Island, off the Washington Coast, while doing survey work for the Coast and Geodetic Survey. No vessel had been able to get anywhere near the island for days because of the wind-driven surf. The man had been alone for a month with scarcely any food. Was he still alive?

The motto of the lifesaving service was: "You have to go out but you don't have to come back."

At precisely 8 a.m. on November 27, the surfboat fell in with the *Manning*, which had steamed in from Port Angeles. The cutter headed out of Juan de Fuca Strait and moved down the coast at a fast clip. The seas were rough but the hardy vessel's sharp bow cut through them easily.

At 2 p.m., the *Manning* was off Carroll Island, rolling and pitching excessively. Her part of the mission was over—now the surfmen had to go into action. They glanced at the sea around them—a heavy mass of liquid brine, colored a dull gray under the ominous, low-hanging clouds. The surf was dashing thirty feet up on the island's rocky shore making it absolutely impossible to land anywhere on the island. It was a difficult sea for the sizable revenue cutter; she could not even hold her position. Still, there was no hesitation on the part of the surfboat crew. They had come a long way to perfect a rescue, and they would succeed, one way or another.

With great difficulty the boat and her doughty crew were lowered into the water on the lee side. A huge sea erupted beneath the little craft as soon as it hit the water, almost crushing it against the side of the cutter. It was nip and tuck, but the skilled oarsmen soon had control and were moving away from the *Manning* with long, hard strokes. They pulled closer to the island, a lonely outcropping in a wrathful ocean. Wind sent a biting spray into the faces of the men but they pursued their task until they were almost in the surf. It was then that a gaunt, tattered figure was seen waving feebly from the rocky beach.

A run through that surf would capsize the boat, or maul it into submission. The only hope for saving the man was to get in as close to shore as possible and throw him a lifeline. The terrified castaway stood on a large wave-swept boulder. One of the crewmen coiled up a line while the oarsmen used all their skill to steady the pulsating boat. The line was heaved but it fell short of the mark. The boat pulled out to sea momentarily and then backtracked for another try.

Again the line went whirring above the maelstrom, and this time it landed within reach of the man. Bracing himself, he jumped into the water until it lapped up under his chin. He then tied the rope around his waist and gave the signal that it was fast. On the other end, two men left their oars and pulled in on the line. Gasping and struggling to keep his face out of the water, the man was pulled toward the craft. Like a hooked fish he was jerked inside, where he lay almost motionless on the bilgeboards.

With precision, the rowers resumed their places, and at the direction of the steersman headed back to the revenue cutter. The surfboat was hauled aboard, lashed securely to the deck, and the castaway placed in a warm berth in sickbay.

Some of the ship's officers gathered about him when he finally opened his eyes. He gave his name as Nels Nordin, and with difficulty he told his story. For several days preceding his rescue he had nothing to eat but coffee and compound grease. He kept repeating with tear-filled eyes that he owed his life to the surfboat crew. But to the rescuers this was just another routine incident in lifesaving. The deserved thanks, however, came in an official document from the office of the Secretary of the Department of Commerce, dated December 15, 1913:

> The Superintendent of the Coast and Geodetic Survey requests that the thanks of this department be tendered . . . for the rescue by Captain George McAfee and the crew of the Neah Bay [Baada Point] Life-Saving Station, under circumstances of great peril, during stormy weather on November 27, 1913, of Nels Nordin, a member of the party of Mr. E. H. Pagenhart, of the Coast and Geodetic Survey, off Carroll Island, where Nordin had been cut off by the storm after his provisions had been exhausted.
>
> It affords me great pleasure to commend this act of courage and skill on the part of Captain McAfee and the members of his crew.
>
> The thanks of the department are also most cordially tendered to the officers of the revenue cutter *Manning* for their prompt efforts to render assistance, and for their inval-

uable aid in obtaining and conveying the life-saving crew and their boat to the locality of the rescue.

WILLIAM C. REDFIELD,
Secretary,
The Secretary of the Treasury

It was unfortunate that the much-needed Baada (earlier Baadda) Point Lifesaving Station was one of the last of its kind established on the West Coast of continental United States. A station there many years earlier would have been the means of saving numerous lives. The scant population in this area, however, brought little pressure in establishing such a station until after the turn of the century.

THE SNOHOMISH

Because Neah Bay was so much closer to the ocean, revenue cutters frequently used it as a secondary port to Port Angeles. One such pioneer cutter which became synonymous with Juan de Fuca's graveyard was the *Snohomish*. After her construction at Wilmington, Delaware, she came around Cape Horn to assume her guardian role. An early annual report of the Treasury Department describes the vessel's role. The act of April 19, 1906, required:

> . . . that there be constructed, for and under the supervision of the Revenue Service, a first-class seagoing tug for service in saving life and property in the vicinity of the North Pacific coast of the United States, which tug shall be equipped with wireless-telegraph apparatus, surfboats, and such other modern life and property-saving appliances as may be deemed useful in assisting vessels and rescuing persons and property from the perils of the sea.

The *Snohomish* is constructed of steel, 152 feet long overall, 29 feet beam, 15.5 feet draft, with a displacement of 880 tons. As required by law, she is equipped with every device of any practical value in the saving of life. Although her headquarters are at Port Angeles, Washington, where she is kept in constant readiness to answer calls for assistance, she spends much of her time at Neah Bay. The vessel is fitted with 1-kw radio set; armed with two 1 pounder semi-automatic guns.

During her long tenure of duty, the *Snohomish* performed many missions of mercy, but like all vessels, she had her trouble-some moments.

Rear Admiral F. A. Zeusler USCG (retired), then executive officer of the vessel, recalled one distressing voyage of the *Snohomish* in the fall of 1920. The ship was headed for Port Angeles after an overhaul and coaling at Seattle. The barometer had been falling since 6 a.m. and the wind had backed from the west to the southwest. There was a change of weather coming. Already a strong breeze was blowing. The *Snohomish* was steaming at twelve knots and was taking some spray over the bow. As she proceeded down the strait, the course change was slight in keeping the wind and sea on the port bow.

Zeusler had seen to it that everything was properly secured. The captain was in his cabin, having left orders to be told if conditions changed for the worse. When they approached Dungeness Spit, the head seas increased and the captain ordered the engines to be slowed down. As the vessel changed course off the spit, an SOS was received from the Chilean bark *W. J. Pirrie,* which was in grave danger south of Cape Flattery. Since it was the job of the *Snohomish* to hasten to the rescue, a course was laid down the strait and speed was increased despite the inclement weather. The ship began taking a real beating. Apart from the heavy lurching, she shuddered from stem to stern as she threw her propeller out of the water on each dive. The vessel worked her way against an increasing westerly sea and a south-west gale.

Everything being shipshape and secured, Zeusler went to the wheelhouse to observe the action. He watched the heights of the water coming to meet the ship; her bow rose and only occasionally did she allow the top of a breaking sea to fall on her forecastle head. The speed had to be cut at times as she burrowed deep into the sea. Sometimes, as a heavy wave passed under and lifted her stern, it looked as though the bow would never rise to meet the high green wall of the next sea. The ship had only headway enough to steer by. Sea water flowed down the two passageways but was relieved by the freeing ports.

The barometer had further dropped and the violence and frequency of the squalls increased. Now off Neah Bay, the *Snohomish* was beginning to get the full impact of the southwesterly sea, diving three times in the heavy, onrushing waves. On the third dive there was also a heavy roll to starboard, filling up the starboard passageway and inundating the fantail. The heavy lashings snapped, badly twisting two stanchions. The coaling board and gratings were swept away from the quarter. The ship did not recover from the next roll and took a sharp thirty-degree list to the starboard. Zeusler hurried aft to attempt to clear up the trouble. He then rushed to the bridge and ordered full ahead and left full rudder to attempt to get the wind and sea on the starboard bow.

In the port gangway aft, there was found six inches of water. The starboard rail was eight inches under water. The ship was "in irons"; that is, she would not respond one way or the other, and the captain hastily ordered the vessel slowed. One coaling board had fouled the after starboard freeing port, and lay across the deck, held by the bitts. Water could not escape, nor could the crewmen remove the plank. They sloshed around in the cold, sloppy water. Then they attempted to swing out the port boats to aid in listing the ship to port, but the heavy motion swung the boat back and forth futilely. The engine continued at slow ahead as the vessel took a position athwart the seas, still listing more than thirty degrees to starboard.

The captain kept nursing the ship by power and rudder when suddenly another sea struck, filling the main deck—the top of it hurling itself over the boat deck and bridge. This called for an immediate change of action. The ship would have to save herself.

While the men were securing the boats, Zeusler asked permission to flood the wardroom, hoping this would right the vessel. The plan was hastily explained to the crew and they immediately went to work to open up the starboard door, raise the hatches into the wardroom, and start the bilge pump. To open the door—which had four feet of water upon it on the starboard side—required considerable effort. A plank was mounted on a foundation built on the two handrails leading to the wardroom. Then a tackle was hooked up and the door was slowly forced open. The water started rushing into the wardroom. With the next roll, a pull was made on the tackle, the door opened about a quarter of the way, and it seemed that the whole ocean poured into the wardroom. On the return roll, the impossible appeared to happen. The four feet of water in the wardroom was enough to right the ship and she remained in that position.

The *Snohomish* was then worked into Neah Bay. There in protected waters the mess was cleaned up, repairs made, and she was on her way again.

THE W. J. PIRRIE CALAMITY

Not so fortunate was the *W. J. Pirrie*. She was bucking the same raging storm farther down the coast. Directly in a no-man's land of violent water, the big iron four-masted sailing vessel was fighting a losing battle. She had earlier taken on a full cargo of lumber at Tacoma and had departed in tow of the Grace Line steamer *Santa Rita*.

Though the *Pirrie* flew the Chilean flag, she had been purchased by the American-owned W. R. Grace & Co., which was economizing by towing the 308-foot sailing ship to Peru and Chile. The former square-rigger, operating as a schooner-barge was one of the holdouts in the day of steam. Only occasionally did she spread her canvas, but she did carry a near-normal crew. With the war days just ended, the more dependable method of towing sailing ships had proved practical, cutting long passages under sail. The *Pirrie* had been built at Belfast, Ireland, in 1883, and was one of the largest sailing vessels of her day.

The storm became so violent that the steamer was obliged to drop the towing hawser and seek shelter, leaving the *Pirrie* on her own. Sail was hoisted on the *Pirrie*, but the wind ripped it to ribbons, rendering her virtually defenseless.

By this time the *Snohomish* was searching the expanse of the heaving ocean but could find no trace of the *Pirrie*. Not until a few days later was there any word. At that time two injured seamen were reported in the care of the Indians near Cape Johnson at an almost inaccessible spot on the Washington coast. Alerted, the *Snohomish* proceeded southward and managed to send a boat party ashore. Through moderating surf they made their landing. Ironically, instead of being gallant savers of life, they found themselves engaged in the grim occupation of grave digging. The party discovered and buried the battered bodies of Captain Alfred B. Jensen, master of the *Pirrie*, his wife and child, plus ten of the crew found at various places along those inhospitable shores.

The two who had survived were still in the care of the Indians. Almost frozen, they had reached shore by clinging to pieces of lumber that had worked loose after the ship reputedly broke up somewhere near Destruction Island. They were eventually taken to Seattle, where they had a slow recovery in the hospital.

CG-52300 TO THE RESCUE

An example of quick action under highly adverse conditions was logged in October of 1965. The Coast Guard was notified of a fishing vessel in distress twenty miles southwest of Cape Flattery. The fifty-two-foot rescue cutter *CG-52300*, stationed at Neah Bay, was ordered out to aid the forty-foot fishboat *Irma G.* of Florence, Oregon. The disabled craft had earlier signalled the *Umatilla Reef Lightship* that she was taking water and had no pump aboard. Full gale winds were lashing the Pacific with gusts to seventy-five knots, but there was no hesitation on the part of Richard B. Kephart, skipper of the craft, or his four-man crew.

The *CG-52300* met the full fury of the gale as she passed out of the strait entrance into the seething ocean. The howling wind sent waves barreling into the small craft with tremendous force, the spume flying. Speed was cut to one knot to keep the craft from being pounded to pieces. Then to complicate the situation there occurred an electrical failure aboard, and all outside contact was lost.

The men hung on tenaciously, their oilskins dripping. They pursued their course against thirty-five-foot waves, the boat dropping deep in abysmal troughs and then rising to the top of liquid mountains—and going back for more. This pattern continued for hours and it was not until 4:45 p.m. on October 6 that the *CG-52300* finally reached the distressed fishing vessel. Meanwhile the Coast Guard had lost all contact with the craft. Fearing she had foundered, they ordered the ocean-going cutter *Klamath*, then in Puget Sound, out to assist.

In the interim, the *CG-52300* finally got alongside the fishboat and in a delicate maneuver put a line aboard. There were three men on the *Irma G*, including skipper Marshall Murray, and all were highly elated that help had come after an arduous wait. The line was made fast and the difficult tow back to Neah Bay got underway. After several hours, the struggling *CG-52300* and her charge were sighted off Waada Island and by ten o'clock that night they had tied up at the Neah Bay dock.

"We didn't think we would be able to make it back after the electric power went out on us," the skipper of the Coast Guard craft said, "but we just kept on going." The job was passed off as routine. The fishboat was pumped out, and the exhausted men on the two vessels turned in for a well-earned sleep.

CANADIAN GUARDIANS

On the Canadian side of Juan de Fuca's graveyard is a life-saving station that has had an important role in safeguarding seafarers along Vancouver Island's west coast. It is located at Bamfield, off Barkley Sound. In existence for over a half century, the station has proved invaluable with its trained crews manning motor lifeboats and surfboats. In the day of the sailing ship, these rescue craft spent the greater part of the winter riding out seas that sent far larger vessels to shelter.

Before the age of radio and electronic communications, the lifeboats were constantly busy. The Department of Transport, under whose jurisdiction they operate, has credited them with saving scores of lives and much valuable shipping. The newly formed Canadian Coast Guard is now operating fast and fully equipped ninety-five-foot patrol boats out of Victoria, in conjunction with helicopters. The new vessels have all the latest electronic communications and lifesaving equipment. This has eased the strain on the smaller forty-foot motor lifeboats at Bamfield and Tofino. The role of the motor lifeboats, however, is still vital.

At this writing, the principal Bamfield lifeboat is painted a brilliant orange-red so that it can be seen from great distances at sea. She was built at Quebec in 1951, and is powered by two 110-horsepower diesel engines. She is self-righting and self-bailing. Equipment includes such lifesaving gear as radiotelephone, direction finder, line-throwing rocket gun, and searchlights.

The Bamfield station maintains constant communication with the light stations at Cape Beale, Pachena and Carmanah, and is ready to put to sea on a moment's notice. As part of the Canadian Coast Guard, this station also works in conjunction with all the other government maritime agencies when emergencies arise. The majority of calls for the Bamfield lifeboat today are from smaller craft hugging the shores, but in bygone days it was not uncommon for them to tackle any kind of job, offshore or inshore, besides attending to most of the needs of the area lighthouses. When the station was established in 1910, open surfboats were used. Gasoline-powered lifeboats were introduced at the station in 1913.

SEARCH FOR THE JESSIE ISLAND NO. 4

Though mercy missions of the Bamfield lifeboats have been legion, not all have had happy endings. Take the case of the *Jessie Island No. 4*. This small Canadian freight packer departed Chemainus, B. C., on a routine voyage to Port Alberni, B. C., on December 26, 1926. When she failed to arrive on schedule the next day, there was much concern. When still unreported the second day, the Bamfield lifeboat was alerted and put out to sea immediately. The waters were rough and a persistent southerly wind made the craft pitch and roll violently. Day after day her crew searched for survivors or wreckage.

The hunt went on until January 5, 1927, when some wreckage was sighted by the lifeboat on the remote shores of Pachena Bay. The men went ashore to investigate and there, battered almost beyond recognition, were the remains of the vessel. The housing was missing and the hull crushed like an eggshell. There was no sign of any of her four crewmen. The search for survivors continued, but to this day not a single clue exists as to the fate of the missing. The Bamfield motor lifeboat returned to her station, mission completed, but the victory belonged to the elements.

Man's ways and means of transportation by sea have greatly changed in the last two hundred years, but the natural elements in Juan de Fuca's graveyard of ships remain virtually unchanged; they still claim their toll in lives and property. In 1967, an early December storm west of Cape Flattery produced winds in excess of a hundred miles an hour and created waves up to sixty feet. The masters of three ships confirmed the size of the waves. The Norwegian cargo ship *Nego Anne* lost more than a million feet of lumber, which comprised her deckload. The Canadian weather ship *Quadra*, 475 miles west of the strait entrance, suffered damage near the eye of the storm, and both her master and the skipper of the *Nego Anne* said that it was the worst storm they had seen in all their years at sea. At Baada Point on Neah Bay, the Coast Guard pier had two hundred feet torn out by surging seas and high winds.

Even as the writer closes this narrative, word comes from Vancouver Island that skin divers have located the remains of the wreck of the big British four-masted steel bark *Pass of Melfort*, which crashed ashore in a gale near the entrance to Ucluelet Harbor in Barkley Sound, December 26, 1905 with the loss of her entire crew of thirty-five. There must be scores of other such remains of ancient and modern vessels from Barkley Sound to the graveyard of Juan de Fuca, just waiting to be explored by curious skin divers.

THE END

APPENDIX

Following are thumbnail sketches of recorded major shipwrecks and serious mishaps in and around the entrance to the Strait of Juan de Fuca often referred to as the "Graveyard of the Pacific."

Active, Canadian sealing schooner, 42 tons, foundered in a gale 30 miles west of Cape Flattery, Washington, April 1, 1887. Captain J. Gutterman and 28 Indians lost their lives. Vessel was built at Mayne Island, B.C., in 1885.

Alaskan, Canadian coastal freighter, wrecked on Seabird Islets between Cape Beale and Pachena Point, B.C., January 2, 1923. All hands, 11 Victoria men, were lost. The vessel sailed January 1, from Victoria with a cargo of salt for the herring salteries at Barkley Sound.

Alice B, American motor vessel, 20 tons, stranded and foundered March 29, 1929, near Neah Bay, Washington. Five crewmen saved. Location 48:23 N. Lat. 124:37 W. Long.

Alice Cooke, American schooner, four-masted, 782 tons, was picked up in 1926 by the tug **Angeles** off Cape Flattery. The schooner was waterlogged and severely damaged off the entrance to Juan de Fuca Strait. She was towed in and repaired. The vessel was built in 1891, and served 34 years in the Pacific Coast-Hawaii service.

Alice Gertrude, American passenger steamer, 413 tons, wrecked in gale on rocks in Clallam Bay, Washington, January 11, 1907.

American Girl, American schooner, two-masted, later converted to three-masted, 225 tons, was lost supposedly off the West Coast of Vancouver Island, disappearing with all hands on a voyage from San Francisco to Port Gamble with an 8-man crew. Owned by Albert Rowe of San Francisco. Parts of the wreck were reported to have been cast up on the beach at Cape St. James in the Queen Charlotte Islands.

Andalusia, Panamanian freighter, steamship, 7,700 tons, ran aground four miles east of Neah Bay, November 4, 1949, after fire broke out on board. Commanded by Captain George Lemos. Fire extinguished in 90 minutes but freighter loaded with 5,000,000 feet of B. C. lumber could not be moved. She eventually broke in two and became a total loss.

Archer, British (iron) bark, 900 tons, dismasted and thrown on her beam ends in gale off Cape Flattery, Victoria for Portland, Oregon, March 16, 1894. Three crewmen drowned. Captain John Dawson and rest of crew clung to the ship's taffrail for several hours before a boat could be swung free. Picked up by ship **John C. Porter.** Derelict found by steamer **Maude** and towed to Clayoquot Sound. Wreck was later towed to Victoria and then to Port Blakely, Washington, where she was converted to a barkentine for American owner Rufus Calhoun. Built at Sunderland, England, in 1876, she was afloat till 1936, when wrecked in the Philippine Islands as the Marie.

Arkansas, French steamship (see SS **Suremico**).

Armin, German bark, en route from B. C. ports to China with a cargo of lumber, was wrecked between Sooke and Port San Juan (Port Renfrew), August 23, 1864, because of fog. Crewmen all escaped in boats and made it to Victoria. Armin was total loss.

Arrogant, motor vessel, lost off Cape Flattery, September, 1945.

Atalanta, American bark, wrecked in gale 50 miles off Cape Flattery, December 16, 1890. In command of Captain Frederick Masher and bound for San Francisco from Port Gamble with lumber. Vessel was dismasted and began to break up but was held afloat by her cargo. The ship had reached the latitude of the Columbia River and was blown all the way back to the Juan de Fuca graveyard. Crew stayed with wreck which came ashore near Clayoquot, Vancouver Island. The natives cared for survivors until picked up by the sealing schooner **Katherine.** The **Atalanta** was built at Amesbury, Massachusetts, in 1851, and was many years in the Liverpool passenger trade.

Aurora, British bark, reputed to be missing somewhere off Cape Flattery in 1886. Unconfirmed. Vessel was of 1,300 tons.

Austria, American bark, wrecked on Flattery Rocks off Cape Alava, January 21, 1887.

Becherdass Ambiadass, British bark, Captain Williams in command, bound for Moodyville, B. C., from Shanghai, was wrecked July 27, 1879, five miles south of Cape Beale, B. C. The wreck was caused by fog. The vessel dragged over the reef and became a total loss. Crew rescued by Captain Spring of the schooner **Favourite.**

Belvidere, American ship, 1,225 tons, in command of Captain J. S. Gibson, with a crew of 19, wrecked on Bonilla Point, B. C., November 29, 1886, while en route from Wilmington, California, to Departure Bay, in ballast. Struck rocks during a heavy fog. Later pulled free by tug **Tyee,** but foundered before the tug could beach her. Owned in San Francisco by Goodall Perkins & Co., and under charter to R. Dunsmuir.

Bering Sea, vessel of this name reported lost off Cape Flattery, 1895. Unconfirmed report. She still appeared to be active in 1898.

Beryl, Canadian tug (steel) struck Nitinat bar, B. C., and was wrecked in 1920.

Beulah, Panamanian motor vessel (freighter), 1,389 gross tons. After weathering a terrific battle with raging seas off the west coast of Vancouver

Island and narrowly averting being swept on the rocks, she managed to make her way to Victoria on a 31-degree list. Shortly after, she sank at her moorings in the harbor, December 27, 1937. She resisted eight attempts at being refloated. Finally, on the ninth try by use of a 15-foot cofferdam, March 12, 1938, salvagers were successful. The vessel was a floating mass of wreckage. She was owned by Flood Bros. of Panama and was eventually rebuilt and repaired for a large sum of money. When she got entangled in the gale in Juan de Fuca's graveyard prior to making Victoria, her steering mechanism was badly damaged. Also first officer Tryve Bragdo was washed overboard and drowned and the boatswain severely injured. The ship was inbound from the South Seas when hit by the gale. She was built in Norway in 1923.

Bianca, five-masted schooner, 2,139 tons, went aground and was totally wrecked near Clallam Bay, Washington, December 15, 1924.

Bibiya, American motor vessel, 29 tons, foundered off Tatoosh Island, near Cape Flattery, September 4, 1948. Vessel was built in 1945, fishing out of Seattle.

Blanco, motor vessel, 18 tons, collided with unknown ship near Umatilla Lightship, August 21, 1936. Two of her three-man crew were lost. Vessel, a fishboat, sank.

Bretagne, motor vessel, lost October 15, 1929, southwest of Cape Flattery.

Cadaretta, American steamship (freighter), 2,648 tons, stranded off James Island, Washington, May 28, 1945. Refloated and beached near Neah Bay, where salvagers under Captain Loring Hyde repaired her temporarily and later refloated her. She was escorted to port and overhauled.

Cambridge, American bark, 255 tons, broke up in a gale 15 miles southwest of Cape Flattery, June 13, 1877. Chinese cook drowned. Remainder of crew escaped. Vessel en route to San Francisco from Port Ludlow with lumber.

Canada Maru, Japanese passenger vessel, 5,700 tons, stranded near Cape Flattery in fog, January 31, 1918. All 176 passengers safely removed. Target of major salvage operation, vessel was refloated in August of 1918.

Carluke, Canadian motor vessel, 15 tons, sank in collision, August 21, 1955, off Nitinat, B. C.

Carol M, Canadian motor vessel, 27 tons, stranded March 12, 1933, near Nitinat, B. C.

Champion, American sealing schooner, wrecked near Nitinat, B. C., in 1887. The vessel capsized while trying to cross the bar. Owned by Chief Peter of Neah Bay. Cultus George, an Indian crewman, was lost in the wreck.

Charles B. Kinney, American bark, sailed from Port Townsend for Australia with lumber, November 20, 1886. Vanished with all hands somewhere off Tatoosh Island. A month later, the lighthouse keeper at Cape Beale reported that an abandoned hulk came ashore near the cape. The seas were heavy and the ship broke up that night, the wreckage drifting away. Among the wreckage on the beach was a broken quarter board with the letters Charles B.

Chesley No. 19, barge, 330 tons, stranded off Pachena Point, B. C., August 31, 1936.

Chitose Maru, Japanese bulk carrier, collided with Danish freighter **Marie Skou,** north of Neah Bay, September 20, 1967; was towed in, badly holed.

Circa, schooner, wrecked near Sombrio Point, B. C., in 1882.

City of San Diego, Canadian schooner, 48 tons, built at San Francisco in 1871. Lost with all hands somewhere south of Cape Flattery in 1902. Some of her wreckage was found on the beach at Ozette, Washington. This vessel was one of the better known units of the Pacific sealing fleet during much of her career. She caught seals until 1895 and came under the British (Canadian) flag in 1893.

C. L. Taylor, American barkentine, 366 tons, formerly U. S. Government steamer **Wenona,** foundered 25 miles southwest of Cape Flattery, February, 1883. Vessel was thrown on her beam ends in a southeast gale. Masts were cut away, and the vessel righted. Captain Alexander Bergman's six-year-old son was then washed overboard. The father jumped over after him but failed to save him. He was pulled back aboard, only to find his wife dead in her cabin. The second mate and six men left the vessel in the ship's boat. The captain, first mate, and cook stayed with the ship and were picked up at 7 p.m., February 21, by the bark Arcturas. The Taylor soon broke up. She had been en route to San Pedro from Port Townsend with lumber.

Coast Trader, American steamship, 3,286 tons, torpedoed and sunk by enemy submarine, June 7, 1942, off Cape Flattery, 48:15 N. Lat. 125:40 W. Long.; 37-man crew escaped. Built in 1920, at Newark, N. J., for U. S. Shipping Board. Last operated by Coastwise Line under Army jurisdiction.

Coloma, American bark, 852 tons, wrecked on rocks off Cape Beale, B. C., December 6, 1906, outbound with lumber from Everett to San Diego. Crew of ten rescued by Canadian government vessel, **Quadra.** The 168-foot vessel was owned by the Pacific Shipping Co.

Columbia, German bark, 2,577 tons. In 1902 she was taken in tow by the SS Hyades off Cape Flattery and brought to Seattle almost completely dismasted from Pacific gales. The vessel also suffered much deck damage while returning in ballast from Japan. She was later rebuilt as the six-masted barkentine **Everett G. Griggs,** and later the **E. R. Sterling** under the American flag.

Colusa, American bark, 1,189 tons, en route to Puget Sound from Hawaii, ran aground on Bonilla Point, B. C., November 1899. She freed herself, drifted west in leaking condition, and was abandoned by her crew, who gained the shore in Barkley Sound. Ship broke up shortly after. Owned by C. Nelson of San Francisco. Part of the wreck reportedly drifted as far north as Alaskan shores.

Commodore, American ship, 1,100 tons, stranded two miles south of Tatoosh Island during a strong westerly gale, January 10, 1877. Commanded by Captain Charles Hastorf. Vessel was bound for Seattle from San Francisco. When the vessel first struck, her rudder was knocked off. The masts were cut away and anchors dropped. The vessel went ashore and broke up. Wreck was sold for $475. Insured for $16,000; no cargo, vessel in ballast.

Condor, HMS, British Naval frigate vanished with all hands en route to Honolulu from Esquimalt, December 2, 1901. She is believed a victim of a gale off Cape Flattery the night of December 2. One report claims she carried 140 victims to a watery grave, another reports only 104.

Continental, sloop, wrecked near Clo-oose in the 1880s.

Cowlitz, American bark, 797 tons, in command of Captain William Hansen, with a crew of 14, sailed from Port Gamble for San Francisco with lumber, January 29, 1893. She vanished with all hands, supposedly in a gale off Cape Flattery.

Crescent, American five-masted schooner, was battered by huge seas off Cape Flattery, January 9, 1914, and entered the Strait of Juan de Fuca with deckload gone and upperworks stove. Repaired and returned to sea.

Cyrus, American brig, Captain Mitchell, wrecked at the entrance to Port San Juan, B. C., December 23, 1858. Vessel was bound from Steilacoom for San Francisco, with cargo of lumber.

Dance, schooner, wrecked between Port San Juan and Sombrio Point, B. C., November 10, 1860. All hands saved.

Dare, American schooner, 259 tons, stranded off Bonilla Point, B. C., December 23, 1890, during a thick fog. The heavy seas knocked the wreck to pieces but the crew made the shore safely. Vessel commanded by Captain F. A. Berry. The three-masted schooner was built in 1882 at North Bend, Oregon, by and for A. M. Simpson.

Dart, American sealing schooner (owned by Indians), wrecked off Carmanah Point, B. C., in April 1895 while sealing. She was manned by Neah Bay Indians. Vessel was built at Lummi, Washington, in 1890.

Delmar, motor vessel, stranded near Carmanah Point, B. C., November 3, 1950.

Discovery, American barkentine, 415 tons, vanished at sea en route to San Francisco from Puget Sound in January 1896; is believed to have been lost somewhere off Cape Flattery with her entire crew.

D. L. Clinch, schooner, wrecked near Sombrio Point, Vancouver Island, November 10, 1860. Just a year earlier, in December 1859, this vessel distinguished herself by taking the first registered cargo from British Columbia to a foreign port. She sailed from New Westminster, B. C. for San Francisco with 60,000 feet of cabinet wood and 50 barrels of cranberries. The vessel was commanded by Captain Bunker.

Duchess of Albany, British ship, stranded at Bonilla Point, B. C., in 1888. No details.

Duchess of Argyle, British four-masted bark, 1,700 tons, inbound to Burrard Inlet from Liverpool, wrecked in fog five miles southeast of Port San Juan, near Sombrio Point, October 11, 1887. Commanded by Captain H. E. Heard.

Duchess San Lorenzo, ship reported lost with all hands off Cape Flattery, March 1854.

Edith, steam-powered vessel stranded on Waada Island, Washington, May 8, 1910. Total loss.

Edwin, American bark, 404 tons, became waterlogged in rough seas off Cape Flattery, December 1, 1874. Vessel was partially dismasted. Captain Hughes' wife, two children, and the Chinese cook were washed overboard and drowned. The Captain and eight men climbed to the foretop of mast and remained for three days as the wreck drifted northward and finally came ashore near Hesquiat, B. C. They were finally rescued by Indians and picked up by the schooner Alert.

Eldorado, American ship, 1,067 tons, foundered off Cape Flattery, April 1, 1887. There were only two survivors. Vessel departed Seattle in tow of tug Tyee and cast off for San Francisco with a cargo of coal. She was commanded by Captain S. L. Humphreys with a crew of 14. Encountered severe southeast gale and began leaking so badly that the pumps could not stem the inflow. At 8 p.m. on the eve of her departure, three huge seas boarded and sent the ship plummeting to the bottom. Two survivors were picked up by schooner Fanny Dutard. Others either drowned with the ship or were swept from wreckage. Vessel owned by A. M. Simpson and others.

Eliza, American schooner, capsized derelict found at entrance to Strait of Juan de Fuca in early March of 1874. The vessel had departed Coos Bay, Oregon, in January, with coal and lumber for California, but was evidently abandoned by her crew. She carried 18 persons and records show no word of their rescue. She was found by the HMS Boxer, which tried to sink her with gunfire as a menace to navigation. Being unsuccessful, the tugs Grappler and Isabel towed the wreck to Esquimalt.

Ella S. Thayer, American bark, 1,098 tons, foundered 15 miles off Cape Flattery, December 16, 1886. She was bound from Tacoma for San Francisco with coal when she encountered severe weather off the cape. All boats but one were destroyed. In this, the weary 15-man crew, headed by Captain Mathson, made their escape. Without food or water, they drifted for 36 hours before the German bark Von Molke, Captain Cox, rescued them and took them to Victoria. The Thayer, built in 1865 at Bath, Maine, was owned by Charles A. Nutson of San Francisco.

Ellen Foster, American ship, 996 tons, wrecked in Neah Bay, Washington, December 22, 1867. Commanded by Captain Anderson, the vessel was in ballast, bound for Utsaladdy, Washington, from Callao, for a cargo of lumber. Vessel was victim of a hurricane from the east southeast inside the strait. She ran for Neah Bay, anchoring in nine fathoms. The blow continued and she dragged across the reef and sank. Crew made shore in ship's boat. They were later taken to Port Townsend by the tug **Cyrus Walker**. The **Foster** was a swift clipper ship, built at Medford, Massachusetts, in 1852, for J. & A. Tirrell of Boston. A bronze cannon recovered from Neah Bay in the 1920s was believed to be from the **Ellen Foster**.

Fawn, Canadian schooner, 58 tons, wrecked near Carmanah Point, B. C., October 1905. Vessel was built at Chemainus, B. C., in 1892. For many years it was a sealing vessel in the North Pacific. (Another account lists the wreck in February 1902, on the west coast of Vancouver Island.)

Florence, American ship, 1,684 tons, vanished with all hands off Cape Flattery in 1902. Vessel was bound for San Francisco from Tacoma. She was owned by California Shipping Co., and was built at Bath, Maine, in 1877, by Goss & Sawyer.

Florencia, Peruvian brig, encountered gale off Cape Flattery, December 8, 1860, and was on her beam ends for three hours. The captain, cook, and a passenger were drowned. The waterlogged wreck drifted to Nootka Sound, where the remainder of the crew escaped. The vessel was en route to Callao from Utsaladdy, Washington, with a cargo of lumber.

Floridian, American steamship (freighter), 6,765 tons, collided with SS **Admiral Fisk**, near **Umatilla Lightship**, September 1, 1928. The **Floridian** went down in deep water. Her crew of 40 were all rescued. The vessel was built at Sparrows Point, Maryland, in 1915, and was owned by the American-Hawaiian Steamship Co., who used her in intercoastal trades.

Flottbek, German ship, 1,972 tons, went on beam ends between Flattery Rocks and White Rock, south of Cape Flattery; was miraculously pulled free by tug and towed to port for repairs. Owned by Knohr & Burchard, Hamburg. Built in 1891 in Newcastle, England. Accident occurred, January 13, 1901. First officer and 12 crewmen took to boat for help and rowed all the way to Neah Bay, almost exhausted from hunger and exposure. Captain Shoemaker, master.

Forest Queen, American bark, 511 tons, Captain Basely, vanished with all hands (11) off Cape Flattery in March 1898, bound to San Pedro from Tacoma with 500,000 feet of lumber and 107,000 lathes. This vessel was built at Port Ludlow, Washington, in 1869, by Hiram Doncaster, and was one of the fastest, most economical, and most profitable carriers in coastwise trades. Last owned by Charles Nelson of San Francisco. In 1877, she hung up the remarkable record of 11 consecutive round trips between Puget Sound and San Francisco, under Captain Burns—the best voyage taking 18 days, the poorest 34. Average was 27 days gross time.

Fort Camosun, Canadian steamship (freighter), 7,126 tons, torpedoed and shelled by an enemy submarine off Cape Flattery, June 19, 1942. Vessel was built by Victoria Machinery Depot and was under operation of the Ministry of War. She was on bareboat charter from the War Shipping Administration; operators were T. & J. Brocklebank. When hit amidships (portside), the vessel was outbound with plywood, zinc, lead, and general cargo. Badly damaged and down by the head, she somehow remained afloat and was towed in and later beached off Neah Bay. Salvage tugs aided her and temporary repairs were made. She was then taken back to Victoria. Yarrows Yard, at Esquimalt, unloaded, repaired, and reloaded her for another try. The vessel was commanded by Captain T. S. Eggleston.

Gale, salmon troller, operated by James Robinson of Seattle, was driven aground two miles south of Cape Flattery on October 18, 1967. The surge of the tide drove the vessel into a rocky wedge, ripping off the keel and knocking a big hole in the bow. The rudder and propeller were also torn off. Robinson abandoned and had to be rescued from the rocks by a Coast Guard helicopter. The boat was beyond salvage and left to the elements. The Gale was reported overdue at Neah Bay the day before the rescue was made.

Gas, American scow, 22 tons, built in 1907, foundered off Cape Flattery, August 25, 1925.

Gem of the Ocean, American bark, 702 tons, struck off Vancouver Island, eight miles southeast of Port San Juan, in August 1879 and became a total loss. Captain Hawse and his crew escaped and reached Port Townsend in a small boat. The vessel was bound from Seattle to San Francisco with coal. She was built as a clipper ship in 1852, at Medford, Massachusetts, by Hayden & Cudworth for William Lincoln of Boston. Last owned by McPherson & Witherbee, San Francisco.

George Thompson, lost 32 miles off Cape Flattery in 1892. No details.

George Walton, American steamship (freighter), 7,229 tons, caught fire following a boiler explosion, 390 miles southwest of Cape Flattery, November 6, 1951. The explosion killed one crew member. The ship got so hot from the fire that she had to be abandoned by Captain Bentzen and his crew. Four crew members were later killed when trying to climb from a lifeboat up the side of the Japanese freighter **Kenkon Maru.** An SOS had earlier brought the Coast Guard vessel **Northwind** to the scene. She later transferred the tow to the tug **Barbara Foss.** The long tow began, as the ship continued to burn, settling ever lower in the water. She finally went down about 50 miles off the Strait of Juan de Fuca, after the towing hawser was cut. The vessel was bound for India from Portland, Oregon, with 9,600 tons of grain and became a victim of the graveyard on November 17, 1951, at 7 p.m.

Glory of the Sea, motor vessel (fishboat), 46 tons, burned outside the breakwater at Neah Bay, November 2, 1951; a total loss. Built in 1926 at Gig Harbor, Washington. A veteran of the fishing banks, the vessel was owned by John Maljich, Jr., of Tacoma, and carried an eight-man crew.

Golden Rod, motor vessel (fishboat), 15 tons, foundered one mile south of Tatoosh Island, September 28, 1955. Was built in 1907 and owned by Harold Rogers, Port Angeles, Washington.

Grace Darling, American ship, 1,042 tons, vanished off Cape Flattery, January 1878. The vessel was coal laden, bound for San Francisco from

Nanaimo. She sailed from Victoria, January 3, and was last sighted off the cape, January 18, hove to in a heavy gale by the ship **Melancthon**. She is believed to have foundered shortly after with her entire crew of 18. She was built in 1854 as a clipper ship by E. & H. O. Briggs at South Boston, for Charles B. Fessendon of Boston. Was later purchased by Baker & Morrell and had many fine passages to her credit.

Graywood, American passenger steam schooner, 915 tons, foundered off the strait in October 1915. She was owned by the Graywood Steamship Co. (Beadle Bros.). Formerly the **Harold Dollar**, the vessel was built in 1904 at Fairhaven, California, by the famous Bendixsen Yard, and was engaged in coastal lumber trade throughout her career . . . Operating out of San Francisco, the **Graywood** had been outbound from the Golden Gate for Vancouver, B. C., when battering seas opened her seams. The Matson steamer **Hilonian** sighted her distress signals, 50 miles south of Cape Flattery and managed to get a line aboard. After removing Captain F. M. Johnson and the crew of the stricken vessel, Captain A. L. Soule, the **Hilonian's** master, tried to take her in tow. Three miles inside the Strait of Juan de Fuca, the hawser broke. The **Hilonian** stood by until October 3, when the **Graywood** foundered. No lives lost.

Green Sea, motor vessel, 20 tons, foundered on July 24, 1931, off Cape Beale, B. C.

Haida (Hai Da), Chinese-owned but British-registered steamship (freighter), 5,000 tons, vanished with all hands (27) off Cape Flattery en route from Seattle to Hawaii and Hong Kong, in October 1937 with sulphur cargo.

Haida Chieftain, Canadian tug, 143 feet long, caught fire off Cape Beale, B. C., January 3, 1965, and was abandoned by her crew of ten who were picked up by the tug **LaPointe** of Vancouver Tug Boat Co., Vancouver, B. C. The brand-new tug **La Reine** on her maiden trip intercepted the **Haida Chieftain,** put out the fire, and towed the vessel to port. The **Haida Chieftain,** one of the largest Canadian tugs, was rebuilt and returned to service.

Harriet G., American brig, 252 tons, capsized off Cape Flattery in 1917, laden with lumber for Hawaii from Puget Sound. The derelict was taken in tow by the halibut schooner **Sumner,** was brought to port, righted, and rebuilt as a three-masted schooner for the copra trade. She was wrecked as a floating cannery at Uyak, Alaska, in 1932. Was built at Norfolk, Virginia, by W. A. Beach in 1878.

Hartfield, British (iron) ship, 1,867 tons. Unconfirmed report said vessel disappeared off Cape Flattery, January 1908. Owned at Liverpool, England, by J. B. Walmsley, and built in 1884, by Whitehaven Shipbuilding Co. in England.

Harvey Mills, American ship, 2,700 tons, foundered 50 miles off Cape Flattery, December 14, 1886. In command of Captain Crawford, she was en route to San Francisco from Seattle but ran into a heavy gale directly off the cape and was on her beam ends all night, December 13. Next day the mizzen was cut away and took the mainmast with it. A half hour later the vessel sank. Eight escaped on two rafts. Twelve went down with the ship. Then one of the rafts broke up and her people drowned. On the other raft, the first mate Cushman and two seamen drifted four days without food or water. Another seaman was found but he went insane and jumped overboard. The three survivors were finally rescued by the ship **Majestic** and taken to San Pedro.

Hat, lost off Cape Flattery in 1898. No details. Believed to be a small schooner.

Hattie C. Besse, American bark, 666 tons, inbound for Burrard Inlet, B. C., from San Francisco, to load lumber for Shanghai, was wrecked November 20, 1871, 20 miles south of Cape Flattery. The vessel got too close to shore in the fog. When breakers were sighted, she dropped her anchors but dragged, struck a rock and broke up amidships. Two crewmen were severely injured. The crew made it to shore but were unable to save anything from the ship. Vessel was in command of Captain James H. Gragg, was valued at $40,000, and insured for only $15,000. Survivors were picked up by steamer **California** before revenue cutter **Lincoln** reached the scene. She was the first four-masted vessel ever to enter the Columbia River.

Hecate, H. M. survey vessel (British), grounded in fog, August 19, 1861, on a reef two miles east of Cape Flattery. Was later refloated by an American power schooner and, leaking badly, was escorted to Esquimalt.

Hecla, American bark, 1,529 tons, while being towed to sea by the tug **Richard Holyoke**, struck Duncan Rock broadside, August 10, 1907, just a few days after the schooner **Winslow** hit the same obstruction near Tatoosh Island. The Hecla, like the Winslow, sustained serious damage. The license of Captain Michael Bourke of the **Holyoke** was suspended for a month as a result of the mishap, causing the Hecla to miss her charter. The damaged sailing vessel was towed back to port where costly damages were repaired. The Hecla was a New England-built sailing vessel dating from 1877.

Henry T. Scott, American steam schooner, 1,596 tons, was rammed in the fog at the entrance to Juan de Fuca Strait, July 16, 1922, by the SS **Harry Luckenbach**. The Scott was bound for Seattle from San Francisco under Captain C. Thorsell, and was struck off Neah Bay. She sank fast, taking four crewmen with her. Twenty-one others, including one woman passenger, were rescued from the water by boats from the 12,000-ton **Harry Luckenbach**. The Scott was built at San Francisco in 1913.

Hodgdon, brig, departed Puget Sound and Victoria for San Francisco in October 1855. She went missing with all hands in a gale off Cape Flattery.

Inlet Queen, pleasure cruiser, about 30 tons, struck Nitinat bar on April 12, 1912. She filled and sank.

Irene, Bolivian brig, abandoned in sinking condition, 30 miles west southwest of Cape Flattery, January 2, 1887. Commanded by Captain William Silberg, the vessel was laden with lumber from Port Townsend for the Fiji Islands. She encountered a heavy gale off the cape and began leaking. The deck load was jettisoned to no avail; the crew had to abandon at 8:30 a.m., January 2. The vessel was described as old and rotten. Survivors were picked up by the ship **Iroquois** and taken to Port Townsend.

Island Cypress, Canadian barge, 325 feet long, converted from a shallow-draft tanker, sank in rough seas in mid-October of 1963, south of Cape Flattery with a full cargo of waste pulp liquor aboard. The barge was being towed from Woodfibre, B. C., to Grays Harbor by the powerful Canadian tug **Sudbury II.** The barge—valued at $250,000—had to be cut loose from the tug. Nobody was aboard.

Island Maple, Canadian barge, 325 feet long, sank south of Cape Flattery on October 22, 1963, in tow of the Canadian tug **Sudbury** under circumstances strangely similar to those that had taken her sister barge **Island Cypress** one week earlier. This barge was also being towed to Grays Harbor with a full cargo of waste pulp liquor from Woodfibre, B. C., and was valued at $250,000.

Ivanhoe, American ship, 1,610 tons, vanished off Cape Flattery after departure from Seattle for San Francisco with coal, September 27, 1894. Lost with the ship were 19 crewmen and 4 passengers. The ship was commanded by Captain Edward D. Griffin.

Iwanowa, American bark, was waterlogged and thrown on her beam ends in heavy squalls off Tatoosh Island, November 24, 1864. Her masts were carried away and three crewmen drowned. The vessel subsequently righted herself and the wreck drifted northward. Four days later she struck a reef at Nootka and broke up. Captain Mortage and six men, the rest of the crew, started for shore on a raft. Three drowned but the others gained the beach and were later rescued by the sloop **Leonede.**

Jane, motor vessel, 33 tons, foundered on September 27, 1959, three miles off Tatoosh Island. Owned by P. H. Taft of Seattle, the vessel—built in 1930—was a commercial fishing craft.

Jane Grey (Gray), American schooner, 112 tons, struck by severe gale off Cape Flattery en route from Seattle for the Bering Sea, May 1898. Badly battered, the wreck drifted northward and later sank off Vancouver Island. Twenty-seven got off in a launch before the vessel sank, but 37 others were lost. The vessel, which was carrying passengers to the Northland, was usually engaged in sealing.

Janet Cowan, British four-masted bark, 2,497 tons, wrecked four miles east of Pachena Point, B. C., December 31, 1895. Vessel was 108 days out of Cape Town bound for Victoria. In a violent gale off Cape Flattery, she was driven northward in a strong southeaster and sought shelter at Barkley Sound. She was caught by inshore currents and forced ashore near Pachena Point. Because it was too rough to launch a boat, a volunteer seaman swam to shore with a line, by means of which 29 seafarers reached the beach safely. While awaiting rescue, however, seven died from exposure, including the ship's master Captain Thompson. Another seaman went insane and later died. The tug **Tyee** finally sighted the wreck and picked up 15 survivors. Seven others, who had found shelter at a nearby government survival cabin, were rescued by a Canadian vessel.

Japanese Junk of 1833, wrecked near Cape Flattery. Survivors were taken captive by the Makah Indians, but were later ransomed. The disabled craft had drifted to northwest shores from Japan.

Jessie Island No. 4, small Canadian motor vessel. Wreck was found at Pachena Bay. The vessel went missing en route to Port Alberni from Chemainus and was located by Bamfield Lifeboat after wide search. No sign of lost crewmen was ever found. She had left port on December 26, 1926, but her wreckage was not discovered till January 5, 1927.

J. M. Weatherwax, American three-masted schooner, 384 tons, waterlogged and dismasted off Cape Flattery in a storm, November 1910. Towed in by steam schooner **Riverside** and taken to Port Townsend, November 23. She was later repaired.

John Marshall, American ship, overcome by a gale off Cape Flattery, November 10, 1860. Parts of the derelict later came ashore near Bonilla Point but the entire crew was lost without trace. Vessel was en route to Port Discovery, Washington, from San Francisco, in ballast. She was to have loaded lumber.

Keweenah, American steam collier, 272 feet long, built of iron, went missing with her entire crew, December 7, 1894, in a gale off Cape Flattery. She was bound for San Francisco from Comox, with a full cargo of coal.

Laura Pike, American two-masted schooner, 145 tons, went ashore near Pachena Point in March 1891, but was refloated and repaired. She was finally lost off Cape Mendocino, California, February 7, 1902, by foundering. Built in 1875, at Eureka, the vessel also survived a stranding on the Humboldt Bar in 1878, which claimed her crew of seven.

Leonore, Chilean bark, torn apart by gale near Umatilla Reef and carried southward to a point three miles north of the Quillayute, near Cape Johnson, where she was totally wrecked, October 4, 1893. Six lives were lost.

Les Adelphus, French sailing vessel, reported in trouble off Cape Flattery in 1905. Was evidently towed to port and repaired.

Lief E., American gas-powered freight boat, 27 tons, lost off Cape Flattery in 1918. Was built at Ballard, Washington, in 1897.

Lillie Grace, Chilean bark, composite vessel of 545 tons, began leaking off Cape Flattery, December 14, 1886, after departing two days earlier from Port Discovery for Valparaiso with lumber. Caught in a terrific gale and heavy seas, she had eleven feet of water in her hold. Captain Charles Wall, the shipmaster, had the crew construct rafts and trail them astern in case the ship broke up. Finally, the deckhouses, galley, and deck gear went over the side. By December 19, the ship had drifted to a spot a few miles north of Grays Harbor. There, the rafts broke up, and in desperation the captain steered the ship for the beach to save his crew. The wreck stranded amid the breakers. The crew held their perches in the rigging and 24 hours later were rescued by friendly Indians. These survivors made their way to Olympia overland.

Lily, American two-masted schooner, 142 tons, reported in trouble off Cape Flattery in 1897. Was towed in and repaired. The vessel, built in 1882, played the role of the Bounty in the motion picture, **Mutiny on the Bounty** (1934).

Lizzie Boggs, American bark, 445 tons, wrecked in fog just south of Cape Flattery, September 1867. In command of Captain Townsend, the vessel was bound for Puget Sound from San Francisco. The crew escaped in boats and made their way to Neah Bay, where they were rescued by the bark **Ava.**

Lizzie Marshall, American bark, 434 tons, Captain Adolph Bergman, lost on Bonilla Point, B. C., February 22, 1884. The vessel was 14 days out from San Francisco when she first sighted Cape Flattery. Fog set in and the wind died, leaving the vessel little steerageway. With a heavy swell running and no foghorn blaring on Tatoosh, the vessel lost her bearings and was carried toward Vancouver Island. Both anchors were dropped in 20 fathoms on February 21, and a boat with four volunteers was sent to Neah Bay for help. When a southeast gale came up, the vessel parted her anchor chains and went broadside on the rocks. A German sailor trying to retrieve personal effects was drowned. The after part of the vessel wedged tight in the rocks and afforded a means of escape for crewmen. The vessel was built on the Sacramento River in 1876.

Lord Raglan, British bark, foundered in the winter of 1852, in a storm off Cape Flattery, laden with piling, lumber, and spars for England. The vessel was en route from Sooke, B. C., carrying eight passengers. Some wreckage washed up on Vancouver Island.

Majestic, American bark, 1,170 tons, reported in sinking condition off Cape Flattery, January 1893. The vessel was registered in San Francisco and had been built at Portland, Maine, in 1866.

Malamute, fishing troller from Seattle, burned and sank two miles off Sekiu, Washington, October 29, 1966. Harry Hebert, the only person aboard, escaped in a skiff. The fire started in the engine room and totally destroyed the craft.

Malina, American fishboat, 165 tons, owned by the San Juan Fishing and Packing Company, Seattle, ran aground off Carmanah Point, B. C., August 29, 1957. The powerful Canadian tug **Sudbury,** of Island Tug & Barge Ltd., was despatched to the scene and managed to get a line aboard the stranded 100-foot vessel. The Malina was on the rocks with her engine room flooded. The tug was forced to maintain a taut line between her towing engine and the stranded ship for 24 hours for the proper high tide. Meanwhile, the captain, mate, and crew were transferred to the tug, in case the Malina should sink. The tug was finally, by brute force, able to drag the vessel a hundred feet across the rocks to a spot where there was sufficient water to get her afloat. She grounded on Thursday and was refloated the following Sunday in a touch-and-go operation. She was one of very few vessels of size to be refloated along this stretch of coast. The **Malina** was originally built at Seattle in 1943, as a unit of the U. S. Army.

Manning No. I, scow, 628 tons, foundered off Clo-oose, November 23, 1949.

Maria J. Smith, American bark, 545 tons, wrecked five miles southeast of Pachena Point, November 7, 1869. In command of Captain David Smith, the lumber-laden ship out of Port Townsend began to leak in heavy seas off Cape Flattery. She drifted toward Vancouver Island after the lumber load had shifted, and even the topsails could not get her offshore. After she grounded, the captain, his wife, child, and the crew got to shore and were picked up by the schooner Surprise. The wreck sold for $950, the cargo for $750, the sails for $300. The wreck was refloated, but while being towed in by the tug **Politkofsky**, she broke loose in a gale in the strait with a skeleton crew aboard. Later they abandoned her and the derelict drifted about for days. She drifted 500 miles to Bella Bella and in March came up on the beach at Millbank Sound and went to pieces.

Marie Skou, Danish freighter, collided with **Chitose Maru**, Sept. 20, 1967.

Marmion, American ship, 823 tons, coal laden, from Departure Bay, B. C., for San Francisco, foundered off Cape Flattery, November 8, 1879. In command of Captain F. W. Jordan, the vessel encountered a strong southeaster and in a cross sea began to leak badly. Pumps became useless as water gained in the hold. The vessel was abandoned and the crew picked up by the **Tam O'Shanter**. The Marmion later foundered under her 1,300-ton cargo of coal.

Marquis of Dufferin, sternwheel steamer, San Francisco for Alaska (for use on the Yukon River), in company with steamer **Progress**, broke up in heavy weather off Cape Beale, June 27, 1898. She sank and the survivors were transferred to the **Progress**. The vessel was valued at $41,000.

Mary N, motor vessel, stranded October 21, 1950, in the Nitinat River, B.C.

Mascotte, Canadian steamer (salvage vessel), totally destroyed by fire, August 16, 1893, while lying at anchor in Pachena Bay, B. C. She was skippered by Captain Edward McCoskrie. The Mascotte was only three years old and one of the best-equipped wreckers in Pacific Northwest waters.

Matilda, American bark, 849 tons, 158 feet long, stranded on the rocks at the western end of Tatoosh Island in September 1897. The night was clear but the old craft got trapped in a powerful, incoming tide. The wind failed to bring her about and she stranded right below the probing shaft of light from Cape Flattery beacon. Though the vessel became a total loss, all hands were rescued. The vessel was old and tender, having been built at Searsport, Maine, in 1857. She was owned by Captain R. C. Calhoun, prominent shipping man of Port Townsend, himself a victim of many tragedies at sea.

Matteawan, American iron steamship (collier), 3,301 tons. Vanished with all hands off Cape Flattery, December 1901, laden with a full cargo of coal for San Francisco from Comox, B. C.

Matterhorn, British iron four-masted bark, 1,839 tons, Captain R. I. Salter, foundered April 27, 1909, 70 miles off Umatilla Reef, Washington, bound

Seas scud over after half of the Panamanian SS *Andalusia*. The vessel suffered a fire off Cape Flattery in November 1949 and was grounded east of Neah Bay, where she eventually broke in two.

George Arnone   *Mac's Foto Service*

Left: Tug crew examines broken halves of the Panamanian freighter *Andalusia*, east of Neah Bay.
Right: In heavy seas in the North Pacific the SS *Japan Mail* heads for the Far East, fully loaded.

Original *Swiftsure Lightship No. 93*, steam powered and equipped with sail, hoisted oil lanterns in a cluster around the crosstrees each night to guide ships.

Powerful Canadian salvage tug *Sudbury II*, of Island Tug & Barge, is seen here in March 1966, towing in the Greek freighter *Lefkipos*, which broke down off Barkley Sound.

from Portland, Oregon, to Ipswich, England, with grain. The mate, steward, and four seamen drowned. The Matterhorn was built by Russell & Co. for C. E. DeWolf & Co. of Liverpool, in 1882, and was 266 feet long.

May Belle, Canadian sealing schooner, 58 tons, built at Victoria, B. C. in 1891, sailed out of Sooke, B. C., for the Pacific sealing grounds in 1896 and went missing with all hands somewhere off Cape Flattery.

Mia, 37-foot pleasure craft, was rammed on July 29, 1967, in fog off Tatoosh Island, by the SS Hawaiian Citizen, commanded by Captain Frank H. Hickler. The impact sheared off the fore part of the pleasure craft, and the owner-operator, Dr. Harry K. Bailey, Oak Harbor, with his son and Lieutenant Commander George Lamm, abandoned the craft. They were subsequently picked up by another small vessel. The remaining portion of the Mia was towed onto the beach but was declared a total loss.

Michigan, American steam schooner, 566 tons, wrecked near Pachena Point, B. C., January 21, 1893, while bound for Puget Sound from San Francisco to load lumber. She grounded near a creek which now bears her name, on the rugged Vancouver Island coast. All hands were rescued. The vessel was in command of Captain Graves and was owned by W. M. and George Colwell. She carried a full cargo of general merchandise. Four days out of California ports, she encountered thick weather and a heavy westerly sea. Strong northerly currents carried the steamer to the rocks about 30 miles northwest of Bonilla Point at 10:50 p.m., January 21. Twenty-one crewmen and four passengers escaped. No contact could be made with Carmanah Lighthouse or Victoria, so Captain Graves and some of his men crossed the strait in a small boat to Neah Bay and contacted tugs. Three American tugs responded, along with the Victoria salvage ship Mascotte. Much of the cargo was saved, but little else. One crewman of the Michigan, delirious from hardships, wandered off and died of exposure.

Millbay A, 19 tons, sank on October 16, 1924, inside the entrance to Nitinat River, B. C.

Mobil Oil Company (oil drilling) rig began leaking badly while off the entrance to the Strait of Juan de Fuca in early June 1966, while being towed to Cook Inlet, Alaska, from San Francisco Bay by two Red Stack tugs. The 3,000-ton, four-columned rig canted to one side until it was almost horizontal with the surface. It was towed to Port Angeles, where it sank inside Ediz Hook about June 14, 1966. A major salvage job was undertaken to raise and repair the all-welded rig. It was built by the Kaiser Products Company of Oakland, just prior to the ill-fated voyage.

Mogul, British (Canadian) tugboat, 123 tons, lost May 12, 1895. In command of Captain Henry Smith, she had towed the British bark Dharra to sea, and after dropping the hawser had come alongside to recover the heaving line. The two vessels collided. The impact sprang the tug's stern and full steam was crowded on in order to beach her before she sank. She was beached in an exposed position two miles east of Tatoosh Island. Tugs rushed to the scene, but shortly afterwards the surf broke up the Mogul. The crew escaped but the vessel was a total loss. Built at Tacoma in 1886 as an American tug, she was later owned by the British Columbia Tugboat Co. of Victoria.

Montserrat, Hawaiian-American registry, steamship (collier), iron built, 2,000 tons, vanished off Cape Flattery in a gale, heavily laden with coal. She was out of Nanaimo for San Francisco, December 7, 1894. All hands were lost.

Morning Star, schooner, wrecked near Bonilla Point, B. C., in November 1860.

Nebraska, lost at Neah Bay, August 1912. No details.

Nellie May, American bark, 699 tons, foundered off Cape Flattery in January 1890. The vessel departed Port Townsend with lumber for San Francisco and vanished with all hands, probably the victim of heavy seas. Her name board was picked up on May 4, off Cape Flattery, by the tug Lorne, and the wreckage of one of her boats was found by Indians at Clayoquot, B. C. The vessel was owned by Captain Axtel Austin; her skipper, W. P. Sayward of Port Madison, and E. M. Harrick of San Francisco. She was built at Newcastle, Maine, in 1867 and carried a crew of 13, including the captain.

Nereus, Greek steamship (freighter), 6,694 tons, wrecked on August 8, 1937, in a heavy fog one mile southeast of Cape Beale Lighthouse. The crew of 34 was rescued but the vessel became a total loss. Capital Iron Works of Victoria managed to salvage some equipment from the wreck before she broke in two and sank. The ship was abandoned as a total loss 48 hours after grounding. She was 472 feet long and was built in Germany in 1913. Her owner was the Nereus Steam Navigation Co. At the time of her loss the vessel was inbound from Moji, Japan, to Port Alberni, B. C.

Nicholas Thayer, American bark, 584 tons, went missing with all hands after rounding Tatoosh Island en route to Seward, Alaska, from Seattle, in January 1906. The vessel was owned by Alaska Packers Assn. of San Francisco and was built at Thomaston, Maine in 1868 by J. W. Small.

Nika, American steamship (freighter), 2,496 tons, caught on fire south of Cape Flattery, February 14, 1923. The crew of 35 was removed by Coast Guard cutter Snohomish, and taken to Port Angeles. The ship continued to burn furiously and finally plunged to the bottom at 48° N. Lat., 125° W. Long., southwest of Umatilla Reef.

North Star, American brig, 409 tons, capsized off Cape Flattery in April 1887, with the loss of all hands. In command of Captain Williams, the vessel departed Seattle for San Diego on April 8, with a cargo of lumber. Several weeks later the capsized hull came ashore off Portland Point on the West Coast of Vancouver Island. The North Star originally came from Boston.

Norway, American schooner, 192 tons, collided with the schooner Fanny Dutard off Clallam Bay, Washington, January 11, 1894. She had to be abandoned by her crew. The wreck drifted ashore and broke up. The Norway was built in San Francisco in 1870 by Jacob Bell and was owned in the Bay City by Andrew Anderson.

Ocean Bird, American bark, capsized on April 3, 1864, off Cape Flattery, en route from Port Madison to San Francisco with lumber. She left port on March 19, in company with the bark **Rival,** and later encountered severe southwest gales. The crew was on the ship's keel six hours before the masts gave way and the vessel partly righted. The after cabin and the forward house had been torn away, but the crew stayed with the wreck for five more days without food or water. They were finally rescued by the steamer **Panama** and taken to Astoria. Captain Blake, master of the Ocean Bird, and three others were in serious condition from exposure, but recovered.

Orpheus, American ship, 1,067 tons, collided with passenger steamer **Pacific,** south of Cape Flattery, November 4, 1875, resulting in one of the worst ship disasters on the Pacific Coast. The Orpheus, damaged, sailed on and later was wrecked near Cape Beale.

Ououkinish, Canadian motor vessel, 31 tons, burned off Cape Beale, B. C., August 22, 1929.

Pacific, American steamship (sidewheel passenger vessel), 875 tons, foundered after a collision, south of Cape Flattery, November 4, 1875, with a loss of 275 persons. Struck by the ship **Orpheus,** she went down in a few minutes. Only two survived.

Palestine, sailing vessel of this name was reported to have been lost south of Tatoosh Island in April 1859.

Paul D, Canadian motor vessel, sank in collision off Pachena Point, July 12, 1949. She was struck by the fishboat **Goodhope II.** No lives were lost.

Pelicano, Nicaraguan ship, 750 tons, stranded on the rocks on the western point jutting out from Neah Bay, at 6 a.m., January 19, 1875. A heavy snowstorm prevailed at the time and the current slammed the ship into the rocks. A northeast gale made it impossible to launch a boat for several hours. They finally made their escape at 10 p.m. The ship bilged and became a total loss. She was valued at $30,000 and was in command of Captain Juan A. Dam. The vessel was en route to Port Townsend from Callao, in ballast.

Penelope, American ex-sealing schooner, 41 tons, dragged anchor at Clallam Bay, March 10, 1904, and dashed ashore.

Penelope, Canadian sealing schooner, 70 tons, built at Yokohama in 1882, was reportedly lost off the entrance to the Strait of Juan de Fuca in 1899—terminating a highly successful sealing career. Her last master was believed to have been Captain Edward Pratt Miner.

Pennsylvania, gas-powered American fishboat, 31 tons, wrecked near Carrol Island on the Washington Coast, May 1948, but wreckage later came up on the beach at Cape Alava. Was owned by Leonard Sandstrom of Juneau; built at Tacoma in 1914.

Persevere, American brig, sprang a leak and began to sink 40 miles off Cape Flattery, September 15, 1861. Bound for Victoria from San Francisco, the ancient, Dutch-built vessel carried merchandise for Chinese storekeepers. She had been idle in San Francisco many months before her last voyage. As soon as she began to sink, the crew made a rush for the boats, leaving everything behind. No sooner had the last man left the ship than she plunged to the bottom. The survivors rowed to Tatoosh Island, where they were picked up by the SS Sierra Nevada, Portland-bound.

Persian, brig, wrecked near Clo-oose Village, B. C., in the 1800s.

Phoebe, yacht, abandoned off Cape Alava in 1962.

P.L.M., Canadian motor vessel, 16 tons, foundered on November 7, 1950, off Carmanah Point, with the loss of two lives.

Prince Arthur, Norwegian (iron) bark, 1,600 tons, wrecked January 2, 1903, 12 miles south of Ozette River, Washington, with the loss of 18 lives. There were but two survivors. The vessel was built at Birkenhead, England, in 1869, as the Houghton Tower.

Puritan, American four-masted schooner, 614 tons, total loss after stranding between Bonilla and Carmanah points, November 13, 1896. The vessel was built at Port Madison, in 1888, by Hans R. Reed for C. A. Hooper of San Francisco. The Puritan had departed San Francisco on November 5, and was inbound to load lumber at Port Gamble, Washington. Indians rigged a lifeline to save the crew.

Rainier, American bark, 499 tons, struck by a furious gale off Cape Flattery, January 3, 1882. In command of Captain John H. Wolf, she sailed from Port Townsend for Honolulu, December 31, 1881. After a northerly gale struck, she began leaking badly. On January 5, while all hands were at the pumps, a gigantic sea stove the cabin, shifted the deckload of lumber, and threw the craft on her beam ends. Captain Wolf was hurled against the mizzen stay and killed; he had broken his back and fractured his skull. The masts were cut away and the vessel righted. The crew lashed themselves to the poop, where they remained till January 24. They survived on five sacks of potatoes, one sack of flour, and a gallon of vinegar. The gaunt survivors were picked up by the brig Orient off the Oregon Coast.

Raita, French power schooner, registered at Papeete, Tahiti, struck the rocks off Clo-oose, B. C., in a driving storm on January 16, 1925. The vessel was commanded by Captain Jean Louis Richam, and owned by A. Leboucher of Papeete. She began to break up soon after striking the rocks. Her 10-man crew, mostly Polynesian natives, reached shore in a boat after an exhausting battle in the surf. The survivors, suffering from exposure, made their way along the beach five miles east to Carmanah Lighthouse, where they were cared for. The Raita was the former American schooner Lucy, built at Fairhaven, California in 1890, as a coastal lumber carrier. She took the French flag in 1919.

Ray Roberts, Canadian motor vessel, 29 tons, stranded off Port Renfrew, B. C., January 24, 1947.

Renfrew, Canadian cannery tender, 24 tons, capsized in November 1918, while crossing Nitinat Bar with 26 cannery employees aboard. Thirteen were drowned. The bodies washed ashore for several days thereafter.

Revere, American bark, 795 tons, wrecked on September 9, 1883, in Port San Juan Harbor, B. C. In command of Captain J. F. Hinds, the vessel was bound for Port Townsend from Honolulu, in ballast. The vessel left the Islands, August 22, and off the entrance to the Strait of Juan de Fuca got into a pea-soup fog. When surf was heard, the anchors were dropped but the vessel crashed ashore broadside and gouged a hole in her bottom planks. The wreck soon became a total loss, but the crew and passengers were rescued and taken to Victoria.

Richard Harding Davis, American steamship, (Liberty freighter), 7,200 tons, ran aground near Cape Beale, June 22, 1944. She remained aground several days until removed in a major salvage effort under U. S. Navy jurisdiction.

Robert Lewers, American four-masted schooner, 732 tons, was wrecked at Pachena Point, B. C., April 11, 1923, en route to Puget Sound from Honolulu. The tug **Humaconna** took off the crew, but the schooner became a total loss. She was built at Port Blakely, Washington, in 1889, by Hall Brothers for Lewers & Cooke of Honolulu. Her entire career was spent in the lumber trade.

Roche Point, Canadian motor vessel, 31 tons, foundered off Cape Beale, August 5, 1930.

Rose, American tug, 15 tons, foundered off Umatilla Lightship, February 9, 1951. The crew was rescued. She was built in 1907 at Astoria.

Rose of Langley, schooner, foundered, February 22, 1859, near the entrance to Juan de Fuca Strait. Two lives were lost.

Rustler, Canadian sealing schooner, 29 tons, was driven ashore near the Nitinat River, December 26, 1887. She became a total loss, the crew escaping. The vessel was commanded by Captain James W. Todd and owned by J. D. Warren. She homeported at Victoria and was built at East Sound, Washington, in 1883.

Ryo Yei Maru, Japanese motor fishing vessel, was picked up 20 miles off Umatilla Reef, by the SS **Margaret Dollar,** October 31, 1927. The 85-foot craft carried a crew of dead men and had been badly mauled by heavy seas after drifting across the Pacific, disabled.

St. Clair, Canadian tugboat, out of Vancouver, B. C., ran aground off Port San Juan, B. C., and became a total loss, January 22, 1949. Two crew members were drowned.

St. Denis, Canadian steamer, 486 tons, lost off Cape Flattery en route to Salina Cruz, Mexico, from Vancouver, B. C., where she was to have been sold to the Mexicans. Lost December 1010. Vessel was carrying too much coal, it was said, which may have had something to do with her loss. Identified wreckage was found weeks later off Cape Scott on the northern tip of Vancouver Island. Twenty-one lives were lost.

St. Stephens, American ship, Seattle for San Francisco with coal, struck by a severe gale off Cape Flattery. Vessel was reported missing with Captain Douglass, his wife, three children, and a crew of 17, early in 1887. Vancouver Island Indians reported that the battered hulk washed up on a reef off Kyuquot Sound, B. C., on April 9, and the following day two Whitehall boats came ashore empty. Still later, a compass case containing the private correspondence of Captain Douglass was discovered in the area.

St. Vincent, ship, Comox, B. C., to San Francisco, reported destroyed in severe weather off Cape Flattery, laden with coal, March 1887. Two survivors were rescued and brought to Port Townsend.

Santa Rita, American steam schooner, 1,600 tons, February 14, 1923, wrecked in a snowstorm off Clo-oose, B. C. Crew of 32 came ashore via breeches buoy and were cared for by villagers. Parts of the steel hull remained in the surf for many years. Vessel was built in San Francisco in 1913 as the **William Chatham** and was at the time of her loss owned by A. F. Mahoney, San Francisco.

Sarah, British (Nova Scotian) bark, 1,142 tons, wrecked near Pachena Point, B. C., November 8, 1891. Commanded by Captain Greenhalgh, the vessel was inbound for Port Blakely from Manila in ballast. She fell victim to a heavy fog and the currents placed her in jeopardy. The crew escaped in lifeboats, but two were lost in effecting a landing through the surf. The captain, his wife, and baby were among the survivors. The vessel was built in 1874.

Sausalito, American schooner, three-masted shoal-draft vessel, 376 tons, purchased by Thomas Crowley of San Francisco from Tidewater Mill Co., Portland, was southbound from San Francisco for installation of a gas engine as auxiliary power, when driven ashore on Waada Island, Neah Bay, December 27, 1915. The surfboat crew from the lifesaving station at Neah Bay sighted distress rockets and put out to sea, successfully rescuing all hands. The schooner broke up shortly after. The **Sausalito** was built at Oakland, California, in 1903 for the coastwise lumber trades.

Sea Witch, American bark, 1,289 tons, abandoned by her crew of 16 in sinking condition in heavy seas several miles off Cape Flattery, December 7, 1906. She was en route to San Francisco with lumber from Port Hadlock, Washington. Crew was rescued by the schooner **Forest Home**. The vessel was owned by the North Atlantic Salmon Company of San Francisco, and was built at East Boston, Massachusetts in 1872.

Seventy Six, sailing vessel, in trouble off Neah Bay in 1881. Reportedly salvaged and repaired.

Sierra Nevada, American bark, 664 tons, sailed from Seattle, September 19, 1886, for San Francisco with a full cargo of coal. In command of Captain F. H. de la Roche, with a crew of 12, she rounded Tatoosh Island September 20, and was never seen or heard of again. She was believed to be a victim of a severe northerly gale sweeping the area. The 23-year-old ship was grossly overloaded with 1,209 tons of coal and probably went down so fast there was no chance for the crew to escape.

Skagit, American barkentine, 506 tons, in command of Captain Louis Rose, was wrecked October 25, 1906, at Clo-oose Point, B. C. The ship's cook, while attempting to save the captain, was drowned along with him. The remaining eight survivors gained the shore in the ship's boat. The vessel had been inbound to Port Gamble, her home port, to load lumber for San Francisco when she grounded. The Skagit was owned by Puget Sound Commercial Co. and was built in 1883 at Port Ludlow, Washington, by Hiram Doncaster. Most of her career was in the Puget Sound-Hawaii lumber trade.

Skagway, American steel steam schooner, 1,838 tons, lost by fire off Tatoosh Island, December 16, 1929. The crew of 27 escaped. The charred hull drifted inshore and foundered among Skagway Rocks near Cape Flattery. The vessel was owned by the Skagway Steamship Co. of Los Angeles and was built in 1908 by the Moran Shipyard of Seattle.

Soquel, American four-masted schooner, 767 tons, Callao for Port Townsend, struck Sea Bird Rocks off the west coast of Vancouver Island, January 22, 1909, when Captain Henningson mistook Pachena Light for Cape Flattery Light. She struck about midnight and shortly afterward a mountainous sea combed the vessel, carrying away two masts and a lifeboat and killing the master's wife and child. The Canadian-Pacific steamer Tees and the Canadian government-chartered steamer **Leebro**—acting as a lighthouse tender—rescued the survivors the following day. The Soquel was a total loss.

Southern Chief, American bark, 1,282 tons, abandoned off Cape Flattery by her crew. She was badly mauled and waterlogged in December 1894 while bound for Australia from Tacoma with lumber. The wreck was later towed in, condemned, and burned.

Southerner, American sidewheel passenger steamer, 338 tons, wrecked ten miles south of Cape Flattery, December 26, 1854. Passengers and crew gained shore safely.

Speedway, Canadian power schooner (rum runner), caught fire off Cape Flattery in February 1925. The crew abandoned ship and were later rescued.

Squamish Queen, Canadian fish packer, 178 tons, foundered on November 6, 1958, between Pachena Point and Cape Beale. She was owned by Anglo-B. C. Packing Co. and was built at Victoria in 1943.

Stockholm, American motor vessel, lost near Cape Flattery in 1911.

Sunbeam, fishboat, 15 tons, stranded on December 4, 1925, off Carmanah Point, B. C.

Suremico, American steamship (freighter), 3,253 gross tons, collided with the French steamship (freighter) **Arkansas,** off Cape Flattery in 1929 in the fog. Both ships were heavily damaged, the Suremico so badly that she was considered too far gone to rebuild. Though the ship was only nine years old, she was cut down to a huge gravel barge. The Arkansas, built in 1899 and owned by the French Line, suffered a giant hole which ripped her starboard bow section wide open. She underwent major surgery at the Todd Dry Dock in Seattle.

Surplus, American motor vessel, 16 tons, burned on October 3, 1961, one and a quarter miles south of Tatoosh Island. Built in 1943, she was a fishing vessel owned by L. Y. Cook of Port Angeles.

Susan Abigail, American brig, came to a tragic end many miles northwest of Cape Flattery in July 1865, when she was captured and burned by the Confederate cruiser **Shenandoah,** which played havoc with shipping in the North Pacific in the latter days of the Civil War. The **Abigail,** a well-known coasting packet, first came around the horn in 1851, and entered Puget Sound and Columbia River trade in 1853, in command of Captain Paul Corno.

Susie M. Plummer, American four-masted schooner, 920 tons, departed Everett, Washington, for San Pedro in December 1909. A couple of days later, the vessel was sighted capsized off Cape Flattery, but no trace of her crew of ten was ever found. The vessel was owned by W. G. Tibbitts of San Francisco. She was built at Thomaston, Maine, in 1890. The lumber-laden vessel was sighted, just before Christmas, off Tatoosh Island, by the NYK steamer **Kaga Maru** and Hill's SS **Minnesota.** She was on her beam ends, dismasted and boats gone. No one was aboard. The cutters **Snohomish** and **Tahoma,** plus the tugs **Tyee** and **Pioneer,** went out to search for the derelict. The wreck eluded the searchers and menaced shipping lanes until January 1910, when she was reported to have gone aground and broken up far to the north at San Josef Bay. She carried a crew of 14 and was commanded by Captain Harry L. Hansen.

Susy Lane, American motor vessel, 30 tons, wrecked by stranding on reef off Tatoosh Island, August 5, 1951. She was a fishing vessel owned by Edgar W. Lane of Seattle and had been built just two years earlier.

Umatilla, American steamship, 3,069 tons, struck unidentified reef off Washington Coast, which later took the name of the ship (Umatilla Reef). The mishap occurred on February 8, 1884. The vessel refloated herself though badly damaged.

Una, British brigantine, driven ashore, December 26, 1851, near Cape Flattery. Crew was rescued by schooner **Damariscove.**

Uncle John, American barkentine, 314 tons, wrecked near Nitinat, B. C., off the locale of Tsusiat Falls, on October 7, 1899. The vessel was inbound from Honolulu for Puget Sound. She was a total loss but the crew gained shore. The **Uncle John** was built at Eureka, California, in 1881, by Charles Murray for John Vance of Eureka.

Unidentified fishboat, sighted by the SS **Meitetsu Maru** afire and abandoned 40 miles northwest of Cape Flattery, November 2, 1957. There were no survivors.

Unidentified iron gunboat, wreckage found on beach at Nitinat near Tsusiat Falls in the 1800s. According to the local Indians, the remains had been there many years prior to 1880, but no positive identification was ever made.

Uzbekistan, Russian steamship (freighter), 4,000 tons, bound for Seattle from Portland, to complete loading war cargo for Vladivostok, was wrecked two and a half miles east of Pachena Point, April 30, 1943.

Valencia, American passenger steamship, 1,598 tons, wrecked three miles east of Pachena Point, B. C., January 22, 1906, with the loss of 117 lives. This was one of the most tragic ship disasters on the North Pacific.

Varsity, American motor vessel, 90 tons, San Francisco for Puget Sound, wrecked by stranding four miles east of Pachena Point, February 5, 1940. The fishing vessel carried seven men, four of whom died in the wreck. The vessel was owned by Joe Cloud of Tacoma, and was built at that city in 1937.

Vesta, American schooner, 285 tons, wrecked near Nitinat, B. C., December 10, 1897. The schooner, owned by Albert Rowe, was built in San Francisco by M. Turner, in 1882.

W. A. Banks, American bark, 323 tons (another source gives 469 tons), wrecked in Clallam Bay, Washington, November 10, 1869. The vessel was built in Maine in 1854, and came out from the East Coast in 1863, under ownership of the Oregon Steam Navigation Co. She was last registered at Utsaladdy, Washington.

Walter Raleigh, American bark, 487 tons, reported in trouble off Cape Flattery in 1872. She was owned by Comstock's Dispatch Line of New York. She was towed in.

Warrimoo, British passenger steamship, 3,326 tons, ran aground in fog, four miles west of Carmanah Point, B. C., August 9, 1895, bound for Vancouver, B. C., from Australia. Averting what could have been a serious disaster, the vessel managed to float free on the next high tide and proceeded to Victoria for repairs. She was owned by the Royal Mail Steamship Co., London, and was built at Newcastle in 1892.

Water Baby, American motor vessel (fishboat), 17 tons, rammed and sunk by the SS *Colorado* in fog, 30 miles west of Cape Flattery, September 29, 1958.

Waterwing, Canadian motor vessel, 57 tons, stranded on December 2, 1948, at Port Renfrew, B. C.

Watson, American passenger steamship, 1,820 tons, stranded in fog on Waada Island, near Neah Bay, Washington, September 1, 1910. Object of a major salvage operation, the vessel was eventually refloated and taken to port for repairs totaling $30,000. She was built at Toledo, Ohio, in 1902.

W. C. Parke, American bark, vanished with all hands off Cape Flattery, bound for Australia from Port Gamble with lumber. She left Puget Sound, August 12, 1877, in command of Captain "Blackie" Blackstone.

Webfoot, British bark, 1,061 tons, departed Tacoma for Callao with 862,-000 feet of lumber, November 10, 1886. In command of Captain Gilbert Yeates, she was off Tatoosh Island next morning, leaking badly from a heavy southwest sea. A portion of the deckload was jettisoned with little result. By November 12, the ship was filling fast, so she came about and headed back into the strait. A pilot was picked up and the vessel headed for Royal Roads. Then fire broke out and spread rapidly. All hands abandoned except the captain and one sailor. They were eventually driven off by the intense heat. They were picked up by the tug **Pilot** and taken to Victoria. The burning, 30-year-old hulk drifted off the strait entrance, and the wreckage washed ashore near Clo-oose.

Wempe Bros., American four-masted schooner, 681 tons, wrecked near Carmanah Point, B. C., October 28, 1903. She was bound for Ballard, Washington from San Pedro. The vessel was built at Aberdeen, Washington, in 1901, and was last owned by Oliver J. Olson of San Francisco.

Wergeland, Norwegian auxiliary five-masted schooner, 2,457 tons, on maiden voyage, was battered by heavy seas off Tatoosh, in the fall of 1917. She lost two masts, her deck load, and sustained serious damage to her hull. The wreck was towed back to Port Blakely, Washington, for repairs. She was built by the Olympia Shipbuilding Co. at Olympia, and was en route to Norway via Portland, Oregon, when hit by the storm. She was in service till 1930.

Western Star, American diesel tugboat, 28 tons, burned at Sekiu, Washington, February 4, 1959. Built in 1920, the vessel was owned by R. A. Busacker of Tacoma.

William, British brig, driven ashore about four miles east of Pachena Point, January 1, 1854. The captain and the cook perished. Fourteen survivors reached shore and were cared for by the natives, who later took them to Sooke by canoe.

William Tell, American ship, 1,500 tons, wrecked, December 23, 1865, on reef three miles northwest of Port San Juan.

Willis A. Holden, American four-masted schooner, 1,188 tons, badly damaged and almost completely dismasted off Cape Flattery in a severe storm in February 1911. The vessel was rebuilt and suffered a similar experience in the North Pacific three years later. The Holden was built at Ballard, Washington, in 1902.

William F. Garms, American four-masted schooner, 1,094 tons, badly buffeted off Vancouver Island's west coast, December 28, 1913, after losing her rudder. Laden with a full cargo of mine timbers for Mexico, she drifted within 600 yards of shore with all anchors out. An effort to launch a boat to go for help failed. When all hope appeared lost, the cutter **Snohomish** and tug **Goliah** came to the rescue and pulled the battered, dismasted vessel to safety. Her deckload was gone, as well as most of her masts and rigging. She was in command of Captain F. Turloff. The vessel was later rebuilt and renamed **Golden State.**

W. J. Pirrie, Chilean four-masted, schooner-barge (bark), 2,516 tons, departed Tacoma with lumber for Chile in tow of Grace Line's SS **Santa Rita,** November 24, 1920. Two days later, near Umatilla Reef in a heavy storm, the steamer was forced to cut her tow loose. The **Pirrie** vanished. Then on the afternoon of November 26, two injured seamen were reported in care of Indians near Cape Johnson. The Coast Guard cutter **Snohomish** landed a party at the cape, where they found the bodies of Captain Jensen, his wife and child, and ten of the crew on the beach. The two survivors who had come ashore on wreckage after the vessel foundered were taken to a Seattle hospital. The 308-foot iron ship was built at Belfast, Ireland, in 1883. A marker with the names of the dead had been erected at the site of the common grave, but vandals pried the plaque from its concrete base and for decades the memorial was faceless. Then, in the summer of 1964, the plaque was replaced by Wayne Merry, a Forest Service ranger.

Winslow, American four-masted schooner, 566 tons, plowed into Duncan Rock near Tatoosh Island, July 28, 1907. She was inbound under a full suit of canvas, Puget Sound from San Francisco, when she was caught in a severe storm while endeavoring to enter the strait. Captain Oscar Friedrich, her master, found visibility reduced to virtually nothing when the Winslow struck the rock, knocking a huge hole in her bows. Water poured in rapidly until the decks were awash. With great skill, the skipper kept his command off the treacherous Vancouver Island shores as they drifted northward. The next day the tug **Tacoma** found the vessel and towed her into Winslow, Washington, where costly repairs were made.

Woodrich, small sailing vessel, reported wrecked near Clo-oose in the 1880s.

Woodside, Canadian steamer, lost her rudder and piled ashore five miles east of Pachena Point, near the Nitinat River entrance, March 12, 1888. She was bound for Port Alberni from Victoria, with four passengers and general cargo. All got ashore safely but the vessel was a total loss. She was built at Sooke, B. C., in 1878, and was 87 feet long.

Zip, Canadian motor vessel, 44 tons, stranded on Bonilla Point reef, October 7, 1936.

INDEX

SHIPWRECKS

List of Shipwrecks

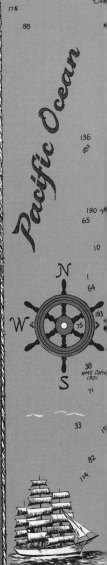

Pacific Ocean

Bo

175
88
136
101
190
65
10
1
64
193
75
38
HMS Cone
1901
71
33
82
114

N
W
S

Map Art by Oliver Bailey

© 1968 BINFORDS & MORT